R Bioinformatics Cookbook

Second Edition

Utilize R packages for bioinformatics, genomics, data science, and machine learning

Dan MacLean

BIRMINGHAM—MUMBAI

R Bioinformatics Cookbook, Second Edition

Copyright © 2023 Packt Publishing

Group Product Manager: Kaustubh Manglurkar

Publishing Product Manager: Deepesh Patel

Book Project Manager: Farheen Fathima

Senior Editor: Nathanya Dias

Technical Editor: Devanshi Ayare

Copy Editor: Safis Editing

Proofreader: Safis Editing

Indexer: Rekha Nair

Production Designer: Jyoti Kadam

DevRel Marketing Coordinator: Nivedita Singh

First published: October 2019

Second edition: October 2023

Production reference: 1181023

Published by Packt Publishing Ltd.

Grosvenor House

11 St Paul's Square

Birmingham

B3 1RB, UK.

ISBN 978-1-83763-427-9

www.packtpub.com

To my daughter, Zoë: Hi! I'm sorry if this is a bit of a dull book but I don't have another one to offer. Or anyone I'd rather dedicate a book to.

Contributors

About the author

Professor Dan MacLean has a PhD in molecular biology from the University of Cambridge and gained postdoctoral experience in genomics and bioinformatics at Stanford University in California. Dan is now an honorary professor at the School of Computing Sciences at the University of East Anglia. He has worked in bioinformatics and plant pathogenomics, specializing in R and Bioconductor, and has developed analytical workflows in bioinformatics, genomics, genetics, image analysis, and proteomics at the Sainsbury Laboratory since 2006. Dan has developed and published software packages in R, Ruby, and Python, with over 100,000 downloads combined.

I want to thank everyone involved with the Sainsbury Laboratory; working with you all has helped me develop the knowledge that has gone into this book.

About the reviewer

Dr. Swarna Kanchan has a doctorate in Bioinformatics with over 15 years of experience in research and academics. He is currently a Staff Scientist at the Department of Biomedical Sciences, Joan C. Edwards School of Medicine, Marshall University, Huntington, West Virginia, USA. He was a Postdoctoral Fellow at INRIA Bordeaux, France; Nencki Institute of Experimental Biology, Warsaw, Poland and Boise State University, Boise, Idaho, USA. He also worked as an Assistant Professor at Presidency University, Bengaluru, India. He has several high-impact research articles, book chapters and books to his credentials.

Support in the review process from Dr. Minu Kesheri, and the research associate at Marshall University, USA, is highly acknowledged.

Table of Contents

2

Loading, Tidying, and Cleaning Data in the tidyverse   23

3

ggplot2 and Extensions for Publication Quality Plots   45

4

Using Quarto to Make Data-Rich Reports, Presentations, and Websites   77

5

Easily Performing Statistical Tests Using Linear Models   97

6

Performing Quantitative RNA-seq   125

7

Finding Genetic Variants with HTS Data   177

8

Searching Gene and Protein Sequences for Domains and Motifs   205

9

Phylogenetic Analysis and Visualization   235

10

Analyzing Gene Annotations   265

13

Turbo-Charging Development in R with ChatGPT   337

Preface

In biology, genetics and genomics data is the driver of discovery. To harness the power of data, bioinformaticians rely on computational tools and none is more powerful in the statistical and visualization world than R. *R Bioinformatics Cookbook, Second Edition*, is designed to help you take control of all manner of bioinformatics analyses and to help you navigate the intricate world of bioinformatics with R.

The *R Bioinformatics Cookbook, Second Edition* book, is a resource for getting good work done quickly. It will help researchers to sharpen their skills and broaden their knowledge of important packages such as the tidyverse for data management, ggplot for visualization, and mlr for machine learning and delves deeply into the comprehensive Bioconductor framework of tools tailored specifically toward the most taxing and common analyses in bioinformatics.

Who this book is for

This book is for bioinformaticians, data analysts, researchers, and R developers who want to address intermediate to advanced biological and bioinformatics problems by learning through a recipe-based approach. Working knowledge of the R programming language and basic knowledge of bioinformatics are prerequisites.

What this book covers

Chapter 1, Setting Up Your R Bioinformatics Working Environment, shows how to set up your computer and toolchain for easy and efficient work.

Chapter 2, Loading, Tidying, and Cleaning Data in the tidyverse, shows how to load and prepare external tabular data for use in complex pipelines.

Chapter 3, ggplot2 and Extensions for Publication Quality Plots, explains the structure of ggplots and how to create attractive and informative plots of many types.

Chapter 4, Using Quarto to Make Data-Rich Reports, Presentations, and Websites, covers how to mix code and written text into literate computing documents in a powerful and flexible way.

Chapter 5, Easily Performing Statistical Tests Using Linear Models, explores how to do the most common tests in bioinformatics in R's powerful statistical model framework.

Chapter 6, Performing Quantitative RNA-seq, uses the latest, most widely used tools for RNA-seq, including EdgeR, DESeq2, and sleuth.

Chapter 7, Finding Genetic Variants with HTS Data, uses powerful Bioconductor packages to work with high-throughput genome sequencing data.

Chapter 8, Searching Gene and Protein Sequences for Domains and Motifs, explores functional sequence features using predictive tools and databases.

Chapter 9, Phylogenetic Analysis and Visualization, looks at carrying out genome and gene alignments and how to create attractive and informative phylogenetic trees.

Chapter 10, Analyzing Gene Annotations, shows how to infer biological properties of gene sets from annotations of those genes.

Chapter 11, Machine Learning with mlr3, explains how to develop effective and useful pipelines for machine learning with the powerful and flexible mlr3 package.

Chapter 12, Functional Programming with purrr and base R, shows how to apply functional programming styles to streamline and empower your analysis pipelines.

Chapter 13, Turbo-Charging Development in R with ChatGPT, explains how to make R code development and testing easier by making use of the latest ChatGPT models.

To get the most out of this book

The book assumes that you have a basic working knowledge of R in the console and that you have a background in biology or life sciences. The book won't try and teach you any biology; instead, we concentrate on applications of R within science. You will learn lots of new things about R that will enhance your bioinformatics research.

Software/hardware covered in the book	Operating system requirements
R 4.2 or greater	Windows, macOS, or Linux
Python 3.8 or greater	Windows, macOS, or Linux

Many individual R packages and some external tools are needed. All these will be discussed in the relevant chapters and recipes so make sure to read the *Getting ready...* sections.

If you are using the digital version of this book, we advise you to type the code yourself or access the code from the book's GitHub repository (a link is available in the next section). Doing so will help you avoid any potential errors related to the copying and pasting of code.

The sample data for this book is provided in an R package that you can install from within R. Look out for advice on how to do that in the relevant chapters and recipes. The code won't work without the sample data, so look out for that.

Download the example code files

You can download the example code files for this book from GitHub at https://github.com/PacktPublishing/R-Bioinformatics-Cookbook-Second-Edition-. If there's an update to the code, it will be updated in the GitHub repository.

We also have other code bundles from our rich catalog of books and videos available at https://github.com/PacktPublishing/. Check them out!

Conventions used

There are a number of text conventions used throughout this book.

`Code in text`: Indicates code words in text, database table names, folder names, filenames, file extensions, pathnames, dummy URLs, user input, and Twitter handles. Here is an example: "Create a README.md file at the root to describe the project."

A block of code is set as follows:

```
/Users/macleand/Desktop/rcookbook/Ch_1/renv/library/R-4.3/aarch64-
apple-darwin20/rbioinfcookbook/extdata/my_project
```

Any command-line input or output is written as follows:

```
install.packages("renv")
```

Bold: Indicates a new term, an important word, or words that you see onscreen. For instance, words in menus or dialog boxes appear in **bold**. Here is an example: "Lastly, check **Open in new session**."

> **Tips or important notes**
> Appear like this.

Get in touch

Feedback from our readers is always welcome.

General feedback: If you have questions about any aspect of this book, email us at customercare@packtpub.com and mention the book title in the subject of your message.

Errata: Although we have taken every care to ensure the accuracy of our content, mistakes do happen. If you have found a mistake in this book, we would be grateful if you would report this to us. Please visit www.packtpub.com/support/errata and fill in the form.

Piracy: If you come across any illegal copies of our works in any form on the internet, we would be grateful if you would provide us with the location address or website name. Please contact us at copyright@packt.com with a link to the material.

If you are interested in becoming an author: If there is a topic that you have expertise in and you are interested in either writing or contributing to a book, please visit authors.packtpub.com.

Share Your Thoughts

Once you've read *R Bioinformatics Cookbook*, we'd love to hear your thoughts! Scan the QR code below to go straight to the Amazon review page for this book and share your feedback.

https://packt.link/r/1-837-63427-0

Your review is important to us and the tech community and will help us make sure we're delivering excellent quality content.

Download a free PDF copy of this book

Thanks for purchasing this book!

Do you like to read on the go but are unable to carry your print books everywhere?

Is your eBook purchase not compatible with the device of your choice?

Don't worry, now with every Packt book you get a DRM-free PDF version of that book at no cost.

Read anywhere, any place, on any device. Search, copy, and paste code from your favorite technical books directly into your application.

The perks don't stop there, you can get exclusive access to discounts, newsletters, and great free content in your inbox daily

Follow these simple steps to get the benefits:

1. Scan the QR code or visit the link below

https://packt.link/free-ebook/9781837634279

2. Submit your proof of purchase
3. That's it! We'll send your free PDF and other benefits to your email directly

1

Setting Up Your R Bioinformatics Working Environment

R is a powerful and versatile programming language that is widely used in bioinformatics, data science, and statistics. One of the key benefits of using R is its rich ecosystem of packages and libraries, which allows users to easily perform complex tasks and analyze large datasets – in particular, the tidyverse packages, which provide a lot of data science functionality, and the Bioconductor packages, which are state of the art in biological analysis, have provided great power. To get the best out of these and make sure that you are working in the most productive ways, it is important to use the best tools and employ a clear and organized project structure to ensure that your work is readable, maintainable, and reproducible.

One of the most important aspects of a good project structure is separating the different parts into different files and directories based on their purpose. For example, it is a good practice to keep your data in a separate directory from your code and to separate your code into different files for different tasks, such as data cleaning, analysis, and visualization. A well-set-up machine and clear project structure that keeps code readable, maintainable, and reproducible benefit the original developer of the code, other developers who may work on the code later, and any future users of the code and the scientific results. It is also crucially useful when we come to writing up results for publication and being organized this way can save a lot of headaches and stress and even repeating of work.

Computing environments, such as renv and Anaconda, are also an important part of a good project structure. These packages allow you to create a virtual environment that is separate from your system-wide R installation, which makes it easy to manage different versions of programs, packages, and dependencies. This is particularly useful when working on multiple projects that require different versions of packages, or when working on a project with other collaborators who may be using different versions of packages. It can also help recreate a project easily when you haven't worked on it for a while. Using virtual environments ensures all collaborators have the same software environment.

Bioconda and Homebrew are package management systems that make it easy to install and manage bioinformatics software on your computer. Bioconda is focused on bioinformatics software and packages, while Homebrew is a general-purpose package management system for macOS and Linux. Both are particularly useful for bioinformatics research as they allow you to easily install and manage the large number of specialized bioinformatics programs and packages needed for various analyses and pipelines.

In this chapter, you'll learn some essential tips and tricks for setting up your computer so that you can work in the most productive way.

In this chapter, we will cover the following recipes:

- Setting up an R project in a directory
- Using the `here` package to simplify working with paths
- Using the `devtools` package to work with the latest non-CRAN packages
- Setting up your machine for the compilation of source packages
- Using the `renv` package to create a project-specific set of packages
- Installing and managing different versions of Bioconductor packages in environments
- Using `bioconda` to install external tools

Technical requirements

We will use renv to manage packages in a project-specific way. To use renv to install packages, you will first need to install the `renv` package. No specific R version seems to be needed for `renv`, though it's a good idea to use the latest version of R. `renv` will automatically record the version of R that you used when you start working with it on a project. Note also that you shouldn't use `renv` directly in the home directory, only in project-level directories. You can see more information on this working structure in the *Setting up an R project directory* and *Using the renv package to create a project-specific set of packages* recipes.

You can do this by running the following command in your R console:

1. Install `renv`:

```
install.packages("renv")
```

2. Next, you will need to create a new renv environment for your project by running the following command:

```
renv::init()
```

This will create a new directory called " `.renv` " in your current project directory.

3. You can then install packages with the following:

```
install.packages("<package name>")
```

4. You can also use the `renv` package manager to install Bioconductor packages by running the following command:

```
renv::install("bioc::<package name>")
```

5. For example, to install the `Biobase` package, you would run the following:

```
renv::install("bioc::Biobase")
```

6. You can use renv to install development packages from GitHub like this:

```
renv::install("<user name>/<repo name>")
```

7. For example, to install the user `danmaclean`'s `rbioinfcookbook` package, you would run the following:

```
renv::install("danmaclean/rbioinfcookbook")
```

You can also install multiple packages at once by separating the package names with a comma. renv will automatically handle installing any required dependencies for the packages you install.

Under `renv`, all packages will be installed into the local project directory and not the main central library, meaning you can have multiple versions of the same package – a specific one for each project.

8. All the sample data you need for this package is in the specially created data package on GitHub: `danmaclean/rbioinfcookbook`. The data will become available in your project after installing that.

For this chapter, we'll need the following packages:

- Regular packages:

    - devtools

    - here

    - renv

    - reticulate

    - usethis

- GitHub:

    - danmaclean/rbioinfcookbook

In addition to these packages, we will also need non-R tools such as `conda`; these will be described when needed.

Further information

Not all the recipes in this section happen in R; some are command-line-based setups. I generally assume a Bash terminal for these bits. Most macOS and Linux machines will have these available in a Terminal application. Windows users will likely not need these specific steps, though various packages for running a Linux subsystem on Windows exist if you wish to search them out.

In R, it is a normal practice to load a library and use functions directly by name. Although this is great in short interactive sessions, it can cause confusion when many packages are loaded at once and share function names. To clarify which package and function I am using at a given moment, I will occasionally use the `packageName::functionName()` convention.

Sometimes, in the middle of a recipe, I'll interrupt the code to dive into some intermediate output or to look at the structure of an object. When that happens, you'll see a code block where each line begins with ## (double hash symbols). Consider the following command:

```
letters[1:5]
```

This will give us the following output:

```
## a b c d e
```

Note that the output lines are prefixed with ##.

Setting up an R project in a directory

R is a command-line tool, and historically, users would work at the command line in order to make use of the language, but as the complexity of a user's tasks increases beyond running a few simple commands, then that interface becomes limiting, and more powerful and flexible tools are needed.

RStudio is an **integrated development environment** (**IDE**) for the R programming language. It provides a user-friendly interface for writing and running R code, as well as tools for data visualization and data manipulation. RStudio includes a variety of other tools, such as code completion, syntax highlighting, and error checking, which can help users to write and debug their code more efficiently. RStudio provides a powerful and flexible environment that can be customized to suit the needs of individual users. It provides many options for customizing the layout of the interface, including the ability to integrate with GitHub, render help and vignettes, and visually inspect R objects.

An R project is a collection of files and directories that are organized together for a specific project or analysis. When you create an R project, RStudio creates a new directory with a file called `.Rproj`

The `.Rproj` file is a special file that is created automatically when you create an R project. This file contains important information about the project, such as the working directory, environment variables, and other settings. It also includes the R version used in the project. This information is stored in a single file, making it easy to share and work on projects with others.

A major advantage of using RStudio and R projects is that it makes it easy to organize and manage files and directories for different projects. When you create an R project, RStudio creates a new directory that contains all the files and directories associated with the project. This allows users to keep their files organized and easily switch between different projects. Additionally, the `.Rproj` file makes it easy to share projects with others and collaborate on projects.

Getting ready

For this recipe, we'll need to have a version of R and a version of RStudio installed. It sounds obvious to say that you'll need R but I do so to draw the distinction between R and RStudio. Installing one does not install the other, so you'll need to make sure R is installed from `https://www.r-project.org/` and RStudio Desktop from `https://posit.co/products/open-source/rstudio/`. Also note that upgrading one does not affect the other, though it's often wise to do both together. We'll also use the `usethis` package.

How to do it...

Setting up is done through the RStudio menu options as follows:

1. Create a new project by using the RStudio menu:

    I.   Select **File | New Project…** from the menu bar (see *Figure 1.1*).

    II.   Select **New Directory** from the pop-up window (see *Figure 1.2*).

    III.   Select **New Project** (see *Figure 1.3*).

    IV.   Pick an informative name for your top-level project folder and type it in the name box.

    V.   Create a Git repository by ticking the box.

    VI.   Use `renv` by ticking the box.

    VII.   Lastly, tick **Open in new session**.

2. Create some useful directories. In the R console, in the new project, type the following:

    ```
    sapply(c("R", "data", "analysis", "src"), dir.create)
    ```

3. Create a README.md file at the root to describe the project:

    ```
    usethis::use_readme_md()
    ```

The first dialog box looks like this:

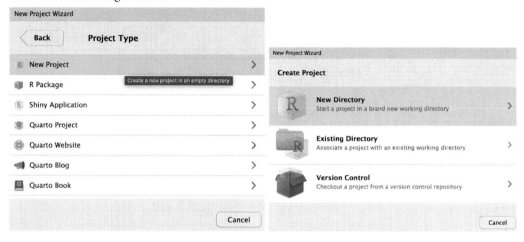

Figure 1.1 – Create Project dialog box

Next, we must choose where to save the project:

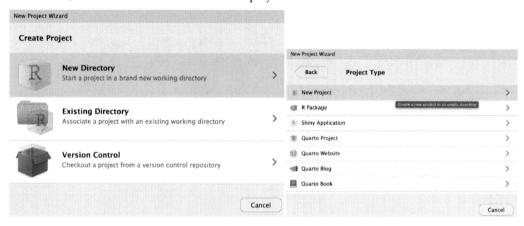

Figure 1.2 – Select the destination dialog box

And then we choose the settings for the project:

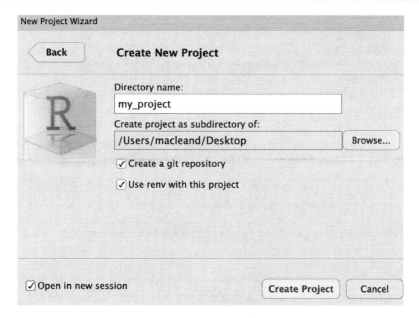

Figure 1.3 – The settings dialog box

And with that, we should have a working, self-contained new R project.

How it works...

In *step 1*, we use the RStudio wizard to create a new project in its own new directory. The wizard sets up all the bits we need, including a .Rproj file for keeping track of the project, and .gitignore, .Rprofile, and the renv folder for more automated use of Git and renv. The correct selections for the boxes can be seen in the preceding figures. Selecting **Use renv with this project** means that any package we install with install.packages() or renv::install() directly will be installed into that renv folder instead of the central library folder R has, so the versions of packages we use in this project will be specific to this project. Opening in a new session means that we get a brand new instance of R in memory without any previously loaded packages or pollution from existing objects.

When the new session opens, it will have its base in the project folder, so all paths can be referenced from this point. Also, every time we want to come back to this project after shutting it down, we can simply click the .Rproj file and an RStudio session will burst into life in the correct project folder.

In *step 2*, we use R in the R console in the new project to create some useful directories: R for R source files containing things such as reused functions; data for raw input data processed by our analysis; analysis for Rmarkdown and other analysis style documents; and src for scripts and things in non-R languages that are also used in the project. We name each of these in a vector and get sapply() to run the dir.create function on each one.

In *step 3*, we create a README.md file using the usethis package use_readme_md() function. This creates a skeleton README file in Markdown format. Here we can add what the purpose of the project is, any date-related information such as progress updates, and generally, any useful information for the user of the project, including ourselves!

There's more...

The usethis package is extremely useful for simplifying the common tasks whenever we set up a new project. Initially, we only really need the README.md file it can create for us, but it has options for many things, including adding project licenses, badges, Git credentials, setting up unit tests, setting up packages, and more.

Using the here package to simplify working with paths

The here package in R is used for managing file paths in a consistent and platform-independent manner. One of the main advantages of using this package is that it allows the user to easily navigate and manipulate file paths without having to worry about the specific file structure of their operating system. The package also provides a number of useful functions for creating and managing directories, which can be particularly useful when working with complex file structures.

The here package allows for more reliable and reproducible code. When working with file paths, it is common to use the setwd() function to set the working directory. However, this can lead to issues when trying to run the same code on different machines or platforms. The here package addresses this problem by providing a consistent way to specify file paths, regardless of the operating system.

The here package also provides a way to handle project-specific file paths with ease. This is particularly useful when working on large projects where the file structure is complex and you need to navigate through different subdirectories. With the here package, the user can specify the project root directory, and all the other file paths can be defined relative to this root directory. This makes it easier to move the project to a different location or share it with others without having to change the file paths in the code. It also helps to handle the differences in path separators on different operating systems, such as the forward slash (/) on Unix-based systems, and the backslash (\) on Windows. This ensures that the file paths are correctly formatted for the specific operating system being used, further increasing the reliability and portability of the code.

Getting ready

For this recipe, we'll need an active R project in a folder (a bit like the one used in the *Setting up an R project* recipe) in a directory and the here package. If you don't want to use an existing project or make the structure yourself, you can pull an example one from the danmaclean/rbioinfcookbook GitHub package. Once that is installed, you can find the place the example folder got copied to on install with the following:

```
fs::path_package("extdata", "my_project", package="rbioinfcookbook")
```

And it will return a path like this:

```
/Users/macleand/Desktop/rcookbook/Ch_1/renv/library/R-4.3/aarch64-
apple-darwin20/rbioinfcookbook/extdata/my_project
```

Copy the file from there to somewhere useful such as your desktop and work from in there.

The directory structure looks like *Figure 1.4*:

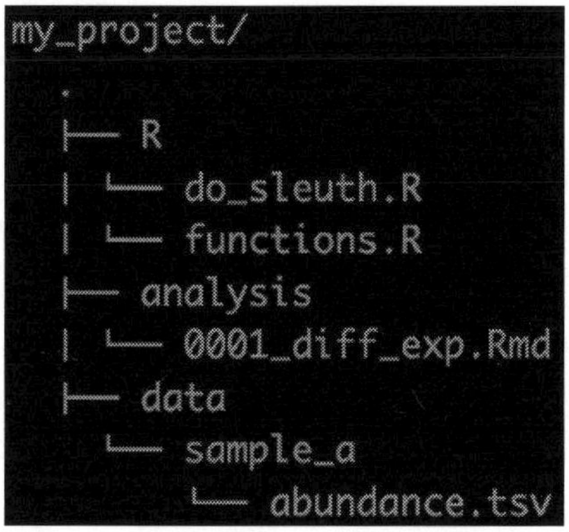

```
my_project/
.
├── R
│   └── do_sleuth.R
│   └── functions.R
├── analysis
│   └── 0001_diff_exp.Rmd
├── data
    └── sample_a
        └── abundance.tsv
```

Figure 1.4 – The current project directory tree

Our aim will be to set up the project under here and set up paths in files appropriately.

How to do it...

Set up the script as follows:

1. Here, we use here in the do_sleuth.R script; at the top of the script, add the following:

    ```
    here::i_am("R/do_sleuth.R")
    ```

2. Add a reference to an input file.

    We will refer to data/sample_a/abundance.tsv inside the do_sleuth.R file:

    ```
    abundance <- here::here("data", "sample_a", "abundance.tsv" )
    readr::read_csv(abundance)
    ```

3. Set up the first code chunk.

4. To use here in the 0001_diff_exp.Rmd file, at the first computation chunk, add the following:

    ```
    here::i_am("analysis/0001_diff_exp.Rmd")
    ```

5.   Load in a set of reused custom functions within that file:

```
source(here::here("R", "functions.R")
```

And that is how we use the here package to help make all references to files relative to a project directory.

How it works...

This slightly repetitive recipe serves to highlight the fact that there are really only two functions used in the here workflow and that the pattern of use is quite straightforward. In the first part of the pattern, the user uses the i_am() function to declare where the script is – this helps here work out the project structure. Then, the here() function itself is used every time we want to use a path. We simply have to think of all our paths relative to the project root – in this case, the my_project folder. Note that all these steps are performed as edits to the respective files and not typed into the console.

In *step 1*, we get our R script to declare its position in the project tree, allowing here to work out the structure.

In *step 2*, we can create a path description for the input file elsewhere in the project file structure, independent of the syntax of the operating system, and the value of getwd() using the here() function. Each element passed to here() is just a step on the path to the file.

In *step 3*, we're simply repeating the initialization we did in *step 1* for this different file – here, an R Markdown document – so the new code must go in the first computed chunk.

And in *step 4*, we use the here() function to build a path to our functions.R file and load its contents for use in the current document.

There's more...

You can use the here() function without arguments to get it to tell you where it thinks the project root currently is. Also, you can use the dr_here() to get it to tell you why it thinks that is the project root.

Using the devtools package to work with the latest non-CRAN packages

A source R package contains the plain text source code for an R package, which can be installed and built on the user's machine. A binary R package, on the other hand, is a pre-built version of an R package that contains pre-compiled code and can be installed and used directly without the need to build the package from the source, and without needing all the tools and programs needed for the compilation progress. When we install packages from CRAN using install.packages(), we are typically getting a pre-compiled binary version of the code.

The devtools R package is a collection of tools that make it easier to develop R packages. It includes functions for creating and installing source packages, building and reloading package documentation, and more. Additionally, it also provides functionality to check packages, build documentation, manage package dependencies, and test package functionality. It allows users to easily share and collaborate on R package development, making it a popular choice among R developers. Here, we will look briefly at its function for installing packages from sources that have not been uploaded to CRAN. Often, this will be newer versions of packages that *are* on CRAN but the developer has added new features or fixes that have not yet made it into a suitable form for the main library.

Getting ready

For this recipe, we'll need the devtools package and we will use some particular branches and **pull requests (PRs)** of the rbioinfcookbook package. Remember to put the default version back at the end after you've run through the recipe for the full functionality of that package.

How to do it...

Working with devtools to install packages follows a basic pattern; we give a repo/username argument to commands like this:

1. Install a source package that lives on GitHub:

    ```
    devtools::install_github("danmaclean/rbioinfcookbook")
    ```

2. Install the example_devtools_ branch:

    ```
    library(rbioinfcookbook)
    '    ## The next line won't work...
    '    rbioinfcookbook::function_from_branch()
    '
    '    ## Now it will
    detach("package:rbioinfcookbook", unload=TRUE)
    '    devtools::install_github(
    "danmaclean/rbioinfcookbook@example_devtools_branch"
    )
    '    rbioinfcookbook::function_from_branch()
    ```

3. Install a specific pull request:

    ```
    ## The next line won't work...
    '    rbioinfcookbook::function_from_PR()
    '
    '    ## Now it will
    detach("package:rbioinfcookbook", unload=TRUE)
    '    devtools::install_github("
    ```

```
danmaclean/rbioinfcookbook#1"
)
'    rbioinfcookbook::function_from_PR()
```

4. Clean up by unloading the package from R memory and then from disk:

```
detach("package:rbioinfcookbook", unload=TRUE)
'    remove.packages("rbioinfcookbook")
```

5. Restart and put back the default version of the package:

```
install.packages("danmaclean/rbioinfcookbook")
```

This whole process has taken us through installing and replacing the rbioinfcookbook package to find functions that only exist in particular branches of the GitHub repository.

How it works...

In *step 1*, we simply install a source package that resides on GitHub, with the install_github() function. The syntax of the argument function is username/repo. By default, the function pulls and installs the latest main branch update. If you've already initialized renv for working on a project, devtools will install into the renv library, though that isn't mandatory.

In *step 2*, we go a step further and install from a specific branch – example_devtools_branch – which adds a function that is not in the main branch, function_from_branch() (note that for cleanliness in memory, we use the detach() function to clear out the previously loaded version from memory each time). We test that function before the installation and after to verify that we get the new code. At some points in installations, R's databases of functions can lose track. Restarting R usually fixes this, so if it doesn't appear to work at this stage, first try using detach() again, and if that doesn't work, try restarting R.

In *step 3*, we specify a pull request from which to install. This likely represents very experimental code that the package maintainers haven't yet incorporated into their package, but when you need the bleeding edge code, this is the way to get it. Here, #1 indicates the number of the specific pull request to get, which provides the function_from_PR function. Again, we test it before and after installation.

In *step 4*, we clean up. The installation and uninstallation of packages can confuse R. If you've used library() at any point, then the code will be in memory and needs to be removed – that's what the detach function does. Then, we actually remove the package from the disk.

In *step 5*, we bring the package back to parity and install the full version, which is good for all the other recipes in this book.

There's more...

This recipe concentrates on installing source packages from GitHub, but there are related functions for other version control systems:

- `install_gitlab()` from GitLab
- `install_bitbucket()` from Bitbucket
- `install_url()` from an arbitrary URL
- `install_git()` and `install_svn()` from an arbitrary Git or SVN repository
- `install_local()` from a local file on disk
- `install_version()` from a specific version on CRAN

Setting up your machine for the compilation of source packages

Compilation of source code is the process of converting human-readable code into machine-readable code that can be executed by a computer. It varies on different chips and operating systems because the machine code that is produced must be specific to the architecture of the target platform. A compiler is a program that performs the compilation process.

Some R packages are written in C or Fortran because they are low-level programming languages that can execute faster than R in certain situations. Additionally, C code can be easily integrated into R packages, allowing for faster computations and improved performance. To take advantage of the better performance, some R packages from the source will need to have their foreign language parts compiled. In this brief recipe, we'll look at tricks and shims for installing code that must be compiled on various platforms.

Getting ready

We don't need anything specific prior to this recipe, as we assume a machine that is not already prepped for compilation.

How to do it...

The steps here sometimes refer to different operating systems; not everything is applicable to all computers. I've marked the operating system that each is designed to be used for:

1. To set it up for Windows, find and install the correct version of `Rtools.exe`. We can get it from `https://cran.r-project.org/bin/windows/Rtools/`, (see *Figure 1.5* and *Figure 1.6*).

The console might look like this:

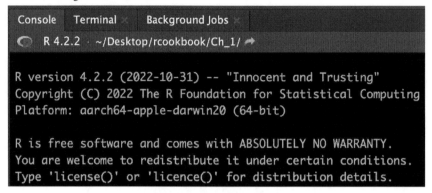

Figure 1.5 – The console in Rstudio; the version number appears on the first line at startup

The web page is a bit spartan and looks like this:

RTools: Toolchains for building R and R packages from source on Windows

Choose your version of Rtools:

RTools 4.3   for R versions from 4.3.0 (R-devel)
RTools 4.2   for R versions 4.2.x (R-release)
RTools 4.0   for R from version 4.0.0 to 4.1.3
old versions of
RTools   for R versions prior to 4.0.0

Figure 1.6 – The web page for RTools; select the right version for your R

2. For macOS, install `xcode command line tools`, in the macOS terminal type:

```
xcode-select --install
```

3. Next, select **Install** in the box that appears:

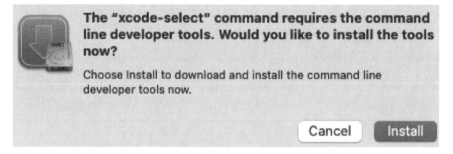

Figure 1.7 – The Xcode install dialog box; confirm the installation to proceed

The following are some further instructions for Apple Silicon machines.

4. Download and install the `gfortran` library in the macOS Terminal:

```
curl -LO https://mac.r-project.org/tools/gfortran-12.0.1-
20220312-is-darwin20-arm64.tar.xz

'sudo tar xvf gfortran-12.0.1-20220312-is-darwin20-arm64.tar.xz
-C /
'

sudo ln -sfn $(xcrun --show-sdk-path) /opt/R/arm64/gfortran/SDK
```

5. Download and unpack OpenMP:

```
wget https://mac.r-project.org/openmp/openmp-12.0.1-darwin20-
Release.tar.gz
'sudo tar xvf openmp-12.0.1-darwin20-Release.tar.gz -C /
```

6. Update some local variables.

    Add the following lines to `"/Users/your_username/.R/Makevars"`, which you should create if it doesn't exist, and make sure you replace `your_username` with your username!

```
CPPFLAGS+=-I/usr/local/include -Xclang -fopenmp
'

LDFLAGS+=-L/usr/local/lib -lomp
'

FC=/opt/R/arm64/gfortran/bin/gfortran -mtune=native
'

FLIBS=-L/opt/R/arm64/gfortran/lib/gcc/aarch64-apple-
darwin20.6.0/12.0.1 -L/opt/R/arm64/gfortran/lib -lgfortran
-lemutls_w -lm
```

These configuration-heavy steps should be what you need to make your computer ready to compile packages. So much for macOS being easier than Windows!

How it works...

Step 1 is a Windows-specific step and it's the only step we need to get the full toolchain for Windows. We simply download and run an installer for the RTools program. Make note of the version of R that you are running and match the version of RTools to it (see *Figure 1.5 and Figure 1.6*). You can see the R version in the console at the start of a new session or at the top of the **Console** window in RStudio.

Step 2 is a general step for macOS machines. `xcode-select` installs a set of tools for development on macOS, and there's a good chance you already have it. If not, go ahead and install it as in *Figure 1.7*.

Step 3 is the first of the steps particular to machines with M1 or M2 Apple Silicon processors. The Apple Silicon `xcode` toolchain lacks a Fortran compiler and some other libraries at the time of writing, and these steps put them in. Here, we download, unpack, and link the compiler using `sudo` for root permissions.

Step 4 is similar in that we download and unpack OpenMP, and *step 5* sets Bash variables that R will load from the `Makevars` script on startup so that it uses the tools correctly.

See also

Naturally, hyperlinks will date and become obsolete over time and toolchains will update; though the links in the recipe are correct at the time of writing, you can check here for changes in the future: `https://mac.r-project.org/`.

Using the renv package to create a project-specific set of packages

In the context of software development, an environment refers to a specific set of dependencies and software versions that is used to run a particular application or project. They are useful for avoiding conflicts between different projects that may require different versions of the same package, and for ensuring that the application runs consistently across different development, test, and production environments. The `renv` R package is a dependency management tool for R projects. It allows the user to create a snapshot of the packages and versions used in a project so that others can easily reproduce the same environment. It also helps in keeping the package's version consistent across different machines and different team members working on the same project. It can help to avoid package version conflicts and can also help in maintaining the reproducibility of the project results. It is particularly useful for managing complex projects with many dependencies. In effect, `renv` creates a custom library in a subdirectory of the current project – called `renv` – and all packages are installed here. `renv` also provides a series of shims for common functions such as `[install-packages()]{custom-style="P - Code"}`, which modifies their behavior such that they interact nicely with the new custom library. In this recipe, we'll look at the `renv` workflow.

Getting ready

We just need the `renv` and `devtools` packages for this recipe.

How to do it...

We follow a series of steps that create a local `renv` package directory and populate that with packages from various sources:

1. Initialize a `project-local` subdirectory:

    ```
    renv::init()
    ```

2. We'll install the common `ggplot2` and `dplyr` packages from the usual CRAN repository:

    ```
    install.packages(c("ggplot2", "dplyr"))
    ```

3. Take a snapshot to save the environment status:

    ```
    renv::snapshot()
    ```

4. Install some development packages:

    ```
    devtools::install_github(
    "danmaclean/rbioinfcookbook@example_devtools_branch"
    )
    ```

5. Decide that the development package wasn't the version you wanted; you want to roll the environment to how it looked at the last snapshot:

    ```
    renv::restore()
    ```

And that is the simple but effective way to manage packages in a `renv` environment.

How it works...

In *step 1*, we create a new environment; in actuality, this creates a number of files and a directory in the current working directory. The `renv` directory is where the packages will be stored. A `renv.lock` file contains a snapshot of the packages – an explicit list of what you want to be installed. The `.Rprofile` file contains commands to activate `renv` on starting the project and a `.gitignore` is created to keep the packages themselves out of your Git repository.

Step 2 is a typical `install.package()` step, but if you are working in RStudio interactively, you may see from the auto-complete that this function is no longer provided by the `base` package, but rather by the `renv` package; `renv` has shimmed this function to add extra functionality.

With *step 3*, we take an explicit snapshot, saving the names and versions of currently installed packages at this point into `renv.lock` such that we can use the list in the file to recreate our environment later, which is especially useful if some package or packages mess things up.

In *step 4*, we install a development package that is suboptimal and that we eventually don't want.

So in *step 5*, we resort to restoring the entire set of packages from the lock file to get to the state we had in *step 3* painlessly.

There's more...

For maximum use across developers, machines, and even just time, `renv.lock`, `.Rprofile`, and `.gitignore` should be committed to version control. Another useful function is `renv::dependencies()`, which will crawl your R files and look for package names, returning a list. Should you need to know what is currently used at the top level, there is `renv::hydrate()`, which will find the R packages used within a project and then install them into the active environment, giving preference to versions already on the system to avoid downloading new stuff.

Installing and managing different versions of Bioconductor packages in environments

Bioconductor is an open source project that provides a collection of R packages for the analysis and comprehension of genomic data. It is focused on the needs of the bioinformatics and computational biology communities. The packages in Bioconductor cover a wide range of topics, including data representation and management, preprocessing and normalization, statistical analysis, and visualization of high-throughput genomic data. Bioconductor exists as a project distinct from R because it addresses the specific needs of the bioinformatics community, and requires different data structures, analysis methods, and visualization techniques to other fields. A user might choose Bioconductor tools because they are specifically designed for the analysis of genomic data and are often more specialized than general-purpose R packages. Bioconductor usually comes with its own installer, but there are other ways to work with specific versions in specific environments, which is what we'll look at in this recipe.

Getting ready

For this quick recipe, we will need the `renv` package.

How to do it...

The use of `renv` for Bioconductor goes as follows:

1. Set up the new environment:

    ```
    renv::init(bioconductor = TRUE)
    'renv::install("Biostrings")
    ```

2. Set up to specify a particular version of Bioconductor:

    ```
    renv::init(bioconductor = "3.15")
    'renv::install("SummarizedExperiment")
    ```

3. Explicitly tell the installer to use Bioconductor at installation, not initialization:

```
renv::install("bioc::ComplexHeatmap")
```

And that is that: declare to `renv` which Bioconductor version you want, and away you go.

How it works...

In *step 1*, we use `renv::init` to initialize the new environment but prime it with the argument to look up Bioconductor repos as well as the standard CRAN ones, so that the `install` step finds the right package.

Step 2 replicates *step 1*, but with an explicit version of Bioconductor, allowing us to specify which version we wish to use. Bioconductor versions are often tied to R versions.

Step 3 tells `renv::install()` to install from Bioconductor using the `bioc::` tag structure. This form can be useful when a project has been initialized without explicitly asking for Bioconductor.

Using bioconda to install external tools

Using environments for packages in R is extremely useful for managing different versions for different projects. Bioinformatics pipelines often have numerous dependencies outside of R, including binary command-line programs and packages from other languages, and it can often be useful to put those under the same sort of management. Tools for that do exist.

Anaconda is a distribution of Python and R that is particularly popular for scientific computing, data science, and machine learning. It includes a large number of pre-installed packages and tools, such as NumPy, SciPy, and Jupyter, making it easy to get started with those technologies. Anaconda also includes the `conda` package manager, which can be used to install additional packages and manage environments. Bioconda is a distribution of bioinformatics software built on top of `conda`. It includes a wide variety of bioinformatics tools and libraries, making it easy to install and manage those tools in a consistent and reproducible way.

These tools make it easy to install and manage software dependencies and provide a consistent and reproducible way to install and manage software, which is important for reproducible research and collaboration.

In this recipe, we'll look at how to create and use software in environments.

swGetting ready

We'll need an installation of `conda` from `https://docs.conda.io/projects/conda/en/latest/user-guide/install/index.html`. Note there are two versions: Anaconda, which gives you all the packages and takes up about 3 GB of disk space, and Miniconda, which takes about 400 MB of disk space. Either will be fine so choose the one that fits well for you. Note that there is a version for commercial users that you'll need to look at if that applies to you (see `https://www.anaconda.com/blog/anaconda-commercial-edition-faq`). We'll also need the R package, `reticulate`.

How to do it...

We'll start this recipe in the command line to set up `conda` and install software into a specific environment, then move into R to run the installed programs from our selected environment:

1. Connect `conda` to the `bioconda` channel at the command line (not the R console):

    ```
    conda config --add channels defaults
    conda config --add channels bioconda
    conda config --add channels conda-forge
    conda config --set channel_priority strict
    ```

2. Create and activate a new environment into which we can install external binaries, again in the command line:

    ```
    conda create --name bioinformatics_project
    conda activate bioinformatics_project
    ```

3. Install the bioinformatics tools:

    ```
    conda install minimap2 gatk samtools==1.15.1
    ```

4. Get the path to the installed binary program in an R script:

    ```
    env_path <- function(env, program = "") {

      df <- reticulate::conda_list()
      b <- df$python[which(df$name == env)]

      if (length(b) == 0) {
        stop("no environment with that name found")
      }

      file.path(dirname(b), program)
    }
    ```

```
'
'minimap2 <- env_path("bioinformatics_project", "minimap2")
'
'system(paste(minimap2, "-h"))
```

With that, we can install `conda` as a package manager, set up the `bioconda` channel to find tools from the bioinformatics community, and run them from within R.

How it works...

Step 1 is done on the command line, not the R console, and the commands configure our new `conda` installation to use `bioconda` as one of its sources for packages. `bioconda` is a community-maintained project outside of Anaconda. The commands here add the channels and prioritize them appropriately.

Step 2 creates a new environment called `bioinformatics_project` and then activates it – that is, makes all subsequent commands operate within that environment. You may see your Terminal prompt change to reflect the change.

Step 3 is an `install` step. We use the command to install three common programs (`minimap2`, `GATK`, and `samtools`) into our new environment. These particular versions will only be accessible when we are inside this environment. Note that `minimap2` and `GATK` are the latest default versions, whereas `samtools` is a specific numbered version.

In *step 4*, we are back in R. We define a custom function that will take an environment name and, optionally, a program name, and return the full path to the environment's `bin` directory or, if a program was specified, the full path to that. The function uses the `reticulate::conda_list()` function to get the details of the environment we are interested in using. In the example, we get the path to the version of `minimap2` that we installed into `bioinformatics_project` as the `minimap2` variable. We can then use that path in our R code in things such as system calls to run the specific versions of programs.

2

Loading, Tidying, and Cleaning Data in the tidyverse

Cleaning data is a crucial step in the data science process. It involves identifying and correcting errors, inconsistencies, and missing values in the data, as well as formatting and structuring the data in a way that makes it easy to work with. This allows the data to be used effectively for analysis, modeling, and visualization. The R tidyverse is a collection of packages designed for data science and includes tools for data manipulation, visualization, and modeling. The `dplyr` and `tidyr` packages are two of the most widely used packages within the tidyverse for data cleaning. `dplyr` provides a set of functions for efficiently manipulating large datasets, such as filtering, grouping, and summarizing data. `tidyr` is specifically designed for tidying (or restructuring) data, making it easier to work with. It provides functions for reshaping data, such as gathering and spreading columns, and allows for the creation of a consistent structure in the data. This makes it easier to perform data analysis and visualization. Together, these packages provide powerful tools for cleaning and manipulating data in R, making it a popular choice among data scientists. In this chapter, we will look at tools and techniques for preparing data in the tidyverse set of packages. You will learn how to deal with different formats and quickly interconvert them, merge different datasets, and summarize them. You will also learn how to bring data from outside sources not in handy files into your work.

In this chapter, we will cover the following recipes:

- Loading data from files with `readr`
- Tidying a wide format table into a tidy table with `tidyr`
- Tidying a long format table into a tidy table with `tidyr`
- Combining tables using join functions
- Reformatting and extracting existing data into new columns using `stringr`
- Computing new data columns from existing ones and applying arbitrary functions using `mutate()`

- Using `dplyr` to summarize data in large tables
- Using `datapasta` to create R objects from cut-and-paste data

Technical requirements

We will use `renv` to manage packages in a project-specific way. To use `renv` to install packages, you will first need to install the `renv` package. You can do this by running the following commands in your R console:

1. Install `renv`:

    ```
    install.packages("renv")
    ```

2. Create a new `renv` environment:

    ```
    renv::init()
    ```

    This will create a new directory called `.renv` in your current project directory.

3. You can then install packages with the following command:

    ```
    renv::install_packages()
    ```

4. You can also use the `renv` package manager to install `Bioconductor` packages by running the following command:

    ```
    renv::install("bioc::package name")
    ```

5. For example, to install the `Biobase` package, you would run the following command:

    ```
    renv::install("bioc::Biobase")
    ```

6. You can use `renv` to install development packages from GitHub like this:

    ```
    renv::install("user name/repo name")
    ```

7. For example, to install the `danmaclean` user `rbioinfcookbook` package, you would run the following command:

    ```
    renv::install("danmaclean/rbioinfcookbook")
    ```

You can also install multiple packages at once by separating the package names with a comma. `renv` will automatically handle installing any required dependencies for the packages you install.

Under `renv`, all packages will be installed into the local project directory and not the main central library, meaning you can have multiple versions of the same package—a specific one for each project.

All the sample data you need for this package is in the specially created `danmaclean/rbioinfcookbook` data package on GitHub. The data will become available in your project after installing that.

For this chapter, we'll need the following packages:

- Regular packages:

  - `dplyr`

  - `fs`

  - `readr`

  - `tidyr`

  - `stringr`

  - `purrr`

- GitHub:

  - `danmaclean/rbioinfcookbook`

- Custom install:

  - `datapasta`

In addition to these packages, we will also need some R tools such as `conda`; all these will be described when needed.

Further information

The packages that require a custom install procedure will be described in the relevant recipes.

In R, it is normal practice to load a library and use functions directly by name. Although this is great in short interactive sessions, it can cause confusion when many packages are loaded at once and share function names. To clarify which package and function I am using at a given moment, I will occasionally use the `packageName::functionName()` convention.

Sometimes, in the middle of a recipe I'll interrupt the code to dive into some intermediate output or to look at the structure of an object. When that happens, you'll see a code block where each line begins with ## (double hash symbols). Consider the following command:

```
letters[1:5]
```

This will give us the following output:

```
## a b c d e
```

Note that the output lines are prefixed with ##.

Loading data from files with readr

The readr R package is a package that provides functions for reading and writing tabular data in a variety of formats, including **comma-separated values (CSV)**, **tab-separated values (TSV)**, and delimiter-separated files. It is designed to be flexible and stop helpfully when data changes or unexpected items appear in the input. The two main advantages over base R functions include consistency in interface and output and the ability to be explicit about types and inspect those types.

This latter advantage can help to avoid errors when reading data, as well as make data cleaning and manipulation easier. readr functions can also automatically infer the data types of each column, which can be useful for a preliminary inspection of large datasets or when the data types are not known.

Consistency in interface and output is one of the main advantages of readr functions. readr functions provide a consistent interface for reading different types of data, which can make it easier to work with multiple types of files. For example, the read_csv() function can be used to read CSV files, while the read_tsv() function can be used to read TSV files. Additionally, readr functions return a tibble, a modern version of a data frame that is more consistent in its output and easier to read than the base R data frame.

Getting ready

For this recipe, we'll need the readr and rbioinfcookbook packages. The latter contains a census_2021.csv file that carries UK census data from 2021, from the UK Office for National Statistics (https://www.ons.gov.uk/). You will need to inspect it, especially its header, to understand the process in this recipe. The first step shows you how to find where the file is on your filesystem.

Note the delimiters in the file are commas (,) and that the first seven lines contain metadata that isn't part of the main data. Also, look at the messy column headings and note that the numbers themselves are internally delimited by commas.

How to do it...

We begin by getting a filename for the sample in the package:

1. Load the package and get a filename:

```
library(readr)
filename <- fs::path_package("extdata",
                             "census_2021.csv",
                             package="rbioinfcookbook"
                             )
```

2. Specify a vector of new names for columns:

```
col_names = c(
            c("area_code", "country", "region",
              "area_name", "all_persons", "under_4"),
            paste0(
seq(5, 85, by = 5),
"_to_",
seq(9, 89, by =5)),c("over_90")
)
```

3. Set the column types based on new names and contents:

```
col_types = cols(
   area_code = col_character(),
   country = col_factor(levels = c("England", "Wales")),
   region = col_factor(levels = c("North East",
                                  "Yorkshire Humber",
                                  "East Midlands",
                                  "West Midlands",
                                  "East of
England",                                          "London",
                                  "South East",
                                  "South West",
                                  "Wales"), ordered = TRUE
                      ),
   area_name = col_character(),
   .default = col_number()
)
```

4. Put it together and read the file:

```
df <- read_csv(filename,
                skip = 8,
                col_names = col_names,
                col_types = col_types )
```

And with that, we've loaded in a file with careful checking of the data types.

How it works...

Step 1 loads the library(readr) package. This package contains functions for reading and writing tabular data in a variety of formats, including CSV. The fs::path_package("extdata", "census_2021.csv", package="rbioinfcookbook") function is used to create a file path to the census_2021.csv file. It simply finds the place where the rbioinfcookbook package was installed and looks inside the `extdata` directory for the file, then it returns the full file path that leads to the file. Quite often, we would see the `system.file()` function used for this purpose. `system.file()` is a fine choice when everything works, but when it can't find the file, it returns a blank string, which can be hard to debug. `fs::path_package()` is nicer to work with and will return an error when it can't find the file.

In *step 2*, a vector of new column names is specified by the code. The vector contains several strings for the first few column names, and then a sequence of strings is created and a long list of age-related columns is created by concatenating two sequences of numbers. The resulting vector is stored in the `col_names` variable.

In *step 3*, we specify the R type we want each column to be. The categorical columns are set explicitly to factors, with the region being ordered explicitly in a rough geographical northeast to southwest way. The `area_name` column contains over 300 names, so we won't make them an explicit factor and stick with it as a general text containing character type. The rest of the columns contain numeric data, so we make that the default with `.default`.

Finally, the `read_csv()` function is used to read the file specified in *step 1* and create a data frame. The `skip` argument is used to skip the first eight rows, which include the metadata in the file and the messy header, the `col_names` argument is used to specify the new column names stored in `col_names`, and the `col_types` argument is used to specify the column types stored in `col_types`.

There's more...

We used the `read_csv()` function for comma-separated data, but many more functions are available for different delimiters:

Function	Delimiter
read_csv()	CSV
read_tsv()	TSV
read_delim()	User-specified delimited files
read_fwf()	Fixed-width files
read_table()	Whitespace-separated files
read_log()	Web log files

Table 2.1 – Parser functions and the type of input file delimiter they work on in readr

For different local conventions on—for example—decimal separators and grouping marks, you can use the locale functions.

See also

The data.table package has a similar aim to readr and is especially good for very large data frames where compute speed is important.

Tidying a wide format table into a tidy table with tidyr

The tidyr package in R is a package that provides tools for tidying and reshaping data. It is designed to make it easy to work with data in a consistent and structured format, which is known as a *tidy* format. Tidy data is a standard way of organizing data that makes it easy to perform data analysis and visualization.

The main principles of tidy data are as follows:

- Each variable forms a column
- Each observation forms a row
- Each type of observational unit forms a table

Data in a tidy format is easier to work with because the structure of the data is consistent, facilitating operations such as filtering, grouping, and reshaping the data. Tidy data is also more compatible with various data visualization and analysis tools, such as ggplot2, dplyr, and other tidyverse packages.

Our aim in this recipe will be to take a wide format data frame where a lot of information is hiding in column names and squeeze and reformat them into a data column of their own and rationalize them in the process.

Getting ready

We'll need the rbioinfcookbook and tidyr packages. We'll use the finished output from *recipe 1*, which is saved in the package.

How to do it...

We have to use just one function, but the options are many.

Specify the transformation to the table:

```
library(rbioinfcookbook)
library(dplyr)
library(tidyr)

long_df <- census_df |>
  rename("0_to_4" = "under_4", "90_to_120" = "over_90") |>
  pivot_longer(
```

```
    cols = contains("_to_"),
    names_to = c("age_from", "age_to"),
    names_pattern = "(.*)_to_(.*)",
    names_transform = list("age_from" = as.integer,
                           age.to = as.integer),
    values_to = "count"
)
```

And that's it. This short recipe is very dense, though.

How it works...

The `tidyr` package has functions that work by allowing the user to specify a particular transformation that will be applied to the data frame to generate a new one. In this single step, we specify a table row-count increasing operation that will find all the columns that contain age information. Next, we split the title of that column into data for two new columns—one for the lower boundary of the age category and one for the upper boundary of the age category. Then, we change the type of those new columns to integer and, lastly, put the actual counts in a new column.

The first function in this pipeline is code from `dplyr`, which helps us rename column headings. Our age data column names are largely consistent, except for the lower bound and the upper one, so we rename those columns to match the pattern of the others, simplifying the transform specification.

The `pivot_longer()` function specifies the transform in the arguments, with the `cols` argument we choose to operate on any columns containing the text `to`. The `names_pattern` argument takes a **regular expression (regex)** that captures the bits of text before and after the `to` string in the column names and uses them as values for the columns defined in the `names_to` argument. The actual counts from the cell are put into a new column called `counts`. The transformation is then applied in one step and reduces the data frames column count to eight, increasing the row count to 6,935, and in the process making the data tidy and easier to use in downstream packages.

See also

The recipe uses a regex to describe a pattern in text. If you haven't seen these before and need a primer, try typing `?"regular expression"` to view the R help on the topic.

Tidying a long format table into a tidy table with tidyr

In this recipe, we look at the complementary operation to that of the *Tidying a wide format table into a tidy table with tidyr* recipe. We'll take a long table and split one of its columns out to make multiple new columns. Initially, this might seem like we're now violating our tidy data frame requirement, but we do occasionally come across data frames that have more than one variable squeezed into a single column. As in the previous recipe, `tidyr` has a specification-based function to allow us to correct our data frame.

Getting ready

We'll use the `tidyr` package and the `treatment` data frame in the `rbioinfcookbook` package. This data frame has four columns, one of which—`measurement`—has got two variable names in it that need splitting into columns of their own.

How to do it...

In stark contrast to the *Tidying a wide format table into a tidy table with tidyr* recipe, this expression is extremely terse; we can tidy the wide table very easily:

```
library(rbioinfcookbook)
library(tidyr)

treatments |>
  pivot_wider(
    names_from = measurement,
    values_from = value
  )
```

This is so simple because all the data we need is already in the data frame.

How it works...

In this very simple-looking recipe, the specification is gloriously clear: simply take the `measurement` column and create new column names from its values, moving the value appropriately. The `names_from` argument specifies the column to split, and `values_from` specifies where its values come from.

There's more...

It is quite possible to incorporate values from more than one column at a time; just pass a vector of columns to the `names_from` argument, and you can format the computed column names in the output with `names_glue`.

Combining tables using join functions

Joining rectangular tables in data science is a powerful way to combine data from multiple sources, allowing for more complex and detailed analysis. The process of joining tables involves matching rows from one table with corresponding rows in another table, based on shared columns or keys. The ability to join tables allows data scientists to gather information from different sources and can also be used to clean and prepare data for analysis by eliminating duplicates or filling in missing values. Note that although the joining process is powerful and useful, it isn't magic and is actually a common source of errors. The user must take care that the operation was successful in the way that they intended and that combining data doesn't create unexpected combinations, especially empty cells and repeated rows.

The `dplyr` package provides functions for manipulating and cleaning data, including a function called `join()` that can be used to join tables based on one or more common columns. The `join()` function supports several types of joins, including inner, left, right, and full outer joins. In this recipe, we'll look at how each of these joins works.

Getting ready

We'll need the `dplyr` package and the `rbioinfcookbook` package, which will give us a short gene expression dataset of just 10 *Magnaporthe oryzae* genes, and related annotation data of approximately 60,000 rows for the entire genome.

How to do it...

The process will begin with loading a data frame from the data package. The `mo_gene_exp`, `mo_go_acc`, and `mo_go_evidence` objects are all available as data objects when you load the `rbioinfcookbook` library, so we don't have to try to load them from the file. You will have seen this behavior in numerous R tutorials before. For our work, this mimics the situation where you will already have gone through the process of loading in the data from a file on disk or received a data frame from an upstream function.

The following will help us to join tables together:

1. Load the data and add terms to genes:

    ```
    library(rbioinfcookbook)
    library(dplyr)

    x <- left_join(mo_gene_exp, mo_terms, by = c('gene_id' = 'Gene
    stable ID'))
    ```

2. Add accession numbers:

    ```
    y <- right_join(mo_go_acc, x, by = c( 'Gene stable ID' = 'gene_
    id' ) )
    ```

3. Add evidence code:

    ```
    z <- inner_join(y, mo_go_evidence, by = c('GO term accession' =
    'GO term evidence code'))
    ```

4. Compare the direction of joins:

    ```
    a <- right_join(x, mo_go_acc, by = c( 'gene_id' = 'Gene stable
    ID') )
    ```

5. Stack two data frames:

```
mol_func <- filter(mo_go_evidence, `GO domain` == 'molecular_
function')
cell_comp <- filter(mo_go_evidence, `GO domain` == 'cellular_
component')

bind_rows(mol_func, cell_comp)
```

6. Put two data frames side by side:

```
small_mol_func <- head(mol_func, 15)
small_cell_comp <- head(cell_comp, 15)
bind_cols(small_mol_func, small_cell_comp)
```

And with that, we have joined data frames into one in most ways possible.

How it works...

The code joins different data frames in various ways. The mo_gene_exp, mo_terms, mo_go_acc, and mo_go_evidence objects are data frames, and they are loaded using the rbioinfcookbook library. Then, the first operation is to add terms to genes using the left_join() function. The left_join() function joins the mo_gene_exp and mo_terms data frames on the gene_id column of the mo_gene_exp data frame and the Gene stable ID column of the mo_terms data frame. Note the increase in rows as well as columns because of the multiple matching rows.

By *step 2*, we're adding accession numbers using the right_join() function to join the mo_go_acc data frame and the result of the first join (x) on the Gene stable ID column of the mo_go_acc data frame and the gene_id column of the x data frame. Ordering the data frames this way minimizes the number of rows; see *step 5* for how the converse goes. Note that the right_join() function returns the full set of rows from the right data frame.

Step 3's inner_join() function demonstrates that only the rows shared are returned. The remaining steps create subsets of the mo_go_evidence data frame based on the component to highlight how bind_rows() does a name-unaware stacking and bind_cols() does a blind left-right paste/concatenation of data frames. These last two functions are quick and easy but do not do anything clever, so be sure that the data can be properly joined this way.

Reformatting and extracting existing data into new columns using stringr

Text manipulation is important in bioinformatics as it allows, among other things, for efficient processing and analysis of DNA and protein sequence annotation data. The R `stringr` package is a good choice for text manipulation because it provides a simple and consistent interface for common string operations, such as pattern matching and string replacement. `stringr` is built on top of the powerful `stringi` manipulation library, making it a fast and efficient tool for working with arbitrary strings. In this recipe, we'll look at rationalizing data held in messy **FAST-All** (**FASTA**)-style sequence headers.

Getting ready

We'll use the *Arabidopsis* gene names in the `ath_seq_names` vector provided by the `rbioinfcookbook` package and the `stringr` package.

How to do it...

To reformat gene names using `stringr`, we can proceed as follows:

1. Capture the ATxGxxxxx format IDs:

```
library(rbioinfcookbook)
library(stringr)

ids <- str_extract(ath_seq_names, "^AT\\dG.*\\.\\d")
```

2. Separate the string into elements and extract the description:

```
description <- str_split(ath_seq_names, "\\|", simplify = TRUE)
[,3] |>
  str_trim()
```

3. Separate the string into elements and extract the gene information:

```
info <- str_split(ath_seq_names, "\\|", simplify = TRUE)[,4] |>
  str_trim()
```

4. Match and recall the chromosome and coordinates:

```
chr <- str_match(info, "chr(\\d):(\\d+)-(\\d+)")
```

5. Find the number of characters the strand information begins at and use that as an index:

```
strand_pos <- str_locate(info, "[FORWARD|REVERSE]")
strand <- str_sub(info, start=strand_pos, end=strand_pos+1)
```

6. Extract the length information:

```
lengths <- str_match(info, "LENGTH=(\\d+)$")[,2]
```

7. Combine all captured information into a data frame:

```
results <- data.frame(
    ids = ids,
    description = description,
    chromosome = as.integer(chr[,2]),
    start = as.integer(chr[,3]),
    end = as.integer(chr[,4]),
    strand = strand,
    length = as.integer(lengths)
)
```

And that gives us a very nice, reformatted data frame.

How it works...

The R code uses the `stringr` library to extract, split, and manipulate information from a vector of sequence names (`ath_seq_names`) and assigns the resulting information to different variables. The `rbioinfcookbook` library provides the initial `ath_seq_names` vector.

The first step of the recipe uses the `str_extract()` function from `stringr` to extract a specific pattern of characters. The `"^AT\dG.*.\d"` regex matches any string that starts with `"AT"`, followed by one digit, then `"G"`, then any number of characters, then a dot, and finally one digit. `stringr` operations are vectorized so that all entries in them are processed.

Steps 2 and *3* are similar and use the `str_split()` function to split the seq_names vector by the `"|"` character; the `simplify` option returns a matrix of results with a column for each substring. The `str_trim()` function removes troublesome leading and trailing whitespace from the resulting substring. The third and fourth columns of the resulting matrix are saved.

The following line of code uses the `str_match()` function to extract specific substrings from the `info` variable that match the `"chr(\d):(\d+)-(\d+)"` regex. This regex matches any string that starts with `"chr"`, followed by one digit, then `":"`, then one or more digits, then `"-"`, and finally one or more digits. The `'()'` bracket symbols mark the piece of text to save; each saved piece goes into a column in the matrix.

The next line of code uses the `str_locate()` function to find the position of the first occurrence of either FORWARD or REVERSE in the `info` variable. The resulting position is then used to extract the character at that position using `str_sub()`. The last line of code uses the `str_match()` function to extract the substring that starts with `"LENGTH="` and ends with one or more digits from the `info` variable.

Finally, the code creates a data frame result by combining the extracted and subsetted variables, assigning appropriate types for each column.

Computing new data columns from existing ones and applying arbitrary functions using mutate()

Data frames are the core data structure in R for storing and manipulating tabular data. They are similar to a table in a relational database or a spreadsheet, with rows representing observations and columns representing variables. The `mutate()` function in `dplyr` is used to add new columns to a data frame by applying a function or calculation to existing columns; it can be used on both data frames and nested datasets. A nested dataset is a data structure that contains multiple levels of information, such as lists or data frames within data frames.

Getting ready

In this recipe, we'll use a very small data frame that will be created in the recipe and the `dplyr`, `tidyr`, and `purrr` packages.

How to do it...

The functionality offered by the `mutate()` pattern is exemplified in the following steps:

1. Add some new columns:

    ```
    library(dplyr)

    df <- data.frame(gene_id = c("gene1", "gene2", "gene3"),
                     tissue1 = c(5.1, 7.3, 8.2),
                     tissue2 = c(4.8, 6.1, 9.5))


    df <- df |> mutate(log2_tissue1 = log2(tissue1),
                       log2_tissue2 = log2(tissue2))
    ```

2. Conditionally operate on columns:

    ```
    df |> mutate_if(is.numeric, log2)
    df |> mutate_at(vars(starts_with("tissue")), log2)
    ```

3. Operate across columns:

    ```
    library(dplyr)

    df <- data.frame(gene_id = c("gene1", "gene2", "gene3"),
    ```

```
                          tissue1 = c(5.1, 7.3, 8.2),
                          tissue2 = c(4.8, 6.1, 9.5),
                          tissue3 = c(8.5, 12.5, 6.5))


df <- df |>
  rowwise() |>
  mutate(mean = mean(c(tissue1, tissue2, tissue3)),
         stddev = sd(c(tissue1, tissue2, tissue3))
         )
```

4. Operate on nested data:

```
df <- data.frame(gene_id = c("gene1", "gene2", "gene3"),
                 tissue1_value = c(5.1, 7.3, 8.2),
                 tissue1_pvalue = c(0.01, 0.05, 0.001),
                 tissue2_value = c(4.8, 6.1, 9.5),
                 tissue2_pvalue = c(0.03, 0.04, 0.001)
                 ) |>
       tidyr::nest(-gene_id, .key = "tissue")

df <- df |> mutate(tissue = purrr::map(tissue, ~ mutate(.x,
value_log2 = log2(.[1]),pvalue_log2 = log2(.[2])) ))
```

These are the various ways we can work with mutate() on different data frames to different ends.

How it works...

In *step 1*, we start by creating a data frame containing three genes, with columns representing the values of each gene. Then, we use the [mutate(){custom-style='P - Code'} function in its most basic form to apply the log2 transformation of the values into new columns.

In *step 2*, we apply the transformation conditionally with mutate_if(), which applies the specified function to all columns that match the specified condition (in this case, is.numeric), and mutate_at() to apply the log2 function to all columns that start with the name tissue.

In *step 3*, we create a bigger data frame of expression data and then use the rowwise() function in conjunction with mutate() to add two new columns, mean and stddev, which contain the mean and standard deviation of the expression values across all three tissues for each gene. If we just use mutate() on the vector, the function will be applied to the entire column instead of the rows. As we need to calculate the mean and standard deviation of the expression values across all tissues, this would be difficult to achieve just by using mutate() on vectors in the standard column-wise fashion.

Finally, we look at using `mutate()` in nested data frames. We begin by creating a data frame of genes and expression values and use the `nest()` function to create a nested data frame. We can then use the combination of `mutate()` and `map()` functions from the `purrr` package, to extract the `tissue1_value` and `tissue2_value` columns from the nested part of the data frame.

Using dplyr to summarize data in large tables

Split-apply-combine is a technique used in data science to analyze and manipulate large datasets by breaking them down into smaller, more manageable pieces, applying a function or operation to each piece, and then combining the results. It's a powerful method for working with data because it allows you to process and analyze data in a way that is both efficient and interpretable. The process can be repeated multiple times to gain deeper insights into the data.

In the tidyverse, the `dplyr` package provides a set of tools for implementing the split-apply-combine technique; we'll look at those in this recipe.

Getting ready

We will need the `dplyr` and `tidyr` packages for this recipe.

How to do it...

The functionality of the `dplyr` package for split-apply-combine techniques is shown in the following steps:

1. Create the initial data frame:

```
chromosome_id <- c(1,1,1,2,2,3,3,3)
gene_id <- c("A1","A2","A3","B1","B2","C1","C2","C3")
strand <- c("forward","reverse","forward","forward",
            "reverse","forward","forward","reverse")
length <- c(2000,1500,3000,2500,2000,1000,2000,3000)
genes_df <- data.frame(chromosome_id,gene_id,strand,length)
```

2. Group on a single column:

```
library(dplyr)

genes_df |>
  group_by(chromosome_id) |>
  summarise(total_length = sum(length))
```

3. Group and summarize on multiple columns:

```
genes_df |>
  group_by(chromosome_id, strand) |>
  summarise(
    num_genes = n(),
    avg_length = mean(length)
    )
```

4. Work on a nested data frame:

```
# Create a nested dataframe
chromosome_id <- c(1,1,1,2,2,3,3,3)
gene_id <- c("A1","A2","A3","B1","B2","C1","C2","C3")
strand <- c("forward","reverse","forward","forward","reverse",
"forward","forward","reverse")
length <- c(2000,1500,3000,2500,2000,1000,2000,3000)
genes_df <- data.frame(chromosome_id,gene_id,strand,length)

genes_df$samples <- list(data.frame(sample_id=1:2,
expression=c(2,3)),
                         data.frame(sample_id=1:3,
expression=c(3,4,5)),
                         data.frame(sample_id=1:2,
expression=c(4,5)),
                         data.frame(sample_id=1:3,
expression=c(5,6,7)),
                         data.frame(sample_id=1:2,
expression=c(6,7)),
                         data.frame(sample_id=1:2,
expression=c(1,2)),
                         data.frame(sample_id=1:2,
expression=c(2,3)),
                         data.frame(sample_id=1:2,
expression=c(3,4))
                        )


genes_df |>
  tidyr::unnest() |>
  group_by(chromosome_id,strand) |>
  summarise(mean_expression = mean(expression))
```

These are a broad set of examples for the use of split-apply-combine in `dplyr`.

How it works...

Step 1 explicitly creates a data frame; we do it this way so that we can easily understand its structure.

In *step 2*, we use the method in its simplest form: the `group_by()` function is used to group the rows of a data frame based on the `chromosome_id`, and then we use `summarise()` to return a summary data frame. *Step 3* is similar but shows how multiple grouping columns can be used to create more granular groups and how more than one summary function can be applied.

Step 4 is more complex; the new data frame is a nested data frame, and the `samples` list column contains a data frame of expression data in each cell. When using `group_by()` and `summarise()` functions on a nested data frame, you first need to access the nested data using the `tidyr::unnest()` function, then group and summarize as usual. Note that when using `tidyr::unnest()`, the new data frame will have multiple rows for each gene, one for each sample, so it's important to group the data frame by the columns of interest.

Using datapasta to create R objects from cut-and-paste data

Being able to paste data into source code documents is useful for all sorts of reasons, not least because it allows for a reproducible example, also known as a *reprex*—a minimal, self-containedexample that demonstrates a problem or a concept. By including data in the source code, others can run the code and see the results for themselves, making it easier to understand and replicate the results.

The R `datapasta` package makes it easy to paste data into R source code documents. It provides a set of functions for converting data to and from R definitions and is extremely useful when creating static data objects in code examples, tests, or when sharing. In this recipe, you will learn how to use `datapasta` to bring external data into your source code documents by typing them in longhand.

Getting ready

We will use the `datapasta` package, though installing it is non-standard. Use this command:

```
renv::install("datapasta", repos = c(mm = "https://milesmcbain.r-universe.dev", getOption("repos")))
```

This should install the package using `renv` and make us ready to go. Remember to install `renv` the usual way if you don't already have it.

How to do it...

The `datapasta` tool is implemented as an add-in for RStudio, so we begin by setting that up:

1. Use the RStudio **Tools | Addins | Browse Addins** menu and then **Keyboard Shortcuts**. You get to choose which key combination you want to use for pasting.

2. Click the middle column next to the operations, as shown in the following screenshot, and press the keys you want to use. The combination in *Figure 2.1* is a good choice:

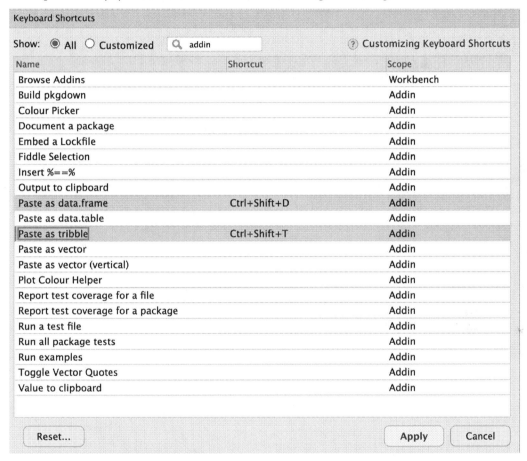

Figure 2.1 – Selecting key shortcuts

3. Get a web table—for example, go to this page on *Wikipedia:* `https://en.wikipedia.org/wiki/Tab-separated_values`—and copy the whole text-based example table using the browser's right-click **Copy** feature. This should put the text table in your copy/paste buffer. It should look like what's shown in *Figure 2.2*:

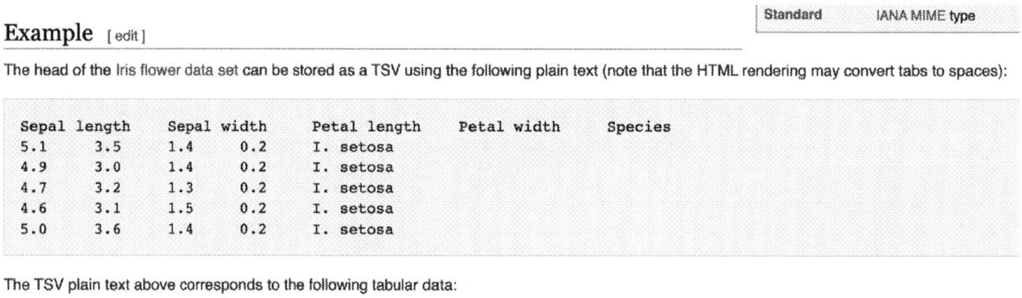

Example [edit]

The head of the Iris flower data set can be stored as a TSV using the following plain text (note that the HTML rendering may convert tabs to spaces):

```
Sepal length    Sepal width     Petal length    Petal width     Species
5.1     3.5     1.4     0.2     I. setosa
4.9     3.0     1.4     0.2     I. setosa
4.7     3.2     1.3     0.2     I. setosa
4.6     3.1     1.5     0.2     I. setosa
5.0     3.6     1.4     0.2     I. setosa
```

The TSV plain text above corresponds to the following tabular data:

Figure 2.2 – Web data on Wikipedia

4. Paste the table now in your copy/paste buffer into an R source document. Place the typing cursor at a suitable place in the source R document you're working in and use the key combo to paste in the table.

So, with the preceding setup, we should be able to quickly take data from varied sources and coerce them into R objects for analysis.

How it works...

The `datapasta` package is really useful. The first step sets up our preferred paste keys for later use; the second step is simple, and we just go somewhere and find some data in the world we would like in our R source; and by the third step, we're selecting the place to put the data definition and pasting it in. Our example goes from a table in a web page to this definition for an R object:

```r
data.frame(
   stringsAsFactors = FALSE,
        Sepal.length = c(5.1, 4.9, 4.7, 4.6, 5),
         Sepal.width = c(3.5, 3, 3.2, 3.1, 3.6),
        Petal.length = c(1.4, 1.4, 1.3, 1.5, 1.4),
         Petal.width = c(0.2, 0.2, 0.2, 0.2, 0.2),
             Species = c("I. setosa","I. setosa",
                         "I. setosa","I. setosa","I. setosa")
)
```

And that powerful little operation is how we can convert web data to source code very easily.

There's more...

It's possible to go the other way around, from some R object to a definition of that object using the `dpasta()` function, which can coerce data frames, tibbles, and vectors into definitions. This is really useful for reproducible examples. This example shows how to actually build the object with code so that we don't have to share the file and everything is in one source document:

```
library(datapasta)
mtcars |>
    dpasta()
```

This shows how the `datapasta` package is a super-useful tool for turning objects from the web and within R into code.

3

ggplot2 and Extensions for Publication Quality Plots

Clear and informative data visualizations are the most important tool that bioinformaticians have to effectively communicate complex data and findings to other scientists in the field. They allow for easy and efficient exploration and understanding of large and complex datasets. The process of creating a good visualization is very iterative, and many drafts of a visualization are discarded before a final one is settled on, so it is important that we have plotting tools that allow for quick and easy plot creation and customization.

ggplot2 is a popular data visualization library in R that provides an elegant solution for bioinformaticians. It is based on the *Grammar of Graphics*, a principle that allows users to easily create complex and customizable visualizations by breaking them down into small, modular components, defined by a consistent interface. These make ggplot2 highly flexible and allow for the creation of a wide variety of visualizations. ggplot2 has been extended in multiple packages, meaning a small ecosystem of ready-to-go visualization types exists that can help us to create more complex and informative visualizations or make them ready for publication through layout and labeling. In this chapter, we'll look at many ways to create publication-ready plots in ggplot2. The data we will use will come from various sources. Sometimes, we will use the palmerpenguins package, which provides measurements of things such as the bill and flipper size of penguins of different species living on different islands off the coast of Antarctica. Other times, we will use gene expression data from the devastating rice pathogen *Magnaporthe oryzae*. All the datasets have the common attribute of being tidy data frames—they have one observation per row and one column per experimental variable being measured. Once loaded, they can all be printed to screen for inspection, should you wish to look at how the structure relates to the plots.

In this chapter, we will cover the following recipes:

- Combining many plot types in `ggplot2`
- Comparing changes in distributions with `ggridges`
- Customizing plots with `ggeasy`
- Highlighting selected values in busy plots with `gghighlight`
- Plotting variability and confidence intervals better with `ggdist`
- Making interactive plots with `plotly`
- Clarifying label placement with `ggrepel`
- Zooming and making callouts from selected plot sections with `facetzoom`
- Composing multiple plots into single plots with `cowplot` and `patchwork`

Technical requirements

We will use `renv` to manage packages in a project-specific way. To use `renv` to install packages, you will first need to install the `renv` package itself. Here's how to install `renv` and then use it to install packages:

1. Run the following command in your R console:

    ```
    install.packages("renv")
    ```

2. Next, you will need to create a new `renv` environment for your project by running the following command:

    ```
    renv::init()
    ```

3. This will create a new directory called `.renv` in your current project directory.

4. You can then install packages with the following command:

    ```
    install.packages("<package name>")
    ```

5. You can also use the `renv` package manager to install Bioconductor packages by running the following command:

    ```
    renv::install("bioc::<package name>")
    ```

6. For example, to install the `Biobase` package, you would run the following command:

    ```
    renv::install("bioc::Biobase")
    ```

7. You can use `renv` to install development packages from GitHub like this:

    ```
    renv::install("<user name>/<repo name>")
    ```

For example, to install the danmaclean user's rbioinfcookbook package, you would run the following command:

```
renv::install("danmaclean/rbioinfocookbook")
```

Some more tips:

- You can also install multiple packages at once by separating the package names with a comma. renv will automatically handle installing any required dependencies for the packages you install.

- Under renv, all packages will be installed into the local project directory and not the main central library, meaning you can have multiple versions of the same package, one specific one for each project.

- All the sample data you need for this package is in the specially created data package on GitHub, danmaclean/rbioinfcookbook. The data will become available in your project after installing that.

For this chapter, we'll need the following packages:

- Regular packages:

  - cowplot

  - dplyr

  - ggdist

  - ggeasy

  - ggforce

  - gghighlight

  - ggplot2

  - ggrepel

  - ggridges

  - palmerpenguins

  - patchwork

  - plotly

- GitHub:

  - danmaclean/rbioinfcookbook

With that, we'll be ready to go. None of the packages should present a particular problem for installation.

Further information

In R, it is normal practice to load a library and use functions directly by name. Although this is great in short interactive sessions, it can cause confusion when many packages are loaded at once and share function names. To clarify which package and function I am using at a given moment, I will occasionally use the `packageName::functionName()` convention.

Sometimes, in the middle of a recipe, I'll interrupt the code to dive into some intermediate output or to look at the structure of an object. When that happens, you'll see a code block where each line begins with ## (double hash symbols). Consider the following command:

```
letters[1:5]
```

This will give us the following output:

```
## a b c d e
```

Note that the output lines are prefixed with ##.

Combining many plot types in ggplot2

The layer model of `ggplot2` is a key feature of the library that allows users to create complex visualizations by building up layers of data, aesthetics, and geoms. Each layer represents a different aspect of the plot, and they are added on top of each other to create the final visualization. In this recipe, we'll use the layer model to create a complex plot of data in the `palmerpenguins` package. It may be helpful to inspect the data in R directly by printing it to the screen. Also, the package is well documented at `https://allisonhorst.github.io/palmerpenguins/`, should you wish to look more into how it was generated.

Getting ready

Install the `ggplot2` and `palmerpenguins` packages.

How to do it...

We can use the layer system to combine multiple plot types as follows:

1. Create the base for the plot:

```
library(ggplot2)
library(palmerpenguins)

p <- ggplot(data = penguins) +
    aes(x = bill_length_mm, y = bill_depth_mm)
```

2. Layer the geoms:

```
p +
  geom_point() +
  geom_smooth(method = "lm") +
  geom_boxplot()
```

3. Order the geoms more helpfully:

```
p +
  geom_boxplot() +
  geom_point() +
  geom_smooth(method = "lm")
```

4. Iterate on new axes:

```
penguins |>
dplyr::filter(!is.na(sex)) |>
ggplot() +
aes(x = species, y = bill_length_mm) +
geom_boxplot(
                position = position_dodge(width = 0.75)
            ) +
geom_dotplot(
                binaxis = 'y',
                stackdir = 'center',
                method = "histodot",
                position = position_dodge(width = 0.75),
                alpha = 0.5,
                dotsize = .5


            )
```

And that is all we need to do for the plot.

How it works...

Step 1 sets up the basic plot object, giving the data and aesthetic layer that form the axes and limits of the eventual plot. The geom layers are not yet added, so viewing this plot (by typing *p*) will show an empty plot with just axes. *Step 2* adds the necessary geoms. Note in *Figure 3.1* how the geoms are layered in the order declared such that the big boxplot completely obscures the rest. We can take control of the order of geoms just by calling them from the bottom up, so in *step 3*, we add the boxplot first and work through the point and smoothed line such that we get a much more visible layering, as seen in *Figure 3.2*:

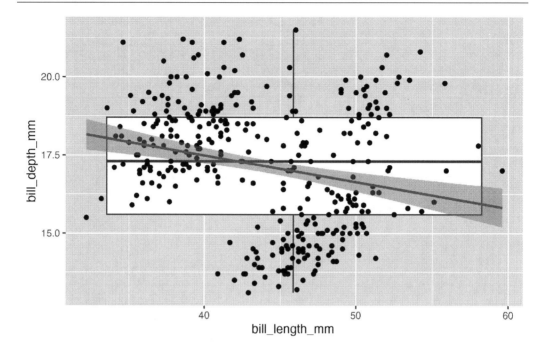

Figure 3.1 – Geoms in layers showing the "bottom-up" render model

The plot itself is of questionable value at this stage and would likely benefit from removing the boxplot and examining the structure in the data caused by other variables such as `species`.

Only geoms that will work with similar data types (that is, discrete or continuous) can be layered effectively in this way, so to look at that extra structure, we restart the base plot in *step 4*. The aesthetic step puts the categoric (discrete) `sex` variable on the *x* axis (and to do so, we must filter out any NA values in the data beforehand) this time. We can now layer geoms per sex and species coloring appropriately using `aes()` to create mappings and `position_dodge(width = 0.75)` to ensure a gap between plot elements. By using layering, we've been able to iterate and stack an informative plot very quickly:

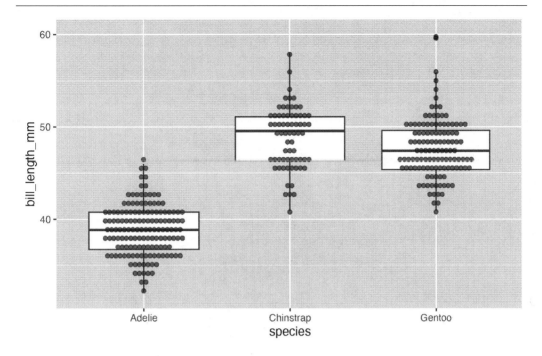

Figure 3.2 – Second iteration with better options and a more reactive layout

And that gives us a plot with many different types combined.

There's more...

The next layer of making `ggplot2` make plots intelligently is to declare mappings between a variable and some visual aspect using an aesthetic, encapsulated in the function called `aes()`. We can use this to map shapes, line colors, fill colors, and point size, among other attributes, to the plot. In our plot, the variable of interest is `species`, so we can add aesthetic mappings to that as follows; note that the global `aes()` for size applies to all geoms, whereas the geom-specific ones apply only within the geom they are declared in.

The following code shows how to do this mapping:

```
penguins |>
  dplyr::filter(!is.na(sex)) |>
  ggplot() +
  aes(x = bill_depth_mm, y = bill_length_mm, size = island) +
  geom_jitter(aes(colour = species)) +
  geom_point(aes(shape = sex), alpha = 0.5 ) +
  scale_colour_brewer(palette = "Set2")
```

The preceding code generates the output shown in *Figure 3.3*:

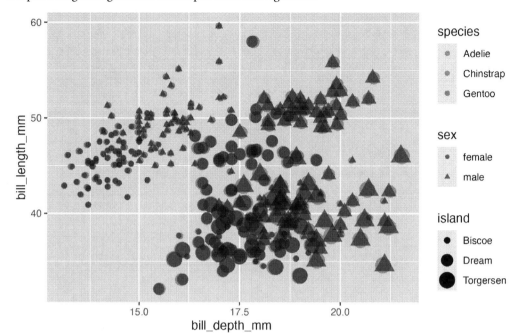

Figure 3.3 – Mapped aesthetics and custom palette

A final modification was done with `scale()` and palettes. In the preceding code, we added a manual color scale with a built-in `ColourBrewer` palette.

Comparing changes in distributions with ggridges

Ridge plots, also known as joyplots, are a visualization tool that allows for the clear comparison of multiple distributions in a single plot. The `ggridges` R package provides an easy-to-use implementation of ridge plots, allowing for the clear comparison of multiple distributions of a single variable by superimposing them on top of each other in a single plot. The package also allows for easy customization of plot features such as color, fill, and theme. The `ggridges` package is particularly useful for comparing the distribution of a single variable across multiple groups or categories. In this recipe, we will look at implementing some useful ridge plots.

Getting ready

We will need the `ggplot2`, `ggridges`, and `palmerpenguins` packages.

How to do it...

We can look at the changes in distributions using the following steps:

1. Plot overlapping distributions:

```
library(ggplot2)
library(ggridges)
library(palmerpenguins)

ggplot(data = penguins) +
        aes(x = bill_length_mm, y = species,
                fill = species,
                color = species) +
                geom_density_ridges(scale = 2,
                        position = "raincloud",
                        alpha = 0.5,
                        jittered_points = TRUE
                        ) +
        theme_ridges()
```

2. Color the peaks with a gradient:

```
ggplot(data = penguins) +
        aes(x = bill_length_mm, y = species,
                fill = stat(x)
                ) +
        geom_density_ridges_gradient(scale = 2,
                        rel_min_height = 0.01,
                        ) +
        theme_ridges()
```

3. Add in quantile markers:

```
ggplot(data = penguins) +
        aes(x = bill_length_mm, y = species,
                fill = factor(stat(quantile))
                ) +
    stat_density_ridges(
        geom = "density_ridges_gradient",
        calc_ecdf = TRUE,
        quantiles = c(0.05, 0.95)
    ) +
    scale_fill_manual(
        name = "Probability",
        values = alpha(c("goldenrod", "gray",
```

```
                         "steelblue"), 0.5),
          labels = c("< 0.05", "0.05 to 0.95", " > 0.95 ")
                         ) +
      theme_ridges()
```

This is all we need to have a nice plot showing differences in the distributions.

How it works...

In *step 1*, we create a basic ridge plot. It's constructed as extra geoms for `ggplot2`, so we build a standard `ggplot` plot description and add the geom to that. The `penguins` plot is set up to show each distribution of bill length against the species and the `geom_density_ridges` geom used to draw the ridge plot. The `position` and `jittered_points` parameters add on the scatter point visualization of the actual points underneath the curve. The `scale` parameter affects the amount of overlap. See *Figure 3.4*:

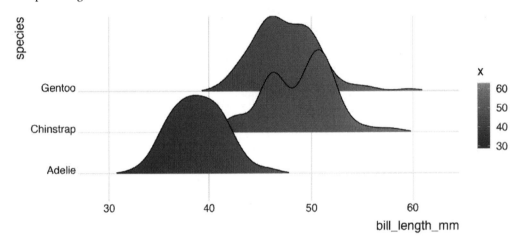

Figure 3.4 – Simple ridge plot

In *step 2*, we create a similar plot colored with a gradient proportional to the bill length. Note that this time, because the fill color must be computed, we must use `stat()` as the fill value and the specific `geom_density_ridges_gradient()` function to handle that. See *Figure 3.5*:

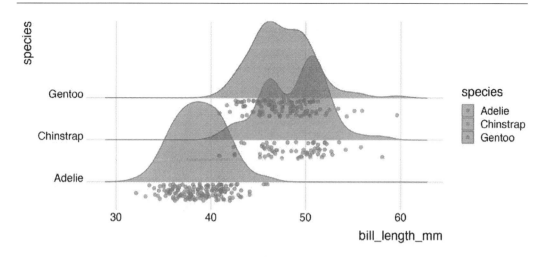

Figure 3.5 – Extending the plot to show points

Finally, in *step 3*, we look at adding quartile intervals into the curves (*Figure 3.6*). This requires that we describe the `fill` parameter as the `factor()` function of the `quantile` stat, which is calculated by the `stat_density_ridges()` function with the given limits in the parameters. The colors are defined and applied by the usual `scale_fill_manual()` function. The `alpha()` function is used here to add a little transparency to the colors as we used named colors. Alternatively, we could use hexadecimal codes here with the alpha channel set on those:

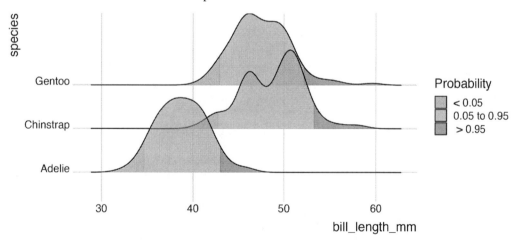

Figure 3.6 – Adding in quartile markers

As we can see, the distributions are now nicely presented and annotated.

Customizing plots with ggeasy

One of the key aspects of customizing plots in ggplot2 is the theme() function, which allows users to customize elements of the plot's overall appearance. Customizing plots in ggplot2 can be a little unintuitive. Although the theme() function is powerful, it does require the user to manually specify each element of the plot, such as axis labels, titles, colors, and shapes. The ggeasy package, built on top of ggplot2, aims to make plot customization more accessible by providing a simpler, more intuitive syntax for many common customization tasks. ggeasy provides a set of simple wrapper functions around theme() that make the important things a lot easier to remember. With this recipe, we'll look at customizing labels, legends, and axes in a plot created initially in ggplot2.

Getting ready

We'll need the ggplot2, ggeasy, and palmerpenguins packages.

How to do it...

We can customize a plot as follows.

Make a base plot:

```
library(ggplot2)
library(ggeasy)
library(palmerpenguins)


p <- penguins |>
  dplyr::filter(!is.na(sex)) |>
  ggplot() +
        aes(x = species, y = bill_length_mm) +
        geom_boxplot(aes(fill = sex),
                            position = position_dodge(width = 0.75)) +
        geom_dotplot(
            aes(fill = sex),
            binaxis = 'y',
            stackdir = 'center',
            method = "histodot",
            position = position_dodge(width = 0.75),
            alpha = 0.5,
            dotsize = .5

        ) +
        theme_minimal()
Customize its appearance
```

```
p +
  easy_legend_at("bottom") +
  easy_labs(title = "Palmer Island Penguin Bill Length",
                  subtitle = "by species and sex",
                  x = "Species", y = "length (mm)") +
  easy_remove_x_axis("title") +
  easy_x_axis_labels_size(18) +
  easy_x_axis_labels_size(18) +
  easy_y_axis_labels_size(14) +
  easy_y_axis_title_size(14) +
  easy_remove_legend_title() +
  easy_plot_legend_size(14)
```

And that is how we add some easy customizations.

How it works...

Step 1 creates a base plot we will go on to modify with ggeasy; the plot is the same one we made in an earlier recipe, layering a dot plot over a boxplot. See *Figure 3.7*:

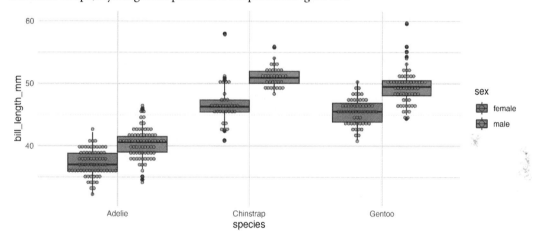

Figure 3.7 – Base plot

The customization part comes with the addition of easy_* functions. With the combination of functions used here and in order used, we move the legend to the bottom to take advantage of the space there and allow the plot to spread. We set the title and subtitle labels and give the axes better-formatted names. Next, we remove the *x* axis title completely because in this case the axis is categorical and the axis is self-describing. Then, we resize the text of all the labels on the axes for greater readability, before removing the self-evident legend title. Finally, we set the size of the legend to take advantage of the greater space left. See *Figure 3.8*:

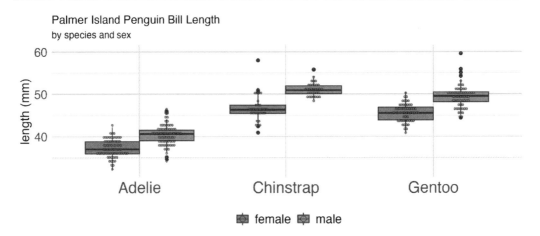

Figure 3.8 – With modified labels

And with that, we have a final plot.

There's more...

If you want to learn which theme() options are being affected by a given easy_* function and the syntax for using it, set the easy_* function argument teach to true, and you'll get a description of what that function is doing.

Highlighting selected values in busy plots with gghighlight

Bioinformatics datasets often comprise measurements of many items. The genomes we analyze have thousands of genes, but usually, we're only interested in the few that respond to particular changes in the experiment we have designed. So, it's of great use to be able to highlight those few in our plots. In this recipe, we'll look at the gghighlight package, which can make that very easy.

Getting ready

We'll need the gghighlight, ggplot2, and rbioinfcookbook packages for the main functions. We'll also use dplyr briefly. The datasets for these are fission yeast wt versus mutant gene expression data and an Arabidopsis treatment timecourse. The columns in the data are for the log 2 ratio of gene expression in mutant versus wt and the *p*-value from a statistical test.

How to do it...

We can highlight selected values in a plot such as a gene expression plot using the following steps:

1. Create a volcano plot, highlighting significant genes:

```
library(rbioinfcookbook)
library(ggplot2)
library(gghighlight)

fission_ge |>
      dplyr::mutate(signif = dplyr::if_else(padj < 0.05, TRUE,
FALSE),
                            scaled_p = -log10(padj)
                            ) |>
ggplot() +
  aes(x = log2FoldChange, y = scaled_p ) +
  geom_point(aes(colour = signif)) +
  gghighlight(scaled_p > 10 ,
                    label_key = id)
```

2. Create a line plot highlighting genes significant in at least one time point:

```
ggplot(ath_ts) +
  aes(x=time, y=logFC) +
  geom_line(aes(colour = target_id)) +
  scale_x_continuous(breaks = c(0,3,6,12), labels = c("0h",
"3h", "6h", "12h")) +
  gghighlight(min(P.Value) < 0.05,
        unhighlighted_params = list(linewidth =0.5,
        colour = alpha("gray", 0.2))
        )
```

And that simple code creates the plot we need.

How it works...

The first example shows us how to create a volcano plot, a common visualization in genomics that plots the p-value against the expression value, allowing us to see the most highly expressed and significant genes. The `fission_ge` data comes with the data package we loaded, and we use `dplyr::mutate()` to add a column called `signif` that marks whether the gene is significant and a column called `scaled_p` that contains a log transformation of the p-value that will scale the values more nicely on the y axis. The plot is straightforward, based on the `geom_point()` representation. We can highlight interesting genes with the `gghighlight()` function. The most important aspect of this function is the first argument, which makes up a logical predicate; data points that pass this predicate will be highlighted and others backgrounded. The predicate here is simply whether the `scaled_p` value is over `10`, and the value for `label_type` tells the function which column to use for labels. `gghighlight()` actively shades the predicate-failing uninteresting genes and puts the rest in the foreground with labels; see *Figure 3.9*:

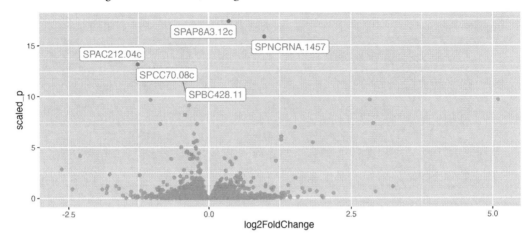

Figure 3.9 – Highlighted volcano plot

The second example is a line plot of gene expression-level changes over time; each line represents a single gene. Again we start by creating a base ggplot using `ath_ts`, which comes in the data package, though this time with the `geom_line()` geom, and we add a more readable *x* axis with `scale_x_continous()` while we're at it. Then, we apply a highlighting filter with `gghighlight()`, specifying the predicate as any gene whose minimum over the whole time course drops below 0.05 (i.e., is significant at any time point). We format the look of the unhighlighted lines with the `unhighlighted_params` argument, which takes a list of settings for `ggplot` aesthetics. See *Figure 3.10*:

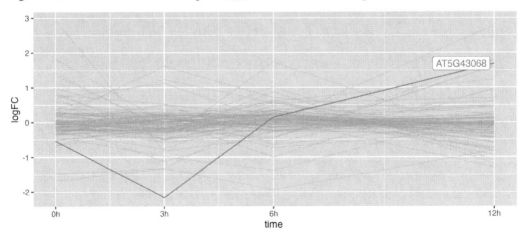

Figure 3.10 – Highlighted time series

Together, these steps show us how to make highlighted plots.

Plotting variability and confidence intervals better with ggdist

Confidence intervals are used to make inferences about a population based on a sample of data. They capture the variability of the data by providing a range of possible values for some parameter, rather than a single point estimate. The interval is a measure of how sure we are that the interval contains the true population parameter. It is common to show distributions and annotate them with range markers or confidence intervals. With this recipe, we will look at how to use ggplot's ggdist extension to make informative and great-looking plots of distributions.

Getting ready

For this recipe, we need the ggdist, ggplot2, and palmerpenguins packages.

How to do it...

We can create plots with confidence intervals as follows:

1. Create a raincloud plot:

```
library(ggplot2)
library(ggdist)
library(palmerpenguins)

ggplot(penguins) +
  aes(x = flipper_length_mm, y = island) +
  geom_dots(side = "bottomleft", aes(colour = island)) +
  stat_slabinterval(aes(fill = island)) +
  theme_minimal()
```

2. Delimit arbitrary regions in a curve:

```
ggplot(penguins) +
  aes(x = flipper_length_mm, y = island,) +
  stat_halfeye(aes(fill=stat( (x > 190 & x < 200) ))) +
  geom_vline(xintercept =  c(190, 200), linetype = "dashed" ) +
  scale_fill_manual(values = c("gray", "steelblue")) +
  theme_minimal()
```

3.   Create a gradient plot:

```
ggplot(penguins) +
  aes(x = flipper_length_mm, y = island) +
  stat_gradientinterval(aes(colour=island, fill=island)) +
  theme_minimal()
```

And that is all we need to make plots with representations of variability.

How it works...

Step 1 shows us how to create a raincloud plot, as seen in *Figure 3.11*. We set up the data and aesthetic layer in ggplot as usual, adding in the geom_dots() function from ggdist, which will add a layer of dots representing each data point to the plot. We set the side parameter to put the dots underneath the line as "bottomleft". The density plot above the line and the range markers in black are added with a stat layer, not a geom layer, as the range and point markers in black need to be calculated from the data before plotting—stat_slabinterval() does this for us. Note that 'slabs' is ggdist's naming convention for distribution glyphs:

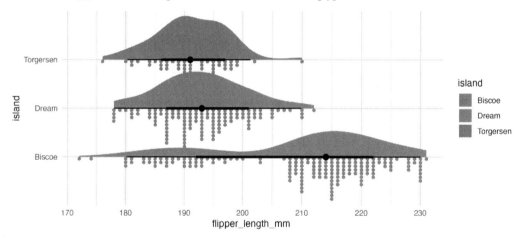

Figure 3.11 – Raincloud plots

Step 2 creates the plot shown in *Figure 3.12*; again, we use a stat_halfeye stat to compute the distributions, passing it a logical predicate to divide the areas of the plot up. We also use the geom_vline() function to add a dashed line to further demarcate the regions across the *y* axis. The last part of this step adds a custom palette:

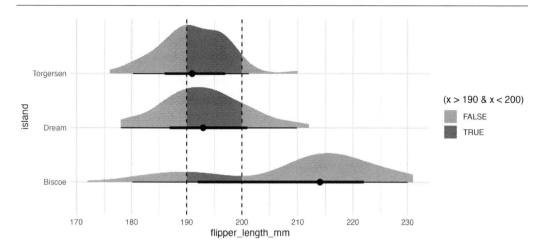

Figure 3.12 – Curve with arbitrary limits marked

Step 3 introduces a completely different way of looking at distributions. We use a gradient of color as a glyph; the deepest areas of color indicate the highest density of data points (*Figure 3.13*). We can compute and add this through the `stat_gradientinterval()` function:

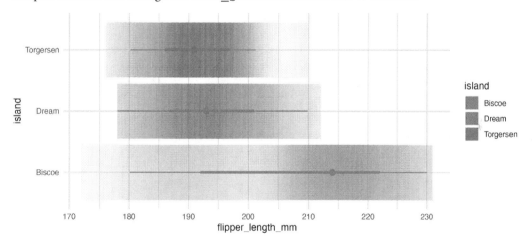

Figure 3.13 – Color gradient plot

These three plots are easily created by the code we just learned.

Making interactive plots with plotly

Interactive plots are great tools for data exploration, allowing users to explore interactively large datasets to gain insights and identify patterns in data. They are useful for programmers wishing to create dashboards for visualizing real-time data and help with interactive presentations that can communicate complex data relationships in an engaging manner. `plotly` is a data visualization library for creating interactive plots in Python, R, and JavaScript. It provides a high-level interface for drawing attractive and informative statistical graphics, and the `ggplotly` package in R allows you to convert static `ggplot2` visualizations to interactive plots through a high-level interface. In this recipe, we'll create a fairly involved `ggplot2` visualization of mutation sites on a genome and then convert it to `plotly` to get a great first-level interaction layer.

Getting ready

We'll need the `ggplot2`, `plotly`, and `rbioinfcookbook` packages for this recipe. The `allele_freq` data object from that is a data frame of allele frequencies of **single nucleotide polymorphisms (SNPs)** from genome sequencing of a bulked population of an Arabidopsis mutant line. The columns give the genomic positions of the SNP, the reference and alternative alleles, and information on the effect of the mutation in the gene.

How to do it...

The steps we need to create an interactive plot are set out as follows:

1. Create a ggplot:

```
library(ggplot2)
library(plotly)
library(rbioinfcookbook)


p <- ggplot(allele_freqs) +
  aes(x = Pos, y = Allele_Freq, label = info) +
  geom_point(aes(colour = type)) +
  facet_grid(Chr ~ ., scales = "free_x", space="free") +
  scale_colour_manual(values = c("steelblue", "gray",
"goldenrod", "red")) +
  theme_minimal()
```

2. Convert it to `plotly`:

```
ggplotly(p, dynamicTicks = TRUE,
            dragmode = "zoom",
            tooltip = c("Chr", "Pos", "info")
            )
```

And those simple steps are all we need for an attractive interactive plot.

How it works...

Step 1 creates a plot using the data, putting the allele frequency on the *y* axis and the position of the SNP on the *x* axis. Note that the aes() function also carries a mapping for the label attribute to the info column; plotly only knows automatically about stuff that is built into the ggplot object, so it needs to have a mapping in this stage. The plot is faceted such that each chromosome gets its own facet, with scales changing to match them. The point color is set to the type column, with the most likely mutations being those that are non-synonymous, in a coding region, and with a CT/GA transition, so these are colored red. Together, this specification creates a plot of SNP type and density across the genome.

When the plot is created, we can go ahead and convert it to plotly to be able to interact with it, which we do with ggplotly(). Setting the dynamicTicks argument allows the scales to redraw under zooming; dragmode allows us to use a drag-box style zoom, and tooltip sets the order of the label items in the on-hover tooltip that appears when a point is selected. Rendering the plot through this function also creates a menu that allows, among other things, resetting the view, highlighting tracks by clicking on the legend, and exporting the current view to a PNG file. A static view of the resulting plot can be seen in *Figure 3.14*:

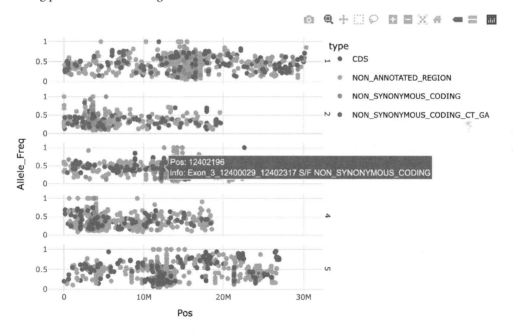

Figure 3.14 – plotly interactive plot from the ggplot specification

The preceding screenshot shows the callout box that appears on a user hover in this interactive plot.

See also

The `plotly` object works really well with Shiny **user interface** (**UI**) elements. Check that package out for a range of checkboxes and sliders that allow you to dynamically alter inputs to the `plotly` object.

Clarifying label placement with ggrepel

Bioinformatics datasets often have many thousands of data points. These can be genomic positions or genes within a genome, and as part of our data analysis, we will frequently want to label positions or genes so that the reader can identify them. A problem arises in that the labels can easily overlap or clash in the plots. The `ggrepel` package provides geoms for `ggplot2` that allow for labels to be positioned much more clearly, incorporating label layout algorithms that make labels and connecting lines repel intelligently. In this recipe, we'll look at the most important options for applying that to a genomics dataset.

Getting ready

We'll need the `ggplot2` and `ggrepel` packages and the fission yeast gene expression dataset in the `rbioinfcookbook` data package. This data frame contains yeast gene IDs in one column, the log 2-fold change of gene expression for that gene, and the *p*-value from a statistical test.

How to do it...

We can create a less noisy plot as follows:

```
library(rbioinfcookbook)
library(ggplot2)
library(ggrepel)

set.seed(44)
fission_ge |>
  dplyr::mutate(
    signif = dplyr::if_else(padj < 0.05, TRUE, FALSE),
    scaled_p = -log10(padj)
  ) |>
  ggplot() +
  geom_text_repel(aes(x = log2FoldChange, y = scaled_p, label = id),
    max.time = 60,
    point.padding = NA,
    arrow = arrow(
        length = unit(0.03, "npc"),
        type = "closed",
        ends = "last",
```

```
        angle = 15
    ),
    force = 10,
    xlim   = c(NA, NA)
) +
geom_point(aes(x = log2FoldChange, y = scaled_p, colour = signif)) +
theme_minimal()
```

This is all we need to apply some tidying to our labels.

How it works...

After loading the libraries, this recipe goes on to set a random seed; this helps with the reproducibility of the plots when using ggrepel as the algorithm for layout has a random component that can make iterating over plot parameters trickier than it needs to be. The dataset has a column called signif added and the *p*-value scaled for the volcano plot we will make. The data passes to ggplot2, and the geom_text_repel() geom is used—note that the aesthetic is declared in the geom with aes() rather than on its own. We must set the label mapping to render the right labels. The parameters for this geom are there to allow maximum readability and space for the labels. The max.time parameter limits the algorithm run time; setting point.padding to NA removes the maximum distance the label can be from the point and allows the label to float far from the point it belongs to. The arrow function defines the properties of the line joining labels and points. The force parameter defines how hard the labels repel (defaulting to 1, so this is strong). The final parameter, xlim, defines a hard boundary on labels on the *x* axis; setting both values to NA means the labels can float outside of the plot area, which is useful as some very busy plots can still run out of room. A corresponding parameter exists for the *y* axis. The plot that is produced can be seen in *Figure 3.15*. A keen-eyed reader will note that most points don't actually have a label. This is because the max.overlaps parameter removes labels that overlap too many things; the default value that we have used implicitly is 10:

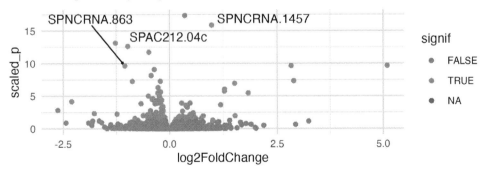

Figure 3.15 – ggrepel labeled plot

As we can see, the plot we have created makes the best use of the space available for the number of labels we want to show.

Zooming and making callouts from selected plot sections with facetzoom

We've already seen in these recipes how bioinformatics datasets can encompass very large scales. Genomes can be thousands of millions of bases long and contain tens of thousands of genes, taxa can have thousands of members, and biomes can have billions of individuals living in areas of a wide range of sizes. Contextual information is therefore often important in analysis and visualization; we may want to see a detail of some subset of data in its original broader context. We can do that by using plots with *callout*-style subplots—zoomed-in areas drawn alongside the wider data. In this recipe, we will look at using the facet zoom functionality in the `ggforce` package to look at an area of interest in a ggplot.

Getting ready

We'll use the `ggplot2`, `ggforce`, `palmerpenguins`, and `rbioinfcookbook` packages for the main part of this recipe. The `allele_freq` and `penguins` datasets will be the basis of our plots. We'll use a little `dplyr` to filter, too.

How to do it...

We can highlight parts of a plot as follows:

1. Zoom in on a particular numeric range:

```
library(rbioinfcookbook)
library(ggplot2)
library(ggforce)

allele_freqs |>
  dplyr::filter(Chr == 1) |>
  ggplot() +
  aes(x = Pos, y = Allele_Freq, label = info) +
  geom_point(aes(colour = type)) +
  facet_grid(Chr ~ ., scales = "free_x", space = "free") +
  scale_colour_manual(values = c("steelblue", "gray",
"goldenrod", "red")) +
  facet_zoom(xlim = c(1000000, 2000000))
```

2. Zoom in on a particular category:

```
library(palmerpenguins)

penguins |>
  ggplot() +
  aes(x = bill_depth_mm, y = bill_length_mm, colour = island) +
```

```
    geom_point() +
    facet_zoom(x = island == "Dream", zoom.data = island ==
"Dream")
```

And that is how we select a region of a plot to highlight in a callout.

How it works...

As usual, the recipe starts by loading the libraries and the data; we then use the `allele_freqs` data to create a scatter plot of allele frequency against genome position, having filtered data so that we are working only on chromosome 1 data. Once the plot is created and colored, we apply a `facet_zoom()` layer from `ggforce` and give it the `xlim` parameter so that the new zoomed facet shows the *x* axis between those points (*Figure 3.16*):

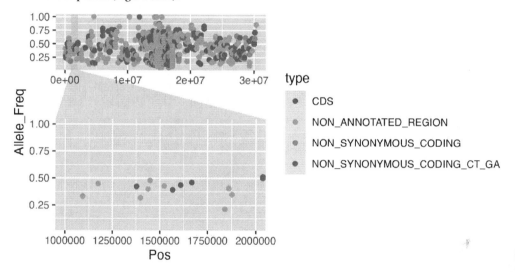

Figure 3.16 – Zooming in by numbers on the x axis

Step 2 looks at pulling out a facet based on categorical data and not just a numeric axis range; in the early part, we build a ggplot on the `penguins` data, coloring a scatter plot by the `island` variable. This time, the `facet_zoom()` function is given a logical expression (`island == "Dream"`) to retain data satisfying the expression in the zoom; `zoom.data` shows only data passing its logical condition in the zoom and not in other panels. Corresponding parameters exist for the *y* axis:

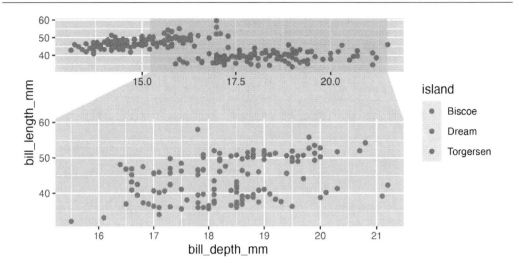

Figure 3.17 – Pulling out a single category

As we can see, the plots highlight particular data effectively.

Composing multiple plots into single figures with cowplot and patchwork

A good plot in a publication or report can greatly enhance the impact of your research results. A well-made plot can convey complex information in a straightforward manner, helping readers to quickly understand and retain key findings. In this recipe, we will go over the basics of composing and formatting plots using the cowplot R package (and, briefly, the patchwork package). These packages provide tools for extracting plot components, reordering them, and labeling them in a way that suits a final plot layout.

Getting ready

The rbioinfcookbook package is needed for some data, as well as the cowplot and patchwork packages for composing plots. To generate our initial plots, we will take inspiration from earlier recipes, repeating some plots with minor modifications. To make those, we'll need ggplot2, ggridges, gghighlight, and ggdist.

How to do it...

We can compose multiple plots into one using the following steps:

1. Compose some plots:

```
library(rbioinfcookbook)
library(palmerpenguins)
library(ggplot2)
library(ggridges)
library(gghighlight)
library(ggdist)


p1 <- ggplot(data = penguins) +
  aes(x = bill_length_mm, y = species,
        fill = factor(stat(quantile))) +
  stat_density_ridges(geom ="density_ridges_gradient",
                    calc_ecdf = TRUE,
                    quantiles = c(0.05, 0.95)) +
  scale_fill_manual(
    name = "Probability",
    values = alpha(c("goldenrod",
        "gray","steelblue"), 0.5),
    labels = c("< 0.05", "0.05 to 0.95", " > 0.95 "),
    guide = guide_legend(nrow = 3, byrow = TRUE)
  ) +
  theme_ridges() +
  theme(legend.position = "bottom")

p2 <- fission_ge |>
  dplyr::mutate(
    signif = dplyr::if_else(padj < 0.05, TRUE, FALSE),
    scaled_p = -log10(padj)
  ) |>
  ggplot() +
  aes(x = log2FoldChange, y = scaled_p) +
  geom_point(aes(colour = signif)) +
  gghighlight(scaled_p > 10 ,
```

```
                         label_key = id) +
    theme(legend.position = "bottom")

  p3 <- ggplot(penguins) +
    aes(x = flipper_length_mm, y = island, ) +
    stat_halfeye(aes(fill = stat((x > 190 & x < 200)))) +
    geom_vline(xintercept = c(190, 200), linetype = "dashed") +
    scale_fill_manual(values = c("gray", "steelblue"),
                      guide = guide_legend(nrow = 2, byrow = TRUE))
  +
    theme_minimal() +
    theme(legend.position = "bottom")


  p4 <- allele_freqs |>
    dplyr::filter(Chr == 1) |>
    ggplot() +
    aes(x = Pos, y = Allele_Freq, label = info) +
    geom_point(aes(colour = type)) +
    facet_grid(Chr ~ ., scales = "free_x", space = "free") +
    scale_colour_manual(
        values = c("steelblue", "gray", "goldenrod", "red"),
        labels = c("CDS", "NON-CDS", "NON-SYN-Coding", "CTGA")
    ) +
    theme(legend.position = "bottom")
```

2. Remove the legends and compose the plots into a column:

```
library(cowplot)
left_column <- plot_grid( p1 + theme(legend.position = "none"),
              p2 + theme(legend.position = "none"),
              p3 + theme(legend.position = "none"),
              ncol = 1, labels = c("A", "B", "C")
              )
```

3. Extract the legends and compose those into a column:

```
l1 <- get_legend(p1)
l3 <- get_legend(p3)

right_column <- plot_grid(l1, NULL, l3,  ncol=1)
```

4.   Compose the two columns and the last plot:

```
two_cols <- plot_grid(left_column, right_column, ncol = 2, rel_
widths = c(0.66, 0.34))
labelled_4 <- plot_grid(p4, labels = "D")

plot_grid(two_cols, labelled_4, ncol = 1, rel_heights = c(0.6,
0.4))
```

And that is all we need to create a plot from multiple plots.

How it works...

Step 1 is a long one, but essentially repeats code discussed earlier in the chapter (for example, the first plot comes from the *Comparing changes in distributions with ggridges* section). Note that in p1 and p3 we modify the legend, using the `guides` function in the `scale_fill_manual()` layer to make sure that the legend will flow over three or two lines (so that there is one legend element per line)—this will be important later as the legend will be extracted into a space of its own.

In *step 2*, we create a plot that comprises p1, p2, and p3 by passing them to cowplot's `plot_grid()` function and setting the number of columns to 1, such that the plots are stacked vertically. We also apply labels for each. Note too that the plots have their legends removed using `theme` before they are stacked; this is because we will apply the legends manually.

Step 3 uses cowplot's `get_legend()` function to extract the legends from the original plots to their own objects; these objects are stacked into a column, again using `plot_grid()`. NULL forces the grid to contain an empty element at that point.

In *step 4*, we compose the two columns we have made (again with `plot_grid()`, this time in two columns in `two_cols`), using the `rel_widths` option to allow the plots to take up 66 percent of the width of the plot area. To finish, we add a label to p4 with—you guessed it—`plot_grid()` and then put that under our previous columns by calling `plot_grid()` for one last time, setting the number of columns to 1 and the relative heights such that the columns take up the majority of space. The final plot looks like the one shown in *Figure 3.18*—or it does when rendered in the small space for plots provided by this book's format. You may see a clearer plot when trying it on your own machine. As R works by rendering into a viewport—a rectangle of a specified size—and trying to fit objects into that, there can be overlap when some objects can't be reduced further. This is a problem in this plot composed of many subplots as some elements can't be shrunk too far—specifically, text must remain large enough to read so when the plot gets too small, it will overlap. There is sometimes a physical limit on how much space we have for plots. The packages we have used give you control over how you can lay out your plot in the margin options:

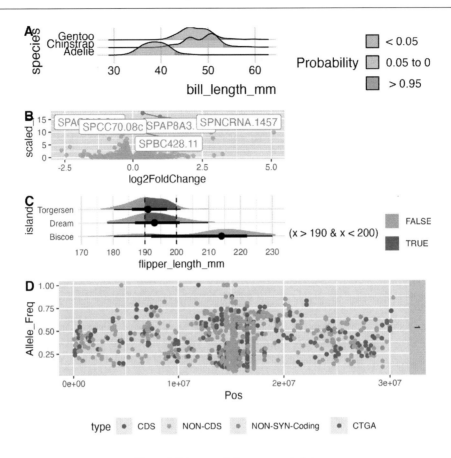

Figure 3.18 – cowplot-composed plot

And with that, we can see how to compose multiple plots into one plot.

There's more...

These plots all have different legends, so we had to accommodate them individually. Many of the plots you will make will share legends and axes. cowplot can help align subplots by axis through the align_plots() function.

See also

The patchwork library offers an alternative take on composing plots, providing a declarative syntax that looks a bit math-like. In the following example, we make two versions of our plots with the legends set to be on two rows, and in the final call, (p1s + p3s) / p4, we create a plot layout that puts two plots on one row, all above a third plot on its own row. Imagine this to be like a math expression , that is, plot1 and plot3, both over plot4. We also add annotation with the plot_annotation()

function; the `tag_levels` argument simply tells the annotation function from which character to start numbering/lettering the panels:

```
library(patchwork)

p1s <-  p1 + scale_fill_manual(
    name = "Probability",
    values = alpha(c("goldenrod", "gray", "steelblue"), 0.5),
    labels = c("< 0.05", "0.05 to 0.95", " > 0.95 "),
    guide = guide_legend(nrow = 2, byrow = TRUE)
  )


p3s <- p3 +  scale_fill_manual(
    values = c("gray", "steelblue"),
    guide = guide_legend(nrow = 2, byrow = TRUE)
    )


(p1s + p3s) / p4 +
  plot_annotation(tag_levels = "A")
```

This code works nicely for a quick composition, giving us the output shown in *Figure 3.19*:

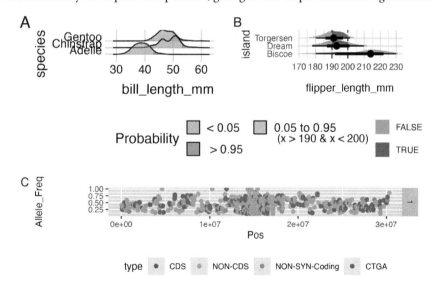

Figure 3.19 – patchwork-composed plot

Figures 3.18 and *3.19* show how different packages can be used to compose the same plots into larger plots.

4
Using Quarto to Make Data-Rich Reports, Presentations, and Websites

Literate computing is the practice of embedding human-readable explanations and annotations within computer code, making it easier for both the author and other developers to understand and reuse the code. The main goal of literate computing is to create readable, reusable code that can be understood not only by machines but by humans as well.

One of the key tools for literate computing is Markdown. Markdown is a simple markup language that allows for the creation of easily readable documents that can be converted to **Hypertext Markup Language** (**HTML**) and other documents, including Word, for display on varied platforms. Markdown is easy to write and understand, even for non-technical users.

R Markdown, a variant of Markdown with R in mind, provides a simple way to embed R code within a document, alongside narrative text and visualizations, to create a complete report. One of the main advantages of using R Markdown is that it makes it easy to create reproducible reports. This means that others can run the same code and obtain the same results, which is essential for scientific and research work. R Markdown also allows for the creation of dynamic reports, as the code and results can be updated automatically when the underlying data changes.

Another benefit of R Markdown is that it makes it easy to format and stylize the document, providing a range of customization options and the ability to use **Cascading Style Sheets** (**CSS**) and HTML to create a polished, professional-looking report. This is particularly useful for creating data-led reports and presentations, where the focus is on presenting information and insights in a clear and engaging way.

Quarto is a multi-language open source scientific publishing system built on top of the Pandoc format conversion tool that has very strong support for R Markdown and other language-literate computing systems, such as Jupyter in Python. In this chapter, we'll take a long look at making full use of the features of Quarto for creating a long list of different document types with embedded dynamic R code.

In this chapter, we will cover the following recipes:

- Using Markdown and Quarto for literate computation
- Creating different document formats from the same source
- Creating data-rich presentations from code
- Creating websites from collections of Quarto documents
- Adding interactivity with Shiny

Technical requirements

You will need to install Quarto, which can be done by selecting the relevant package for your operating system at this link: `https://quarto.org/docs/get-started/`.

1. Quarto has a dependency on LaTeX, but once Quarto is installed, it can install a version of that for you. To install that, use the following command:

```
quarto install tool tinytex
```

From the command line, after you've installed Quarto, all should be ready.

To render, we'll use the command-line options, and I'll make this explicit in each recipe. If you want to take advantage of Quarto's integration into RStudio, you'll need to make sure that you have installed RStudio version 2022.07 or later, which has support in the **integrated development environment** (**IDE**) for Quarto. Install that from here: `https://rstudio.com/products/rstudio/download/`.

2. We will use `renv` to manage packages in a project-specific way. To use `renv` to install packages, you will first need to install the `renv` package. You can do this by running the following command in your R console:

```
install.packages("renv")
```

3. Next, you will need to create a new `renv` environment for your project by running the following command:

```
renv::init()
```

This will create a new directory called `.renv` in your current project directory.

4. You can then install packages with the following command:

```
install.packages("<package name>")
```

5. You can also use the `renv` package manager to install Bioconductor packages by running the following command:

```
renv::install("bioc::<package name>")
```

6. For example, to install the `Biobase` package, you would run this command:

```
renv::install("bioc::Biobase")
```

7. You can use `renv` to install development packages from GitHub like this:

```
renv::install("<user name>/<repo name>")
```

For example, to install the `danmaclean` user's `rbioinfcookbook` package, you would run the following command:

```
renv::install("danmaclean/rbioinfcookbook")
```

Here are some other tips for installation:

- You can also install multiple packages at once by separating the package names with a comma. `renv` will automatically handle installing any required dependencies for the packages you install.

- Under `renv`, all packages will be installed into the local project directory and not the main central library, meaning you can have multiple versions of the same package, one specific one for each project.

- All the sample data you need for this package is in the specially created data package on GitHub: `danmaclean/rbioinfcookbook`. The data will become available in your project after installing that.

For this chapter, we'll need the following packages:

- Regular packages:

  - `ggplot2`

  - `knitr`

  - `palmerpenguins`

  - `rmarkdown`

  - `tidyverse`

- GitHub:

  - `danmaclean/rbioinfcookbook`

These should all install easily, and then we are good to go.

Further information

We will generally call Quarto from the normal command line (Bash or Windows) in the recipes but alternatives do exist. The RStudio IDE contains render buttons, and there are functions in the `quarto` package that can be used in the R console. Feel free to use whichever works for you.

In R, it is normal practice to load a library and use functions directly by name. Although this is great in short interactive sessions, it can cause confusion when many packages are loaded at once and share function names. To clarify which package and function I am using at a given moment, I will occasionally use the `packageName::functionName()` convention.

Sometimes, in the middle of a recipe, I'll interrupt the code to dive into some intermediate output or to look at the structure of an object. When that happens, you'll see a code block where each line begins with ## (double hash symbols). Consider the following command:

```
letters[1:5]
```

This will give us the following output:

```
## a b c d e
```

Note that the output lines are prefixed with ##.

Using Markdown and Quarto for literate computation

A very common task in bioinformatics is writing up our results in order to communicate them to colleagues or to have a good record in our laboratory books (electronic or otherwise). A key skill is to make the work as reproducible as possible so that we can rerun it ourselves when we need to revisit it or when someone else needs to replicate the process. One very popular way to solve this problem is to use literate programming techniques and executable notebooks that are a mixture of human-readable text, analytical code, and computational output rolled into a single document. In R, the R Markdown extension of the Markdown syntax and the Quarto command-line tool (and R package) allow us to combine code and text in this way and create output documents in a variety of formats. In this recipe, we'll look at the large-scale structure of a typical document that can be rendered into multiple formats with Quarto.

Getting ready

We'll need the Quarto command-line tool mentioned at the start of the chapter and a text editor. Optionally, you can install the R `quarto` package. The Markdown we create here should be saved into a file with a `.qmd.` extension—for example, `example_quarto.qmd`.

How to do it...

Developing reusable workflows and reports can be done using the following steps:

1. In the `example_quarto.qmd` file, add a YAML header:

    ```
    ---
    title: "R Markdown in Quarto Report"
    author: "AN Rwizard"
    date: "17 April, 2023"
    output: html_document
    ---
    ```

2. Then, add some text and code to be interpreted:

    ```
    You are reading a document created with Rmarkdown and rendered
    in Quarto.

    This document includes a mixture of text and code. The code
    below is wrapped in back ticks and at render-time the code will
    be executed and the  result inserted into the document


    ```{r}
    library(palmerpenguins)
    x <- penguins$bill_length_mm
    y <- penguins$bill_depth_mm

    lm(y ~ x)
    ```
    ```

3. Text can be formatted using Markdown's minimal markup tags:

    ```
    We can format any text using Markdown, simple inline text
    elements convey the formatting

    ## Hashes at the start of a line make it a heading.

    Two hashes gives a Level 2 heading, three hashes a Level
    3 heading. Headings go from Level 1 (biggest) to Level 6
    (smallest)

    We can create text formats including _italics_ and **bold**.

    We can make lists:
        1. First item
        2. Second item
    ```

```
We can make hyperlinks [a link to Google](https://www.google.
com)
Apply further options and carry over object state between code
blocks
The whole document acts as a single R session  - so objects
created in earlier
blocks can be used later.


Plots are inserted into the document.
```

4. Set some options for a particular block:

```
Options for code blocks can be set at the top after a `#|` (a
hash and a pipe).

```{r}
#| fig-width: 6
#| fig-cap: "A plot, yesterday."

plot(x,y)
```
```

5. After saving, render the .qmd file in the terminal:

```
quarto render example_quarto.qmd
```

And with that done, we should have a nicely formatted code-interpreted output HTML document.

How it works...

The code in this recipe is special in that it must be run from inside an external document; it won't run in the R console. The compilation step reads the whole document, formats the marked-up text, runs the code, and inserts the result into an HTML document to create a unified output.

In *step 1*, we create the YAML header that describes how the document should be rendered, including output format and a dynamic date, by running format on the output of Sys.time(). A global level 1 heading is created by the title declaration and forms a title.

In *step 2*, we actually create some content; the first line is plain text and will pass into the rendered document as normal paragraph text. The section within the block demarked by three backticks (```) is code to be interpreted. Options for the block go inside the curly brackets; here, {r} means this should be an R code block (though other languages are supported, including Python and Bash). The code in the block is run in an isolated R session dedicated to the rendering of the document that is closed when rendering is done. Output is captured and inserted immediately after the code block that created it.

In *step 3*, we look closer at the Markdown tags, exploring how markup such as _text_ and **text** can make formats, lists can be generated by using space and numbers or bullets, and links can be specified.

In *step 4*, we do some more code and set options for the code block by setting options at the top of the block demarked by the #| (hash-pipe) symbol. We set a figure width and a caption for the figure. Note that the code in this block refers to variables created in an earlier block; this is thanks to the shared but new session all blocks in a document are executed in.

In *step 5*, we move out of the document and save it with a .qmd extension for this file type. We then render it on the command line. The final document is an HTML document with the same name as the input.

If you need to get the full example file for this recipe, you can extract it from the rbioinfcookbook package, as described in the following *There's more...* section.

There's more...

The whole example document is provided in the data package; you can copy it to somewhere useful on your system with the following code, but remember to change the destination to somewhere that actually exists:

```
qmd_path <- fs::path_package("extdata", "example_quarto.qmd",
                             package="rbioinfcookbook")
file.copy(qmd_path, 'somewhere/on/your/system/quarto.qmd')
```

This will help you see the whole structure of the document and save you some typing.

Creating different document formats from the same source

The Quarto system is based on the versatile and powerful Pandoc tool for converting documents between different formats. One of its most useful features is the ability to translate between various markup languages, such as HTML and LaTeX, and Markdown and Microsoft Office formats, making it a valuable tool for writers, researchers, and developers alike. This means that if you have a document written in one format, you can easily convert it to another format without having to manually reformat the entire document. Pandoc can also perform various transformations, such as adding footnotes, tables, and images, making it a great tool for formatting and preparing documents for publication. For example, if you need to prepare a report for submission to a journal, you can use Pandoc to convert your R Markdown document to PDF or Word, add images and tables, and format it according to the journal's specifications. Formats are specified by options in YAML headers or configuration files rather than in the markup itself, so prepping a document to be rendered into multiple output formats from the same source is simply a matter of setting the configuration correctly. In this recipe, we'll look at how to do that, specifically for HTML, PDF, and Word document outputs.

Getting ready

We'll need a sample R Markdown document provided by the rbioinfcookbook package, so install that, the fs package, and the ggplot2 package, if you haven't got it already. You'll also need to have followed the instructions for installing Quarto at the start of the chapter. Make sure you have also installed TinyTeX, which is needed by Quarto, also discussed at the start of the chapter.

How to do it...

We can prep a marked-up document for rendering to various formats as follows:

1. Save the example file somewhere accessible:

    ```
    qmd_path <- fs::path_package("extdata", "mtcars.qmd",
                                 package="rbioinfcookbook")
    file.copy(qmd_path, 'somewhere/on/your/system/mtcars.qmd')

    bib_path <- fs::path_package("extdata", "mtcars.bib",
                                 package="rbioinfcookbook")
    file.copy(bib_path, 'somewhere/on/your/system/mtcars.bib')
    ```

2. In your editor, add a YAML header for HTML:

    ```
    ---
    title: "mtcars Analysis"
    subtitle: "an analysis in many formats"
    author: "anrwizard@email.com"
    date-modified: "`r format(Sys.time(), '%d %B, %Y')`"
    email-obfuscation: javascript
    bibliography: mtcars.bib
    execute:
      echo: true
      warning: false
    format:
      html:
        theme: cyborg
        toc: true
        toc-location: left
        html-math-method: katex
        css: styles.css
        number-sections: true
        cap-location: top
        code-fold: true
        code-line-numbers: true
        citations-hover: false

    ---
    ```

3. Run that on the command line:

```
quarto render mtcars.qmd --to html
```

4. Get a **Citation Style Language** (**CSL**) file to determine how references will be formatted:

```
csl_path <- fs::path_package("extdata", "bioinformatics.csl",
                              package="rbioinfcookbook")
file.copy(csl_path, 'somewhere/on/your/system/bioinformatics.
csl')
```

5. Extend the YAML to include a PDF block; *note*—add this under the existing HTML code:

```
pdf:
    pdf-engine: xelatex
    papersize: A4
    documentclass: report
    toc: true
    toc-title: "Workflow"
    lof: true
    mainfont: Arial
    monofont: Courier
    fontsize: "24"
    colorlinks: true
    cap-location: margin
    csl: bioinformatics.csl
```

6. Render the document:

```
quarto render mtcars.qmd --to html,pdf
```

7. Get a Microsoft Word .docx file to act as a style template for the Microsoft Word doc:

```
docx_path <- fs::path_package("extdata", "custom-reference-doc.
docx",
                                 package="rbioinfcookbook")
file.copy(docx_path, 'somewhere/on/your/system/custom-reference-
doc.docx')
```

8. Extend the YAML header for .docx output:

```
docx:
    reference-doc: custom-reference-doc.docx
    fig-align: center
    fig-width: 20
    number-sections: true
    citeproc: true
```

9. Do the final render:

```
quarto render mtcars.qmd --to html,pdf,docx
```

This will give us three output files in `html`, `pdf`, and `docx` from one input.

How it works...

Although this recipe is long, it is really straightforward; all we are doing is setting global and format-specific options and extracting some pre-prepared files from the support package to assist. In *step 1*, we save the base YAML-less `mtcars.qmd` file somewhere we can use it on our machine, such as the desktop. We do the same with the bibliography file we need. `bibliography.bib` contains a BibTeX description of a reference. In *step 2*, we add YAML to the top of the document that says how the document should be formatted. Those key-value pairs in the top level (for example, `title`) are applied to all document formats we want to render. Most of these are obvious; `title` sets the title—a level 1 heading by default, `date-modified` is set to a piece of R code that will generate the date dynamically, `email-obfuscation` chooses a method for scrambling email addresses to prevent harvesting by bots, especially on websites, and `bibliography.bib` sets the path to the references. The HTML-specific options all appear in an indented block under the `format` and `html` tags. Here, we use key values to set the theme from one of the built-ins (`cyborg`). This is a distinctive black one that will be obvious if it has been applied. We turn on a `toc` table of contents and set it to the left with `toc-location`, choose options for rendering math, and give an optional external CSS file for custom styles. We also choose some options that will affect the rendering of code. Experiment with values for these to learn what they do. In *step 3*, we go on to render the document; this is done on the command line. The result should be a `mtcars.html` file and a supporting folder of images and other files. Look at these in a web browser.

In *step 4*, we start with PDF formatting our document, first extracting a `bioinformatics.csl` CSL file that describes reference formatting in documents. The code again extracts it from the support package and puts it somewhere useful on your machine. Then, in *step 5*, we set up the PDF output options, choosing a specific `pdf-engine` renderer, some document type options, more table of contents options, and some specific font choices. These should be clear when you browse the rendered document. The CSL file is specified by the `csl` key. Note that this whole text is in addition to the YAML already added, and its indentation should match that of the `html` block. The whole section should be after the `html` section and before the three closing dashes (−). In *step 6*, we render the two formats together. Compare the outputs to each other and observe how the format-specific options affect each.

With Microsoft Word documents, styles are defined by a reference `.docx` file. Again, there is one in the support package, but you can create your own by going into Word and setting styles however you like, then simply saving the file to act as a template. In *step 7*, we copy the package example reference somewhere accessible. In *step 8*, we set some options. The most important is `reference-doc`, which gets the path to our style reference document. Also important is the `citeproc` key, which turns on the reference formatter. Finally, in *step 9*, back at the command line, we render all three formats of the document.

Creating data-rich presentations from code

Presenting data to audiences of other scientists is a key task; it is vital for us to be able to understand and discuss our results and methods. Creating slides that assist our presentations is usually a manual task that requires the insertion of figures and methods into documents and is one that can consume a lot of a researcher's time. Various presentation formats exist. Microsoft Office PowerPoint is one of the most commonly used presentation tools. It is a user-friendly GUI program and provides a wide variety of templates, animations, transitions, and multimedia features. However, it requires a lot of manual editing. Conversely, Beamer is a LaTeX-based presentation system used for academic and scientific presentations. It's a powerful tool and especially useful for presentations that include mathematical equations, formulas, and algorithms. However, Beamer requires some knowledge of LaTeX, which can make it less accessible. Reveal.js is an open source, web-based presentation system that uses HTML, CSS, and JavaScript, designed to be highly customizable and for interactive presentations. Reveal.js requires a good level of understanding of its underlying technologies.

The great advantage of using Quarto with an R Markdown document is that our presentations can become self-updating when the data changes. In this recipe, we'll look at how to format a Markdown document containing R code so that we can render it as a presentation in the three formats mentioned.

Getting ready

We'll need the `rbioinfcookbook` package and the `fs` package for our template files. We'll also need to have pre-installed Quarto, as described at the start of the chapter, and the `ggplot2` packages for the pages themselves to run.

How to do it...

Setting up a Markdown document for eventual rendering as a presentation might go like this:

1. Set up the first slide as a second-level heading:

    ```
    ## Method

    ::: {.incremental}

    - Exploratory plot
    - Statistical modelling

    :::
    ```

2. Set up the second slide to render a plot but no code:

    ```
    ## Relationship between cylinder count and Miles Per Gallon

    ```{r, point1, echo=FALSE}
    ```
    ```

```
library(ggplot2)

p <- ggplot(mtcars) +
  aes(cyl, mpg) +
  geom_point() +
  geom_smooth(method = "lm")


p
:::
```

3. Set up a third slide with code and result, two-column layout, and presenter notes:

```
::: {.cell}

```{.r .cell-code}
## Linear Modelling

 :::: {.columns}

 ::: {.column width="35%"}
 ```{r, point2, echo=FALSE}
 p
 :::
 ::: {.column width="65%"} {r, point2_model}
lm(mpg ~ cyl, data=mtcars) :::
 ::::
 ::: {.notes} Discuss the negative slope... :::
 :::
```

4. Set up the header to render a title slide and select formats:

```
::: {.cell}

```{.r .cell-code}
---
title: "Motor Cars"
author: "AN Rwizard"
format:
  pptx:
    incremental: true
    reference-doc: reference_presentation.pptx
  revealjs:
    incremental: true
    theme: blood
```
```

```
beamer:
    incremental: true
    theme: AnnArbor
    colortheme: lily
---
```

5. Render from the command line:

```
quarto render presentation.qmd
```

This should generate a presentation document.

How it works...

The recipe is quite straightforward, though there are some new syntax members here. In *step 1*, we create a basic slide; each slide is created by a second-level heading (recall that in Markdown, this is ##). Ostensibly, our first slide describes our method. It is implemented as an incremental list; the three colon delimiters (: : :) mark the beginning and end of the list, and the .incremental bracketed tag marks this as an incrementally revealed list that will display one item at a time (.nonincremental is also available).

In *step 2*, we create a second slide with R code. The output is a plot, and that is shown, but by setting the eval=FALSE R block option, we can stop the code itself from passing through to the eventual presentation.

In *step 3*, we create a more complicated slide with a two-column layout. The four colon delimiters mark the limits of the column layout, and the three colon delimiters the content of each column. We use the width option to set the relative widths of each column. The columns each act as an independent area; the left column prints the plot again, and the right column shows some model code and its result (note the eval option is not set this time). At the very bottom, we use the three colon-delimited .notes tag to add some notes that only the presenter will see.

Now that all our slides are defined, we can set the configuration YAML. This is shown in *step 4*, and the text here should go at the top of the file. The presentation title and author are set here, and the options for each presentation system are set. The incremental tag turns on incremental lists. The theme tag lets you select one of the built-in themes in Reveal.js and Beamer. The reference-doc tag lets you specify a reference PowerPoint PPTX file from which to take styles, as we saw with rendering Word documents in an earlier recipe. If you don't want to render all formats, simply delete the ones you don't want.

Finally, in *step 5*, we render on the command line. The output will go to a .pptx file for PowerPoint, a .html file for Reveal.js, and a .pdf file for Beamer.

There's more...

If you need to get the full example file for this recipe, you can extract it from the `rbioinfcookbook` package like this:

```
qmd_path <- fs::path_package("extdata", "presentation.qmd",
                                 package="rbioinfcookbook")
file.copy(qmd_path, 'somewhere/on/your/system/presentation.qmd')


ref_path <- fs::path_package("extdata", "reference_presentation.pptx",
                                 package="rbioinfcookbook")
file.copy(ref_path, 'somewhere/on/your/system/reference_presentation.
pptx')
```

This, again, should help you see the document in one go and save you some typing.

Creating websites from collections of Quarto documents

Pandoc is a versatile tool that can convert documents between many different formats, including Markdown, HTML, LaTeX, and PDF. It can be used to convert a collection of Markdown documents into a static website. The basic workflow is to write the content in Markdown files, use Pandoc to convert the Markdown files to HTML files, and then serve the HTML files using a web server. Quarto enables this workflow by providing style templates, a series of extra markup, and rendering configurations that simplify the render through Pandoc.

The produced website can be hosted like any other. Of particular, but perhaps not obvious, utility for bioinformaticians is GitHub, which can be used as a hosting platform for the static website. GitHub allows users to create a repository to store the rendered sites, and then use GitHub Pages to host the static website. GitHub Pages is a free service that can host static websites that are built from a GitHub repository. Quarto also provides various tiers of web hosting for your site.

In this recipe, we'll look at how to configure and render multiple Markdown documents into a site using Quarto.

Getting ready

We'll need a set of sample R Markdown documents that constitute the individual pages of the website. Some useful ones are provided by the `rbioinfcookbook` package, so install that. For utility, we'll also need the `fs` package that we'll use to locate our sample files. You'll also need to have followed the instructions for installing Quarto at the start of the chapter. Make sure you have also installed TinyTeX, which is needed by Quarto, also discussed at the start of the chapter.

How to do it...

In order to make a Quarto website from pre-existing Markdown documents, we create a `_quarto.yml` file, put it in the same project folder as our Markdown documents, and fill it with the configuration as follows:

1. Set up the Markdown documents:

    ```
    ws_path <- fs::path_package("extdata", "sample_website",
                                package="rbioinfcookbook")
    fs::dir_copy(ws_path, 'somewhere/on/your/system')
    ```

2. Create a `_quarto.yml` header:

    ```
    project:
      type: website
      output-dir: docs

    website:
      title: "Bioinformatics Report"
      navbar:
        left:
          - href: index.qmd
            text: Index
          - contact.qmd

    format:
      html:
        theme: cosmo
        css: styles.css
        toc: true
    ```

3. Render the site:

    ```
    quarto render
    ```

4. Add sidebar navigation:

    ```
    sidebar:
      search: true
      contents:
        - section: "Intro to Bioinformatics"
          contents:
            - 01-intro.qmd
        - section: "Sequence Data and its uses"
          contents:
    ```

```
        - 02-nucleotide-sequence.qmd
        - 03-amino-acid-sequence.qmd
  - section: "Conclusions"
    contents:
      - 04-wrap-up.qmd
```

5. Re-render the site:

```
quarto render
```

This will give us a nice website with code interpreted and rendered nicely.

How it works...

In *step 1*, we use the familiar `fs` package to pull out a directory name from the `rbioinfcookbook` package and save it somewhere we can see it in our system. The directory is full of example qmd files that we can use as the basis for our website.

In *step 2*, we create a file called `_quarto.yml` in the directory we pulled from the package; this file contains all the configuration information we need in YAML format. The code should be saved in the file. The first stanza in the `_quarto.yml` file is the project definition; here, we're telling Quarto we're building a website and that the output rendered HTML files should go in a sub-directory called `docs` (the name can be anything you want; `docs` is the default for GitHub Pages.)

The second stanza defines stuff about the website; we give a title and set up the names of the pages that are included as links in a page top navigation bar. The important file is the `index.qmd` file. Quarto websites need this one; it will be the front page that people reach when they come to your site. The `text` attribute tells Quarto what text to use to refer to the index page.

The final stanza defines the output types in the render; here, we set `html` (though other types such as `pdf` can be rendered at the same time) and choose our themes and CSS files for the website.

In *step 3*, we actually render the site. The command is issued in the command line/terminal (not the R console) and will be familiar from other recipes. Note that this time, we don't explicitly state a rendering type as that's done in the `_quarto.yml` file. The output goes to the directory you specified—in this case, `docs`. Browse there and load `index.html` to view the site.

In *step 4*, we add another layer of navigation. Larger websites are advantaged by sidebar navigation, so the code here sets that up, defining section titles and the pages that belong to each section. The use of numbers at the front of each page isn't required but is useful for organizing files in the filesystem. Again, this stanza should be entered into `_quarto.yml`, but pay attention to adding it into the file at the same indentation as the navbar code.

Finally, in *step 5*, we render the whole thing.

There's more...

If you need a full copy of the `_quarto.yml` file, one is provided in the directory as `_quarto.yml.bak`.

See also

There's a lot more you can do with Quarto websites; once you've got the basic one running, you can add tools such as commenting, headers, social metadata, Google Analytics, search, and different reader and download modes, just by adding options to the configuration. Check the Quarto documentation (`https://quarto.org/docs/guide/`) for details.

Adding interactivity with Shiny

Shiny is an R package that allows users to build interactive web applications and dashboards with R code. The package provides a framework for building **user interfaces** (**UIs**) using R functions and allows users to write server-side logic to respond to user input and update the UI in real time.

The basic structure of a Shiny application consists of two main components: the UI and the server-side logic. The UI is built using R functions that define the layout and structure of the web page, including input controls and output elements. The server-side logic is written in R code and runs on the server in response to user input. When a user interacts with the web page, the input is sent to the server, which processes the input and updates the UI in real time.

Shiny elements can be incorporated into R Markdown documents alongside other text and R code, enabling us to make our analyses interactive if needed. Quarto can render and serve these documents. In this recipe, we'll look at how to incorporate some basic interactivity elements into a Quarto document.

Getting ready

As for the other recipes here, we'll need to have installed the Quarto tool, as described at the start of the chapter. We'll also need the `rmarkdown` package and the `palmerpenguins` package.

How to do it...

Creating a Quarto document with Shiny widgets begins by creating an appropriate YAML header and then creating a document with code that creates the layout of widgets and code that runs on the server:

1. Create a header:

    ```
    ---
    title: "Penguin Exploration"
    format: html
    ```

```
server: shiny
---
```

2. Create a panel for input widgets:

````
```{r}
#| panel: sidebar
num_vars <- c("bill_length_mm", "flipper_length_mm", "body_
mass_g")
cat_vars <- c("species", "island", "sex")

selectInput("x", "Variable on X", num_vars)
selectInput("y", "Variable on Y", num_vars)
selectInput("colour", "Colour by", cat_vars)
```
````

3. Create a panel for the dynamic plot:

````
```{r}
#| panel: fill
plotOutput("scatter_plot")
```
````

4. Create the server code:

````
```{r}
#| context: server

library(ggplot2)
library(palmerpenguins)
output$scatter_plot <- renderPlot({

  ggplot(penguins) +
    aes_string(input$x, input$y) +
    geom_point(aes_string(colour = input$colour)) +
    theme_minimal() +
    scale_color_brewer(palette = "Set2")

})
```
````

5. Start the server:

```
quarto serve shiny.qmd
```

And that should start an interactive document in our browser window.

How it works...

The recipe starts in *step 1* by creating a YAML header so that Quarto will know that the code in this page is for running in the server environment that the Shiny widgets need. The YAML header sets the title and output format (which must be `html` and the server type).

In *step 2*, we set up the layout. The R block in the Quarto document takes the special option after the hash-pipe symbols (`#|`), telling Quarto that this bit of code goes in a sidebar layout. The R code that follows then creates two vectors that hold the names of the variables we will use as options in our dynamic plot. Next, we use the `selectInput()` Shiny function to create dynamic input drop-down selectors. The first argument for each is the name that will be used to refer to this element in the code, the second is the label for the element in the rendered page, and the third is a list of values that the element will show in the rendered page—note we are using the values in `num_vars` and `cat_vars`.

Step 3 sets up the layout further, adding a panel that will hold a rendered figure. We use the `plotOutput()` function to state that a plot will eventually be rendered here; the only argument to this function is the `scatter_plot` name that will be used to refer to the element in the code.

In *step 4*, we get into the actual processing and plotting code. The `#| context: server` option tells Quarto that this must be run on the server side, not in the page per se, and that this will need to run every time elements on the page are updated. Making it work is quite simple; after loading the libraries for data and plotting, we use the `renderPlot()` function to create a dynamic plot. The only argument is the plotting code—this is multiline code, so must be wrapped in an anonymous code block using `{ }` to make it a single thing of itself. The code block uses `ggplot` to create a plot. Note that the built-in Shiny `input` object is where the values from the input elements go; each member of the `input` object corresponds to an element we created in our sidebar in *step 2*. We must use `aes_string` to get around `ggplot`'s use of non-standard evaluation and use values stored in variables, rather than variable names themselves. Once the plot is created, we assign it to the built-in Shiny `output` object using the name we selected (`scatter_plot`) in *step 3*.

Once our document is created and saved (for example, in a file called `shiny.qmd`), in *step 5*, we can serve it. This step is done on the command line. The output is an address on the local machine, which can sometimes be clicked or cut and pasted into the web browser address bar to view the running interactive page.

There's more...

If you need to get the full example file for this recipe, you can extract it from the `rbioinfcookbook` package like this:

```
qmd_path <- fs::path_package("extdata", "shiny.qmd",
                             package="rbioinfcookbook")
file.copy(qmd_path, 'somewhere/on/your/system/shiny.qmd')
```

So, you can easily see the structure of the document and hopefully save some typing.

See also

These pages can't be hosted on platforms such as GitHub Pages as they need an active web server program to process dynamic server-side updates. Look at `shinyapps.io` or RStudio for hosting options.

5

Easily Performing Statistical Tests Using Linear Models

Linear models are a statistical tool used to model the relationship between a dependent variable and one or more independent variables. They are based on the assumption that the relationship between the variables is linear, meaning that the change in the dependent variable is proportional to the change in the independent variables.

Linear models are widely used in many fields, including bioinformatics. In bioinformatics, linear models can be used to analyze large datasets, such as gene expression data. For example, linear models can be used to identify differentially expressed genes between different experimental conditions or to predict the expression of genes based on other variables, such as clinical data.

Linear models are closely related to statistical tests, such as t-tests and **analysis of variance** (**ANOVA**). In fact, t-tests and ANOVA can be seen as special cases of linear models. For example, a two-sample t-test is equivalent to a linear model with a binary independent variable, indicating the two groups being compared. Similarly, ANOVA is a generalization of the t-test, where there are more than two groups being compared. In this chapter, we will learn how to take a unified approach that teaches a common way of understanding and applying lots of common statistical tests.

In this chapter, we will cover the following recipes:

- Modeling data with a linear model
- Using a linear model to compare the mean of two groups
- Using a linear model and ANOVA to compare multiple groups in a single variable
- Using linear models and ANOVA to compare multiple groups in multiple variables
- Testing and accounting for interactions between variables in linear models
- Doing tests for differences in data in two categorical variables
- Making predictions using linear models

Technical requirements

We will use `renv` to manage packages in a project-specific way. To use `renv` to install packages, you will first need to install the `renv` package. You can do this by running the following commands in your R console:

1. Install `renv`:

    ```
    install.packages("renv")
    ```

2. Create a new `renv` environment:

    ```
    renv::init()
    ```

    This will create a new directory called `.renv` in your current project directory.

3. You can then install packages with the following:

    ```
    renv::install_packages()
    ```

4. You can also use the `renv` package manager to install Bioconductor packages by running the following command:

    ```
    renv::install("bioc::package name")
    ```

5. For example, to install the `Biobase` package, you would run the following:

    ```
    renv::install("bioc::Biobase")
    ```

6. You can use `renv` to install development packages from GitHub with this command:

    ```
    renv::install("user name/repo name")
    ```

7. For example, to install the user `danmaclean` package `rbioinfcookbook`, you would run the following:

    ```
    renv::install("danmaclean/rbioinfcookbook")
    ```

    You can also install multiple packages at once by separating the package names with a comma. `renv` will automatically handle installing any required dependencies for the packages you install.

    Under `renv`, all packages will be installed into the local project directory and not the main central library, meaning you can have multiple versions of the same package, one specific to each project.

All the sample data you need for this package is in the specially created data package on GitHub at `danmaclean/rbioinfcookbook`. The data will become available in your project after installing that.

For this chapter, we'll need the following packages:

- Regular packages:

  - dplyr

  - ggplot2

  - multcomp

  - rcompanion

- GitHub:

  - danmaclean/rbioinfcookbook

In addition to these packages, we will also need some R tools such as Conda. All these will be described when needed.

Further information

Not all the recipes in this chapter happen in R; some are command line-based setups. I generally assume a bash terminal for these bits. Most macOS and Linux machines will have these available in a terminal application. Windows users will likely not need these specific steps, though various packages for running a Linux subsystem on Windows exist if you wish to search for them.

In R, it is normal practice to load a library and use functions directly by name. Although this is great in short interactive sessions, it can cause confusion when many packages are loaded at once and share function names. To clarify which package and function I am using at a given moment, I will occasionally use the packageName::functionName() convention.

Sometimes, in the middle of a recipe, I'll interrupt the code to dive into some intermediate output or to look at the structure of an object. When that happens, you'll see a code block where each line begins with ## (double hash symbols). Consider the following command:

```
letters[1:5]
```

This will give us the following output:

```
## a b c d e
```

Note that the output lines are prefixed with ##.

Modeling data with a linear model

Linear models are a type of statistical model used to analyze the relationship between a dependent variable and one or more independent variables. In essence, they seek to fit a line that best describes the relationship between these variables, allowing us to make predictions about the dependent variable based on the values of the independent variables. The equation for a simple linear model can be written as follows:

$$y = \beta_0 + \beta_1 x + \varepsilon$$

where y is the dependent variable, x is the independent variable, β_0 and β_1 are coefficients that represent the intercept and slope of the line, respectively, and ε is the error term.

The output of a linear model typically includes the coefficients of the model, which describe the strength and direction of the relationship between the variables, as well as measures of the model's goodness of fit, such as the R-squared value.

Linear models have many applications in bioinformatics, including gene expression analysis, where linear models can be used to identify genes that are differentially expressed between two or more conditions, such as healthy and diseased tissues. Quantitative trait analysis is where linear models can be used to identify genetic variants that are associated with complex traits, such as height or disease risk, and Metabolomics where linear models can be used to identify metabolites that are associated with a particular biological process or disease state based on their levels in biological samples.

In this recipe, we'll look at putting together a linear model for numerous variables and examining the quality of the model to assess whether it is going to be useful.

Getting ready

For this recipe, we'll need the built-in `PlantGrowth` dataset, which describes plants' weights under different treatment regimes.

How to do it...

We follow quite a terse set of commands. Building the model is one of R's great strengths and is extremely easy to do:

1. Load in and look at a summary of the `PlantGrowth` data:

    ```
    data("PlantGrowth")
    summary(PlantGrowth)
    ```

2. Specify a linear model for expression based on the other variables:

    ```
    model_1 <- lm(weight ~ group, data = PlantGrowth)
    summary(model_1)
    ```

3. Plot some diagnostics:

```
plot(model_1, which=1)
```

And with that, we've done all we need to do for the building of a linear model. However, interpreting it is much more difficult, so let's look at that closely by breaking it down.

How it works...

Step 1 uses summary(), a generic function that shows us what our PlantGrowth dataset looks like. It generates the following output:

```
##      weight          group
##   Min.   :3.590    ctrl:10
##   1st Qu.:4.550    trt1:10
##   Median :5.155    trt2:10
##   Mean   :5.073
##   3rd Qu.:5.530
##   Max.   :6.310
```

It shows us that we have a continuous weight variable and a categoric group variable that has 3 levels, with 10 measurements in each.

In *step 2*, we build the model using the lm() function, which takes the standard R formula syntax, putting the thing to be modeled (weight) and then the variables we want to use to model with, along with the data object these variables will be found in. Using summary() on the result shows us a lot of information:

```
## Call:
## lm(formula = weight ~ group, data = PlantGrowth)
##
## Residuals:
##     Min      1Q   Median      3Q     Max
## -1.0710 -0.4180 -0.0060  0.2627  1.3690
## Coefficients:
##               Estimate Std. Error t value Pr(>|t|)
## (Intercept)     5.0320     0.1971  25.527   <2e-16 ***
## grouptrt1      -0.3710     0.2788  -1.331   0.1944
## grouptrt2       0.4940     0.2788   1.772   0.0877 .
## ---
## Signif. codes:  0 '***' 0.001 '**' 0.01 '*' 0.05 '.' 0.1 ' ' 1
##
## Residual standard error: 0.6234 on 27 degrees of freedom
##
```

```
## Multiple R-squared:  0.2641, Adjusted R-squared:  0.2096
## F-statistic: 4.846 on 2 and 27 DF,  p-value: 0.01591
```

There are four blocks:

- **Model call**: This is a restatement of the function we called.

- **Residuals**: This is a set of measures of the distribution of the residuals. We'll look at this later.

- **Coefficients**: These are the terms of the equation and their statistics, meaning the intercept and the coefficient of each of the levels of the variables.

- **Estimate**: (computed values of those). We also see columns of statistics for each The model level statistics summary - some statistics that apply to the whole mode

Let's start at the bottom and look at the model-level summary.

Residual standard error is a measure of how well the line fits the data. In essence, residual standard error is the average distance from each real data point to the line. The further the points are from the line (the worse the fit), the bigger the residual standard error. If you look at the plots again with those distances drawn in, you can see quite clearly that the residual standard error for the second model is much bigger than for the first.

R^2 is another measure of how well the model fits the data. If you're thinking about the correlation coefficient here, then you're in the right area. R^2 describes the proportion of variance in the values that can be explained by the values. It always falls between zero and one. A value closer to one is usually better, but it is very domain and dataset-dependent. With small biological datasets, we don't always see values close to one because of the noise of the system. The proper one to use in most cases is the adjusted R-squared.

The F statistic is an indicator of a relationship between the output and input values of the model. In effect, F-tests show how much better the relationship is in your model than in a model where the relationship is completely random. It's a ratio such that when F is one, the relationship is no stronger than a random relationship. The further above one it is, the more likely it is that there is a real relationship in the model. The p-value here is the frequency at which this size of F would occur in a random relationship with a similar dataset size. As with the other statistics, the significance of the actual size of is dependent on the domain and data being analyzed.

Along with these model-level statistics, linear modeling with `lm()` gives us a set of statistics per input variable (called here the coefficients and in that block in the output). These measure the effect that each coefficient has on the output variable. Basically, a significant coefficient is one that has a non-zero slope and is an important determinant of the value of the output value. `Estimate` is the actual value of the coefficient from the model. These are given in the units of the data. `Std. Error` is a measure of the variability of the strength of the effect, so if some data points give more pronounced values at similar coefficient values, you get a higher variability of the strength. Generally, a lower standard error of the coefficient is good. The t-value is an estimate of how extreme the coefficient value is, meaning how many standard deviations away the estimated coefficient is from the center of a presumed normal distribution with a mean of zero. It is absolutely a t-test t-value, and like in a t-test, we want it to be high. The higher the t value is, the more likely the coefficient is not zero. $Pr(> |t|)$ is a weird shorthand expression that gives the probability of getting a value larger than the p-value. This comes from a t-test within the model and takes into account the dataset size and variability. You can think of it as the p-value of a test that asks whether the coefficient is equal to zero. If p is less than some magical value (e.g. 0.05), you can say that the value of the coefficient is not likely to be 0 and therefore is having an effect on the model.

There's more...

Assessing the model by these statistics is only the first level. The next level should always be to generate and analyze diagnostic plots. This is easily achieved with `plot(model_1, which=1)`, which generates up to six diagnostics, specified by the number next to the `which` argument. The first, using `which=1`, looks like the plot in *Figure 5.1* and is called a **residuals versus fitted** plot. This plot is used to work out whether the residuals (the distance between the data points and the eventual fitted line of the model) have any pattern. There should be no pattern here since the distances should essentially be random. Any pattern indicates that the model does not fit the data well and may not be good. The flat line indicates that the residuals are fine in this model:

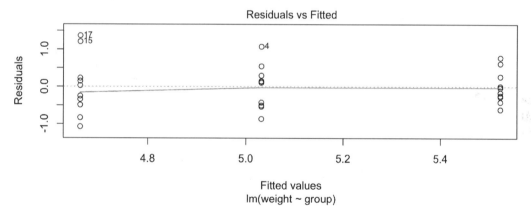

Figure 5.1 – A residuals versus fitted plot on the PlantGrowth dataset

The second plot, using `which=2`, is a **normal Q–Q plot**, as seen in *Figure 5.2*. This plot shows how well the data itself fits to an ideal normal distribution. The closer the points fit to the line, the better, though some slight deviation at the extreme ends is fine. The points at the end in *Figure 5.2* look good enough:

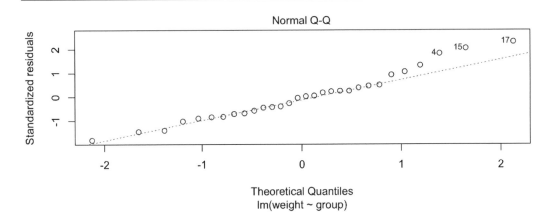

Figure 5.2 – A normal Q–Q plot on the PlantGrowth dataset

The third plot, using `which=3`, is a **scale-location plot**, as seen in *Figure 5.3*. The plot shows how the variance changes across the range of the fitted data. The linear model assumes that the variation should be equal across the data, so if the line stays flat (as it does here), then we have met that assumption. If not, it's reason to be suspicious of the usefulness of the model.

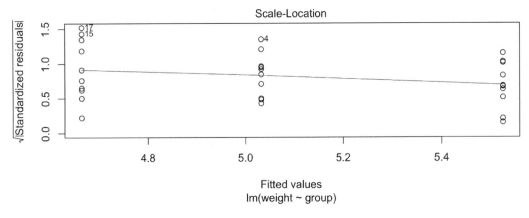

Figure 5.3 – A scale-location plot on the PlantGrowth dataset

The next plot I have shown, which uses `which=5`, is a **Cook's distance plot** that shows the change in fitted value and helps identify outliers in the input data. Any data point with values much larger than others indicates that this value is having a perhaps undue influence on the fit of the model and should be examined carefully.

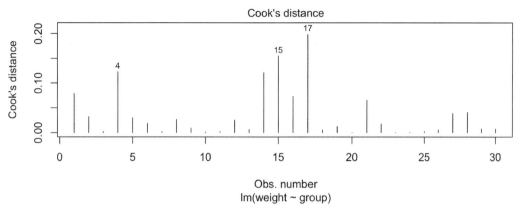

Figure 5.4 – A Cook's distance plot on the PlantGrowth dataset

And that is how we build and diagnose a linear model object.

Using a linear model to compare the mean of two groups

The t-test is a statistical method used to help us decide whether there is likely to be a difference between the means of two groups. t-tests are probably the most widely used tests in bioinformatics and biology, usually applied without consideration as to whether the assumptions of the test hold and can be intepreted without criticism. By learning how to do the t-test through building a linear model, you will be able to test whether the assumptions hold since a well fit model implies a good fit to the assumptions. The t-test is a special case of the linear model because it can be framed as a linear regression problem with a binary predictor variable.

In the linear model, we try to fit a linear equation that describes the relationship between a response output variable (dependent variable) and one or more predictor input variables (independent variables). In the case of a t-test, we have one binary predictor variable, which represents the two groups being compared.

Suppose we want to compare the mean dry weight of plants grown under two different treatments, a test (B) and a control (A). We can set up a linear model where the response variable is the weight and the predictor variable is a binary variable for treatment. The linear model equation can be written as follows:

$dryWeight = \beta_0 + \beta_1 \cdot treatment + \epsilon$

where β_0 is the intercept, β_1 is the coefficient associated with the binary predictor variable *treatment*, and ϵ is the error term.

The t-test can be derived from this linear model by testing whether the coefficient β_1 is likely to be zero. If it is not, then there is evidence of a significant difference in the mean dry weight between the two treatments.

Getting ready

We'll use a modified version of the `PlantGrowth` data, available in the `rbioinfcookbook` package. We'll also use `dplyr`.

How to do it...

We proceed to do the t-test by building a linear model and interpreting its outputs. Take the following steps:

1. Load the data and examine it:

```
library(rbioinfcookbook)
summary(plant_growth_two)
```

2. Build the linear model:

```
model_1 <- lm(weight ~ group, data = plant_growth_two)
summary(model_1)
```

3. Manually work out the group mean difference:

```
library(dplyr)
group_means <- plant_growth_two |>
  group_by(group) |>
  summarize(mean_wt = mean(weight))

group_means

difference_in_means <- group_means$mean_wt[1] - group_means$mean_wt[2]

difference_in_means
```

These few steps are all we need.

How it works...

Step 1 clarifies to us that we have just two treatments in our data loaded from `rbioinfcookbook`. The `summary()` function shows that there are ten measurements in each. Note that the t-test can't be done on data with more than two groups. If you try to do this evaluation with data with more groups, the interpretation falls apart.

Step 2 builds the model in the same manner that we saw in the *Modeling data with a linear model* recipe. The code is nearly identical, but the interpretation of the output is the key, so let's look at that:

```
## Call:
## lm(formula = weight ~ group, data = plant_growth_two)
##
## Residuals:
##     Min     1Q Median     3Q    Max
## -0.862 -0.410 -0.006  0.280  1.078
##
## Coefficients:
##              Estimate Std. Error t value Pr(>|t|)
## (Intercept)    5.0320     0.1637  30.742   <2e-16 ***
## grouptrt2      0.4940     0.2315   2.134   0.0469 *
## ---
## Signif. codes:  0 '***' 0.001 '**' 0.01 '*' 0.05 '.' 0.1 ' ' 1
##
## Residual standard error: 0.5176 on 18 degrees of freedom
## Multiple R-squared:  0.2019, Adjusted R-squared:  0.1576
## F-statistic: 4.554 on 1 and 18 DF,  p-value: 0.04685
```

In this output, in the `Coefficients:` block, we can see that the coefficient between the two groups is 0.494, indicating that the mean of `trt2` is about half a gram greater than the mean of the `ctrl`. We also see that the *Pr(> |t|)* is 0.0469. We already know that the value *Pr(> |t|)* (or the p-value of the coefficient) tells us the probability that we would see the slope observed or greater in random samples if the real difference were zero, so we can interpret this value as the p-value of t-test. In this case, we see a value less than the typical cutoff of 0.05, indicating that the slope size would not likely happen by chance. Together, these suggest that the difference between the two group means is not likely to be zero, so can be interpreted as being significant.

In *step 3*, we use a little `dplyr` code to evaluate the difference between the group means as a confirmation of the coefficient:

```
## # A tibble: 2 × 2
##   group mean_wt
##   <fct>   <dbl>
## 1 ctrl     5.03
## 2 trt2     5.53
```

The difference between `ctrl` and `trt2` is -0.494, corresponding to the value of the coefficient observed in *step 2*.

There's more...

Don't forget to use `plot(model_1)` to generate diagnostic plots to evaluate the fit of the model, as described in the *Modeling data with a linear model* recipe. A good fit indicates that the assumptions of the model and t-test are met and the result is reliable.

Using a linear model and ANOVA to compare multiple groups in a single variable

ANOVA is a statistical method used to test whether there is a significant difference between two or more groups. ANOVA compares the variance within groups to the variance between groups to determine if there is a statistically significant difference in the means of the groups. ANOVA is commonly used in experiments where a response variable is measured across several groups under different experimental conditions.

ANOVA can be used to compare gene expression levels across multiple samples under different experimental conditions, the response variable is the gene expression level, and the categorical variable is the experimental condition. ANOVA can also be used in clinical trials to compare the effectiveness of different treatments or interventions for a disease or medical condition.

Linear models can be used to perform ANOVA by fitting a linear model to the data with a categorical variable that represents the groups. The linear model equation can be written as follows:

$$y_i = \beta_0 + \beta_1 x_{1,i} + \beta_2 x_{2,i} + \ldots + \beta_{k-1} x_{k-1,i} + \epsilon_i$$

where y_i is the response variable for the i-th observation, $x_{j,i}$ is the j-th categorical variable for the i-th observation (j = 1, 2, …, k-1), and ϵ_i is the error term.

To perform ANOVA, we compare the variability between the groups to the variability within the groups. The F-test is used to test whether the differences between the group means are statistically significant. The F-statistic is calculated as the ratio of the variance between groups to the variance within groups.

In this recipe, we'll look at the simplest type of ANOVA, the one-way ANOVA, which has multiple groups in a single variable.

Getting ready

We'll use built-in base functions and the `multcompt` package. The recipe needs only built-in datasets. We will again use the full `PlantGrowth` data. Recall that it has three groups in `weight`.

How to do it...

The statistical power of R shines again in these few but powerful steps:

1. Build the model:

```
model_1 <- lm(weight ~ group, data = PlantGrowth)
summary(model_1)
```

2. Perform a basic ANOVA and Tukey's post hoc test:

```
library(multcomp)
tested <- glht(model_1, linfct = mcp(group = "Tukey"))
summary(tested)
```

Again, just a couple of steps are all we need for a powerful analysis.

How it works...

Step 1 sets up the model in a familiar fashion. The `summary()` of the model looks like this:

```
## Call:
## lm(formula = weight ~ group, data = PlantGrowth)
##
## Residuals:
##     Min      1Q  Median      3Q     Max
## -1.0710 -0.4180 -0.0060  0.2627  1.3690
##
## Coefficients:
##             Estimate Std. Error t value Pr(>|t|)
## (Intercept)   5.0320     0.1971  25.527   <2e-16 ***
## grouptrt1    -0.3710     0.2788  -1.331   0.1944
## grouptrt2     0.4940     0.2788   1.772   0.0877 .
## ---
## Signif. codes:  0 '***' 0.001 '**' 0.01 '*' 0.05 '.' 0.1 ' ' 1
##
## Residual standard error: 0.6234 on 27 degrees of freedom
## Multiple R-squared:  0.2641, Adjusted R-squared:  0.2096
## F-statistic: 4.846 on 2 and 27 DF,  p-value: 0.01591
```

We can see from the overall *p*-value that there is something going on in the model, and it looks like it might be significant, but the individual coefficients are not significant. There are also only two coefficients, which is correct, but there are three possible group contrasts. By default, the linear model takes one group (the first in the dataset) as a common reference and won't automatically cycle through all possible contrasts. For ANOVA, we have to be specific about the contrasts in a post hoc test.

We do exactly that in *step 2*, using the `multcomp` package to do a general linear model hypothesis test through the `glht()` function. The function is more flexible with respect to which designs and contrasts you can get out than the built-in `TukeyHSD()` function, though it is a little more complicated. The basic case is straightforward though. The `linfct()` option just takes a specification of the things to be tested, and the `mcp()` function helps generate the comparison based on a text description, here that the variable group should be analyzed by `Tukey`. The output looks as follows:

```
##    Simultaneous Tests for General Linear Hypotheses
##
## Multiple Comparisons of Means: Tukey Contrasts
##
##
## Fit: lm(formula = weight ~ group, data = PlantGrowth)
##
## Linear Hypotheses:
##                  Estimate Std. Error t value Pr(>|t|)
## trt1 - ctrl == 0  -0.3710     0.2788  -1.331   0.3909
## trt2 - ctrl == 0   0.4940     0.2788   1.772   0.1980
## trt2 - trt1 == 0   0.8650     0.2788   3.103   0.0121 *
## ---
## Signif. codes:  0 '***' 0.001 '**' 0.01 '*' 0.05 '.' 0.1 ' ' 1
## (Adjusted p values reported -- single-step method)
```

By printing the summary, we see the contrast hypotheses written explicitly (e.g. the probability that the difference between `ctrl` and `trt1` is zero). The conclusion is that there is no evidence to suggest either treatment is different from the control, but the difference we observe between `trt1` and `trt2` occurs by chance only about 1.2% of the time, so it is deemed significant.

And that's it! That was a properly done and specified use of the linear model and a subsequent ANOVA with Tukey's post hoc used to determine differences.

There's more...

In *step 1*, we generated a model, and R decided what the baseline should be. If we wish to, we can specify that explicitly using the `relevl()` function and the `ref` option as follows:

```
df <- PlantGrowth
df$group<- relevel(df$group, ref="trt2")
model_2 <- lm(weight ~ group  , data = df,)
summary(model_2)
```

In the `summary()` output, we can see the comparisons are all done based on that new reference. We don't do this as a method for generating all comparisons as it gets tedious quickly and generates multiple comparison errors. The `multcomp` package is cleaner, offers many more options for different types of comparisons, and corrects *p*-values for multiple hypothesis tests.

Using linear models and ANOVA to compare multiple groups in multiple variables

Two-way ANOVA is a statistical method used to analyze the effects of two categorical independent variables, also known as factors, on a continuous dependent variable. The two independent variables can be either fixed or random.

The main purpose of two-way ANOVA is to examine whether there is a significant interaction between the two independent variables, as well as to determine the main effects of each independent variable on the dependent variable.

The analysis involves calculating the sum of squares for each of the effects and the interaction and comparing these values to their respective degrees of freedom to obtain F ratios. The F ratios are then compared to critical values from an F-distribution to determine whether the effects are statistically significant.

Like the one-way ANOVA seen in the *Using a linear model and ANOVA to compare multiple groups in a single variable* recipe, the basis is a linear model, and by assessing that, we can help to ensure that the assumptions of the test are met.

Getting ready

We'll again use the `multcomp` package and a synthetic expression dataset in the `rbioinfcookbook` package called `compost`. Note that the aim isn't to find individual differentially expressed genes, but rather to assess whether the expression level of genes in general is affected by `Replicate` or `Treatment`.

How to do it...

The method is remarkably similar to one-way ANOVA but with complications for potential interactions and more explicit comparisons:

1. Summarize and model the new data:

    ```
    library(rbioinfcookbook)
    summary(expression)
    model_1 <- lm(Expression ~  Treatment + Replicate, data =
    expression)
    summary(model_1)
    ```

2. Perform Tukey's post hoc test:

```
library(multcomp)
tested <- glht(model_1,
               linfct = mcp(Replicate = "Tukey",
                            Treatment = "Tukey"))
summary(tested)
```

3. Compare the test output with a plot:

```
library(ggplot2)

ggplot(expression) +
  aes(Treatment, Expression) +
  geom_boxplot() +
  geom_jitter(aes(colour = Replicate))
```

And that's all we need to do to complete a multi-variable ANOVA. However, the interpretations here are more difficult than for the one-way method, so let's look at them:

How it works...

Step 1 is by now a very familiar model creation step. This is elaborated by the addition of a second variable in the formula, which is added using the + operator. This is therefore a simple additive model and more complicated formulations are needed if you are checking for or want to model interactions between variables. The summary(expression) shows us that we have six genes, three treatments, and three replicates. The following summary(model_1) shows us that there is a likely effect of Treatment on expression, though it isn't clear what. Also, the p-value is a model-level value, so while there are some significant coefficients, it isn't clear which:

```
## Call:
## lm(formula = Expression ~ Treatment + Replicate, data = expression)
##
## Residuals:
##     Min      1Q  Median      3Q     Max
## -3.9665 -1.7154 -0.0843  1.7505  5.0958
##
## Coefficients:
##               Estimate Std. Error t value Pr(>|t|)
## (Intercept)     4.8093     0.7081   6.792 1.39e-08 ***
## TreatmentDrugA  2.3096     0.7757   2.978  0.00451 **
## TreatmentDrugB  1.6672     0.7757   2.149  0.03657 *
## Replicate2      0.3843     0.7757   0.495  0.62250
```

```
## Replicate3        -0.3078       0.7757   -0.397   0.69322
## ---
## Signif. codes:   0 '***' 0.001 '**' 0.01 '*' 0.05 '.' 0.1 ' ' 1
##
## Residual standard error: 2.327 on 49 degrees of freedom
## Multiple R-squared:  0.173,  Adjusted R-squared:  0.1054
## F-statistic: 2.562 on 4 and 49 DF,  p-value: 0.04995
```

In *step 2*, we perform Tukey's post hoc test with `glht()`, elaborating the variables more clearly and receiving the following output:

```
##     Simultaneous Tests for General Linear Hypotheses
##
## Multiple Comparisons of Means: Tukey Contrasts
##
##
## Fit: lm(formula = Expression ~ Treatment + Replicate, data =
## expression)
##
## Linear Hypotheses:
##                            Estimate Std. Error t value
## Pr(>|t|)
## Replicate: 2 - 1 ==
## 0            0.3843       0.7757   0.495    0.9835
## Replicate: 3 - 1 ==
## 0           -0.3078       0.7757  -0.397    0.9929
## Replicate: 3 - 2 ==
## 0           -0.6921       0.7757  -0.892    0.8727
## Treatment: DrugA - Control ==
## 0    2.3096     0.7757   2.978    0.0243 *
## Treatment: DrugB - Control ==
## 0    1.6672     0.7757   2.149    0.1707
## Treatment: DrugB - DrugA ==
## 0    -0.6424     0.7757  -0.828    0.8997
## ---
## Signif. codes:   0 '***' 0.001 '**' 0.01 '*' 0.05 '.' 0.1 ' ' 1
## (Adjusted p values reported -- single-step method)
```

It is clear that we have a significant effect of `DrugA` on Expression but not any effect of other Drugs or Replicates.

Finally, in *step 3*, we do a very sensible sanity check by plotting the data in the same way as we modeled it in order to check whether the results from the test match up with intuition from the plot, as seen in *Figure 5.5*:

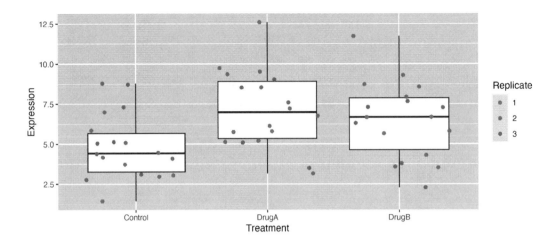

Figure 5.5 – A basic plot for the data for cross-referencing with the test output

And that gives us a sensible and easy way to approach ANOVA with a linear model and compare the results with a plot.

Testing and accounting for interactions between variables in linear models

An interaction between variables occurs when the effect of one predictor variable on the response variable depends on the level of another predictor variable. In other words, the effect of one variable is not constant across different levels of the other variable. The interaction can occur between different drug regimes in medical trials or generally multiple experimental conditions being changed.

Linear models can model interactions by including interaction terms in the model formula. An interaction term is the product of two or more predictor variables, where each predictor variable is centered to have a mean of zero.

Suppose we have a linear regression model with two predictor variables, x1 and x2, and we want to examine their interaction. The interaction term can be included in the model as follows:

$$y = \beta_0 + \beta_1 x_1 + \beta_2 x_2 + \beta_3(x_1 \times x_2) + \epsilon$$

In this model, y is the response variable; x_1 and x_2 are predictor variables; β_0 is the intercept; β_1 and β_2 are the coefficients for x_1 and x_2, respectively; β_3 is the coefficient for the interaction term between x_1 and x_2; and ϵ is the error term.

These models are complicated, and you need to take particular care to interpret them and prevent confounding real results and making wrong conclusions from the data. In this recipe, we will look at how to detect a potential interaction using a simple graphical method and how to model it in a straightforward way. We will keep in mind that large interaction models can sometimes be very complex and may require us to seek the advice of statisticians, but the approach here is useful for first-level analysis and to guide further questions.

Getting ready

In this recipe, we'll use a plant yield size dataset from `rbioinfcookbook` called `compost` and the `dplyr` and `ggplot2` packages.

How to do it...

The first step to take when testing for an interaction is to plot. Then, we can start to model:

1. Check for a potential interaction:

    ```
    library(rbioinfcookbook)
    summary(compost)

    interaction.plot(compost$compost, compost$supplement,
    compost$size,
                    xlab="Compost Type", ylab="Size", trace.label =
    "Supplement"
                    )
    ```

2. Add an explicit interaction column:

    ```
    compost_int <- dplyr::mutate(compost,
        compost_supp = interaction(compost, supplement)
    )
    ```

3. Model the interaction as a separate variable:

    ```
    model_1 <- lm(size ~ compost_supp, data=compost_int)
    summary(model_1)

    library(multcomp)
    tested <- glht(model_1,
                  linfct = mcp(compost_supp = "Tukey")
    )
    summary(tested)
    ```

4.   Create a plot:

```
library(ggplot2)
ggplot(compost) +
  aes(compost, size) +
  geom_jitter(aes(colour = supplement), position=position_
dodge(width=0.5))
```

With these steps, we have a fairly straightforward way of checking and modeling an interaction between variables.

How it works...

In *step 1*, we first examine the data with summary() to familiarize ourselves with it. Then, we create an interaction plot using the function interaction.plot(), which takes vectors as input rather than the entire data frame. We must use the $ subsetting on our column names. The resulting plot in *Figure 5.6* shows the lines that join the means of the groups in the data. When we see crossed lines, we can suspect the presence of an interaction:

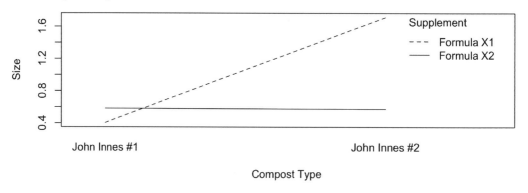

Figure 5.6 – An interaction plot

We must move on to start to model that interaction. While it is possible to specify the interaction in the lm() step with the formula syntax, the interpretation can become difficult and the implementation can become complex. You may require input from statisticians, who may not be readily available. Instead, we take an easier but less powerful approach. In *step 2*, we use the interaction() function and mutate() to create a column compost_supp that describes the interaction between the compost and supplement. Then, in *step 3*, use that new column in the model directly. The post hoc test from the glht() function enumerates all the pairwise interactions possible, as described in the compost_supp column.

The output appears as follows:

```
##    Simultaneous Tests for General Linear Hypotheses
##
## Multiple Comparisons of Means: Tukey Contrasts
##
##
## Fit: lm(formula = size ~ compost_supp, data = compost_int)
##
## Linear Hypotheses:
##                                                                Estimate
Std. Error t value Pr(>|t|)
## John Innes #2.Formula X1 - John Innes #1.Formula X1 ==
0  1.30865    0.13666    9.576    <1e-04 ***
## John Innes #1.Formula X2 - John Innes #1.Formula X1 ==
0  0.17780    0.13666    1.301    0.570
## John Innes #2.Formula X2 - John Innes #1.Formula X1 ==
0  0.17044    0.13666    1.247    0.603
## John Innes #1.Formula X2 - John Innes #2.Formula X1 == 0
-1.13085    0.13666    -8.275    <1e-04 ***
## John Innes #2.Formula X2 - John Innes #2.Formula X1 == 0
-1.13821    0.13666    -8.329    <1e-04 ***
## John Innes #2.Formula X2 - John Innes #1.Formula X2 == 0
-0.00736    0.13666    -0.054    1.000
## ---
## Signif. codes:  0 '***' 0.001 '**' 0.01 '*' 0.05 '.' 0.1 ' ' 1
## (Adjusted p values reported -- single-step method)
```

This shows that three of the interaction contrasts are likely significant. In *step 4*, we create a simple plot (*Figure 5.7*) using ggplot that serves as a check for these conclusions:

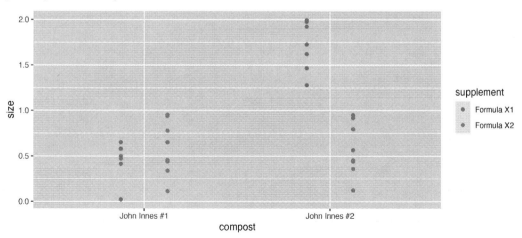

Figure 5.7 – A plot of the data

And that is how we perform a test for an interaction and plot to check our conclusions against the representation of the data.

Doing tests for differences in data in two categorical variables

Categorical output variables, also known as response variables or dependent variables, are variables that take on discrete values from a finite set of possible outcomes. We can consider that there are two types of categorical variables: nominal and ordinal.

Ordinal variables have a natural ordering among the categories. Examples of ordinal variables include education level, income bracket, and satisfaction ratings. In linear models, ordinal variables can be represented using their numerical values or by assigning each category a numerical rank. For example, in a linear model predicting job satisfaction based on salary, the ordinal variable income bracket could be assigned a numerical rank from one to five based on the size of the income range. Ranking helps us to use the linear model framework fairly easily.

Nominal variables are variables that have no inherent order or ranking among the categories. Examples of nominal variables include gender, race, and occupation. In linear models, nominal variables are often represented using dummy variables or one-hot encoding. Dummy variables are binary variables that indicate whether an observation belongs to a particular category or not. For example, in a linear model predicting income based on gender, a male might be assigned a value of 1 for the male gender dummy variable, while a female is assigned 0. Modeling these gets tricky and requires us to build and compare different models. So instead of modeling in the way we've done previously, we will look at using proportional tests to analyze data of this sort. A typical proportional test people in bioinformatics are familiar with is the chi-squared (χ^2) test, which is a special case of a 2x2 category test.

In this recipe, we shall look at ordinal and nominal cases.

Getting ready

To examine ordinal categoric data, we shall use some data on plant disease scoring. The data frame contains information on three strains of a pathogen (control, mild, and deadly), some replicate information, and a categoric score from a visual disease scoring exercise. For the nominal case, we will use tabulated frequencies of side effects reported by patients after different test treatment regimes. Both datasets are from the rbioinfcookbook package. We will also use some methods from dplyr, multcomp, and rcompanion.

How to do it...

Let's look at the ordinal case first, considering how to build a data frame to ensure R knows about the order in the data:

1. Set the type of values explicitly:

```
library(rbioinfcookbook)
library(dplyr)

scores <- disease_scores |> transmute(
    strain = as.factor(strain),
    replicate = as.factor(replicate),
    score = as.factor(score)
)
```

2. Set the ordering and rank the scores:

```
scores <- scores |> transmute(
    score = factor(score, levels = c("1","2","3","4"), ordered =
TRUE),
    rank_score = rank(score),
    strain,replicate
)
```

3. Model and conduct ANOVA on the ranked scores:

```
model <- lm(rank_score ~ strain, data = scores)
library(multcomp)
summary(glht(
    model, linfct = mcp(strain = "Tukey")
))
```

4. Load in the nominal side effects data and tabulate and perform a proportion test:

```
library(rcompanion)
tabulated <- xtabs(frequency ~ treatment + side_effect, data =
side_effects)

tabulated
pairwiseNominalIndependence(tabulated, method = "fdr")
```

5. Create a balloon plot for the data:

```
library(ggplot2)
ggplot(side_effects) +
  aes(treatment, side_effect) +
  geom_point(aes(size = frequency))
```

We end up with a good view of the categoric data and how it varies by group.

How it works...

In the first part of the recipe, we look at ordinal data. The data we load is disease scores, which are given numbers for the categories. This is a clear source of confusion; although the categories look like numbers, we can't treat them as such, as they don't behave like that. For example, a score of four doesn't indicate twice as much disease as a score of two. In *step 1*, we explicitly make the numbers into factors, which will help R to treat them as they should be. In *step 2*, we use `transmute()` to change the score column of the data frame in place to the ordered form using `factor()` with the `ordered` option set. We then create a column stating the rank of the observation throughout the data. Note that `transmute()` quietly discards columns that aren't mentioned, so we add the names of the columns we want to keep (but not change) to the end of the function. We can now model in the way that we are used to, and we do so in *step 3*. The results of the modeling and ANOVA appear as follows:

```
##    Simultaneous Tests for General Linear Hypotheses
##
##    Multiple Comparisons of Means: Tukey Contrasts
##
##
##    Fit: lm(formula = rank_score ~ strain, data = scores)
##
##    Linear Hypotheses:
##                          Estimate Std. Error t value Pr(>|t|)
##    deadly - control == 0   5.5000     0.9129   6.025  0.00211 **
##    mild - control == 0     3.5000     0.9129   3.834  0.02017 *
##    mild - deadly == 0     -2.0000     0.9129  -2.191  0.15164
##    ---
##    Signif. codes:  0 '***' 0.001 '**' 0.01 '*' 0.05 '.' 0.1 ' ' 1
##    (Adjusted p values reported -- single-step method)
```

We can see that the deadly and mild strains show significantly greater evidence of disease than the control, though they do not differ from each other.

In *step 4*, we change over to looking at some nominal, non-ordered data. There's no way to systematically convert these categories to numbers (e.g., by ranking), and while it is possible to examine them with linear models in the way we do in the earlier steps, it is much more complicated. So, we take advantage of proportion tests. First, we must tabulate the input data frame using `xtabs()`, which takes a formula syntax input for collapsing the data. It looks like this:

```
##               side_effect
## treatment   headache nausea none
##    regime_a       30    110  100
##    regime_b       32    120   70
##    regime_c       30    142    0
```

Then, we pass the `tabulated` object to the `pairwiseNominalIndependence()` function, which will carry out a range of tests. The `"fdr"` option tells it which method to use to adjust the *p*-value. The results show us that `regime_a` and `regime_b` don't show any differences in their side effects (at *adj.p* < = 0.05) but that `regime_c` differs from the others:

```
## Comparison p.Fisher p.adj.Fisher p.Gtest p.adj.Gtest p.Chisq p.adj.
Chisq
## regime_a : regime_b 7.81e-02      7.81e-02  0.0773  0.0773  7.81e-
02      7.81e-02
## regime_a : regime_c 1.66e-28      4.98e-28  0.0000  0.0000  1.89e-
21      5.67e-21
## regime_b : regime_c 5.26e-20      7.89e-20  0.0000  0.0000  3.38e-
15      5.07e-15
```

When we make a balloon plot of the data in *step 5*, by mapping frequency to spot size (*Figure 5.8*), we can see clearly why this is. `regime_c` has fewer patients reporting that they suffered no side effects:

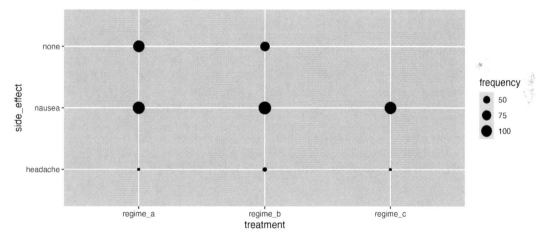

Figure 5.8 – A balloon plot of categoric data

With this, we have a way of identifying differences in categoric data.

Making predictions using linear models

Linear models are commonly used in bioinformatics for prediction tasks due to their simplicity, interpretability, and ability to handle high-dimensional datasets. In bioinformatics, researchers often work with large datasets that have a large number of features (such as gene expression data or sequence data), making it challenging to analyze them with more complex models. Linear models offer a straightforward and computationally efficient way to analyze these datasets. Linear models can help researchers identify genes or genetic variants that are associated with a particular trait or disease. They can also be used in feature selection, which is an important step in bioinformatics data analysis. Feature selection aims to identify the most relevant features (genes, proteins, etc.) that are associated with the outcome of interest (disease, drug response, etc.). Linear models can be used to rank features based on their importance and select the most relevant ones for further analysis, the assumption being that the subset of variables that gives the strongest prediction of the actual data is the best for analyzing that data.

In this recipe, we'll take a look at doing tasks such as predicting new data on our response variable given some input values.

Getting ready

For this recipe, we'll use a dataset built into ggplot2 called txhousing.

How to do it...

We'll begin by creating a model of house prices based on the txhousing:

1. Build a model relating the median house price to city, year, and month of sale:

    ```
    library(ggplot2)
    str(txhousing)
    model <- lm(median ~ city + year + month, data = txhousing)
    ```

2. Create a data frame of possible values from which to predict:

    ```
    new_values <- data.frame(city = c("Abilene"), year = c(2000),
    month = c(2))
    ```

3. Predict the house price for that city/year/month combination:

    ```
    predict(model, newdata=new_values)
    ```

4. Get a confidence interval for the prediction:

    ```
    predict(model, newdata=new_values, interval =  'predict')
    ```

And that is all we need to predict.

How it works...

The recipe is really simple because, again, we are doing something that really plays to R's strengths. In *step 1*, we create a linear model using the house price data, expecting that the `city`, `year`, and `month` variables are going to be important. We then create a new data frame of values for those variables that don't necessarily exist in the original data (*step 2*) and use the `predict()` function to get an estimate of what the median price would be (*step 3*), which is reported as follows:

```
##            1
## 65392.3
```

The elaboration in *step 4* adds the `interval` option, which allows us to specify that we would like a prediction confidence interval. By default, it is a 95% confidence interval:

```
##          fit      lwr        upr
## 1 65392.3 37290.63 93493.96
```

And that is how we build a linear model and use it to predict values.

See also

The basic idea of feature selection (finding the best/most useful variables) is that the ones that give the strongest predictions are the best. The topic is broad and there are many approaches. It is a big topic in machine learning; looking at the `mlr` and `caret` packages is a good start.

6

Performing Quantitative RNA-seq

RNA-Seq has revolutionized the study of gene expression by providing highly accurate estimates of transcript abundances through high-sensitivity detection and high-throughput analysis. Bioinformatic analysis pipelines that use RNA-Seq data typically start with a read quality control step, followed by either alignment to a reference or assembling sequence reads into longer transcripts *afresh*. After that, transcript abundances are estimated with sequence read counting and statistical models, and differential expression between samples is assessed. There are many technologies available for all steps of this pipeline. Quality control and read alignment will usually take place outside of R, so analysis in R will begin with a file containing transcript or gene annotations (such as GFF and BED files) and a file of aligned reads (such as BAM files).

The tools in R for performing analysis are powerful and flexible. Many of them are part of the Bioconductor suite and integrate very well. The key question researchers wish to answer with RNAseq is usually, *which transcripts are differentially expressed?* In this chapter, we'll look at some recipes for that in standard cases, where we already know the genomic positions of the genes (that is, we have a reference genome), and in cases where we need to find unannotated transcripts. We'll also look at other important recipes that help answer *How many replicates are enough?* and *Which allele is expressed more?*

In this chapter, we will cover the following recipes:

- Estimating differential expression with `edgeR`
- Estimating differential expression with DESeq2
- Estimating differential expression with Kallisto and Sleuth
- Using Sleuth to analyze time course experiments
- Analyzing splice variants with `SGSeq`
- Performing power analysis with `powsimR`
- Finding unannotated transcribed regions

- Finding regions that show high expression ab initio with `bumphunter`
- Differential peak analysis with `csaw`
- Estimating batch effects using SVA
- Finding allele-specific expression with `AllelicImbalance`
- Presenting RNA-Seq data using `ComplexHeatmap`

Technical requirements

We will use `renv` to manage packages in a project-specific way. To use `renv` to install packages, you will first need to install the `renv` package. You can do this by running the following commands in your R console:

1. Install `renv`:

   ```
   install.packages("renv")
   ```

2. Create a new `renv` environment:

   ```
   renv::init()
   ```

   This will create a new directory called `.renv` in your current project directory.

3. You can then install packages with the following command:

   ```
   renv::install_packages()
   ```

4. You can also use the `renv` package manager to install Bioconductor packages by running the following command:

   ```
   renv::install("bioc::package name")
   ```

5. For example, to install the `Biobase` package, you would run the following:

   ```
   renv::install("bioc::Biobase")
   ```

6. You can use `renv` to install development packages from GitHub, like so:

   ```
   renv::install("user name/repo name")
   ```

7. For example, to install the `danmaclean` user's `rbioinfcookbook` package, you would run the following:

   ```
   renv::install("danmaclean/rbioinfcookbook")
   ```

You can also install multiple packages at once by separating the package names with a comma. `renv` will automatically handle installing any required dependencies for the packages you install.

Under `renv`, all packages will be installed in the local project directory and not the main central library, meaning you can have multiple versions of the same package, one specific one for each project.

All the sample data you need for this package is in the specially created data package on GitHub called `danmaclean/rbioinfcookbook`. The data will become available in your project once you've installed it.

For this chapter, we'll need the following packages:

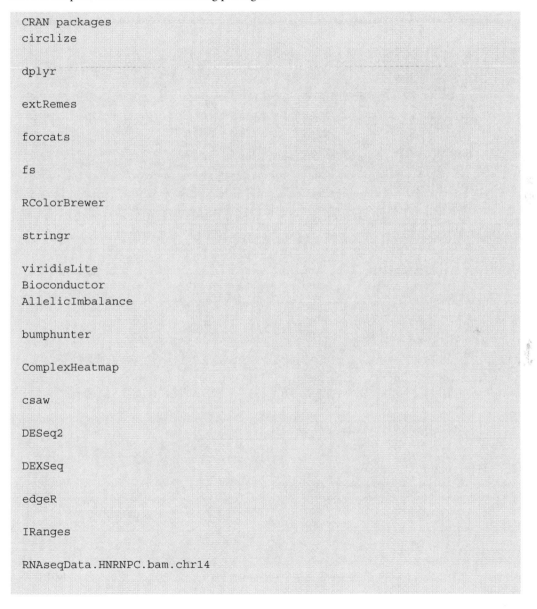

```
CRAN packages
circlize

dplyr

extRemes

forcats

fs

RColorBrewer

stringr

viridisLite
Bioconductor
AllelicImbalance

bumphunter

ComplexHeatmap

csaw

DESeq2

DEXSeq

edgeR

IRanges

RNAseqData.HNRNPC.bam.chr14
```

```
Rsamtools

rtracklayer

SGSeq

SummarizedExperiment

sva

TxDb.Hsapiens.UCSC.hg19.knownGene

VariantAnnotation
GitHub
bvieth/powsimR

danmaclean/rbioinfcookbook

pachterlab/sleuth
```

That's a long list, but it should be everything you need. Some further instructions are provided in specific recipes.

Further information

In R, it is normal practice to load a library and use functions directly by name. Although this is great in short interactive sessions, it can cause confusion when many packages are loaded at once and share function names. To clarify which package and function I am using at a given moment, I will occasionally use the `packageName::functionName()` convention.

Sometimes, in the middle of a recipe, I'll interrupt the code to dive into some intermediate output or to look at the structure of an object. When that happens, you'll see a code block where each line begins with ## (double hash symbols). Consider the following command:

```
letters[1:5]
```

This will give us the following output:

```
## a b c d e
```

Note that the output lines are prefixed with ##.

Estimating differential expression with edgeR

The `edgeR` package in Bioconductor is a tool for identifying differentially expressed genes from RNA-Seq data. It offers a range of normalization methods for correcting differences in library size and sequencing depth, including the **trimmed mean of M-values** (**TMM**) method. TMM is a popular normalization method that uses the mean of log-transformed expression values to scale the data, taking into account the differences in library size between samples.

In addition to normalization, `edgeR` also provides a range of statistical models for testing differential expression. One of the main models used in `edgeR` is the negative binomial model, which is a type of **generalized linear model** (**GLM**) that is well-suited for modeling count data such as RNA-Seq data. The negative binomial model allows for the estimation of the mean and dispersion of the expression counts, and can account for overdispersion, which is common in RNA-Seq data. Overall, `edgeR` is a powerful and widely used tool for differential expression analysis of RNA-Seq data, offering a range of normalization and statistical modeling options to help researchers identify significant changes in gene expression between sample groups.

In this recipe, we'll look at some options, from having the read counts in an object to identifying the differentially expressed features in a genome. So that we can concentrate on the differential expression analysis part of the process, we'll use a prepared dataset. Other chapters in this book will show you how to go from raw data to this stage if you're looking for that step.

We will use the `modencodefly` data from the NHGRI **ENcyclopedia of DNA elements** (**ENCODE**) project for the model organism *Drosophila melanogaster*. You can read about this project at www. modencode.org. The dataset contains 147 different samples for *D. melanogaster*, a fruit fly with an approximate genome of 120 Mbp, annotated with about 15,000 gene features.

Getting ready

The data is provided as a count DataFrame, similar to what we might load in from a text file, and an `ExpressionSet` object. A Bioconductor `ExpressionSet` object is a data structure that's used to store and manipulate gene expression data in R. It is a list-like object that contains the raw expression data and associated metadata, such as sample annotations and feature annotations.

How to do it...

We will see two ways of estimating differential expression with `edgeR` from two different starting datasets.

Using edgeR from a count table

Often, we will receive or have prepared transcript count data and have it in something such as a DataFrame, perhaps loaded originally from a text file or we have received it from another R function.

In this example, we have two prepared DataFrames in the `rbioinfcookbook` package – `count_dataframe`, which contains the actual counts for transcripts, and `pheno_data`, which is a metadata DataFrame that provides information about the samples. Refer to the following steps:

1. Begin by loading the count data and converting it into a matrix:

    ```
    library(rbioinfcookbook)
    genes <- count_dataframe[['gene']]
    count_dataframe[['gene']] <- NULL
    count_matrix <- as.matrix(count_dataframe)
    rownames(count_matrix) <- genes
    ```

2. Then, specify experiments of interest:

    ```
    experiments_of_interest <- c("L1Larvae", "L2Larvae")
    columns_of_interest <- which(
      pheno_data[['stage']] %in% experiments_of_interest
      )
    ```

3. Form the grouping factor:

    ```
    grouping <- pheno_data[['stage']][columns_of_interest] |>
      forcats::as_factor()
    ```

4. Form subset of count data:

    ```
    counts_of_interest <- count_matrix[,counts = columns_of_
    interest]
    ```

5. Create the DGE object:

    ```
    library(edgeR)
    count_dge <- edgeR::DGEList(
      counts = counts_of_interest,
      group = grouping
    )
    ```

6. Perform differential expression analysis:

    ```
    design <- model.matrix(~grouping)
    eset_dge <- edgeR::estimateDisp(count_dge, design)
    fit <- edgeR::glmQLFit(eset_dge, design)
    result <- edgeR::glmQLFTest(fit, coef=2)
    topTags(result)
    Coefficient:  groupingL2Larvae
                   logFC    logCPM          F       Pvalue
              FDR
    FBgn0027527 6.318665 11.148756 42854.72 1.132951e-41 1.684584e-
    ```

```
37
FBgn0037424 6.417770  9.715826 33791.15 2.152507e-40 1.518091e-
36
FBgn0037430 6.557774  9.109132 32483.00 3.510727e-40 1.518091e-
36
FBgn0037414 6.337846 10.704514 32088.92 4.083908e-40 1.518091e-
36
FBgn0029807 6.334590  9.008720 27648.19 2.585312e-39 7.688200e-
36
FBgn0037224 7.055635  9.195077 24593.62 1.102456e-38 2.732070e-
35
FBgn0037429 6.623619  8.525136 24122.44 1.400960e-38 2.975840e-
35
FBgn0030340 6.176390  8.500866 23111.55 2.380783e-38 4.424983e-
35
FBgn0029716 5.167089  8.977840 22556.01 3.218122e-38 5.316695e-
35
FBgn0243586 6.966873  7.769756 21465.47 5.945208e-38 8.839930e-
35
```

> **Use the right result!**
>
> Note that FDR is the more important of the significance columns and likely a better choice
> than P-Value.

Using edgeR from an ExpressionSet object

Often, when working within the Bioconductor ecosystem, we will get transcript abundances as an
ExpressionSet object. The ExpressionSet object is a data structure that represents a collection
of gene expression measurements, typically stored in a matrix with rows representing genes and columns
representing samples. In this example, we'll perform an edgeR analysis from that starting point:

1. Inspect the ExpressionSet data, as follows:

    ```
    head(modencodefly.eset)
    ExpressionSet (storageMode: lockedEnvironment)
    assayData: 6 features, 147 samples
      element names: exprs
    protocolData: none
    phenoData
      sampleNames: SRX007811 SRX008180 ... SRX008276 (147 total)
      varLabels: sample.id num.tech.reps stage
      varMetadata: labelDescription
    featureData
      featureNames: FBgn0000003 FBgn0000008 ... FBgn0000018 (6
    total)
    ```

```
  fvarLabels: gene
  fvarMetadata: labelDescription
experimentData: use 'experimentData(object)'
Annotation:
```

2.   Then, specify experiments of interest:

```
experiments_of_interest <- c("L1Larvae","L2Larvae")
columns_of_interest <- which(
  phenoData(modencodefly.eset)[['stage']] %in%
    experiments_of_interest
)
```

3.   Form the grouping factor:

```
grouping <- droplevels(
  phenoData(modencodefly.eset)[['stage']][columns_of_interest]
)
```

4.   Form the subset of count data:

```
counts_of_interest <- exprs(modencodefly.eset)[,columns_of_
interest]
```

5.   Create the DGE object:

```
eset_dge <- edgeR::DGEList(
  counts = counts_of_interest,
  group = grouping
)
```

6.   Perform differential expression analysis:

```
design <- model.matrix(~ grouping)
eset_dge  <- edgeR::estimateDisp(eset_dge, design)
fit <- edgeR::glmQLFit(eset_dge, design)
result <- edgeR::glmQLFTest(fit ,coef=2)
topTags(result)
Coefficient:  groupingL2Larvae
               logFC     logCPM         F         PValue
          FDR
FBgn0027527 6.318665 11.148756 42854.72 1.132951e-41 1.684584e-
37
FBgn0037424 6.417770  9.715826 33791.15 2.152507e-40 1.518091e-
36
FBgn0037430 6.557774  9.109132 32483.00 3.510727e-40 1.518091e-
36
FBgn0037414 6.337846 10.704514 32088.92 4.083908e-40 1.518091e-
```

```
36
FBgn0029807 6.334590   9.008720 27648.19 2.585312e-39 7.688200e-
36
FBgn0037224 7.055635   9.195077 24593.62 1.102456e-38 2.732070e-
35
FBgn0037429 6.623619   8.525136 24122.44 1.400960e-38 2.975840e-
35
FBgn0030340 6.176390   8.500866 23111.55 2.380783e-38 4.424983e-
35
FBgn0029716 5.167089   8.977840 22556.01 3.218122e-38 5.316695e-
35
FBgn0243586 6.966873   7.769756 21465.47 5.945208e-38 8.839930e-
35
```

That is how we use count tables and expression sets in edgeR.

How it works...

In this recipe, we saw two ways of estimating differential expression with edgeR. In the first half of this recipe, we used edgeR to load data from a count table, and in the second, we did the same analysis from an ExpresssionSet object. Let's break them down in turn.

Using edgeR from a count table

Step 1 loads the rbioinfcookbook library, which is required to access the count_dataframe object. The count_dataframe object is then modified by extracting the gene column and storing it in a separate object called genes, and then removing the gene column from count_dataframe. The modified count_dataframe object is then converted into a matrix using the as.matrix() function and the resulting matrix is stored in an object called count_matrix. The row names of count_matrix are then set to the values in the genes object using the rownames() function.

Step 2 defines an object called experiments_of_interest that contains the L1Larvae and L2Larvae character strings. Another object called columns_of_interest is created by using the which() function to identify the indices of the columns in pheno_data, where the 'stage' column is equal to one of the experiments of interest.

Step 3 creates a grouping factor called grouping using the forcats::as_factor() function from the forcats package. The grouping factor is created by extracting the 'stage' column from pheno_data for the columns of interest and converting it into a factor. We need to create a grouping vector, each index of which refers to a column in the counts table. In the following example, the first three columns in the data would be replicates of a different sample, and so on. We can use any symbols in the grouping vector to represent the groups. The more complicated the grouping vector, the more complicated the experiment design can be. In our recipe, we'll use a simple test/control design, like this:

```
numeric_groups <- c(1,1,1,2,2,2)
letter_groups <- c("A","A","A", "B","B","B")
```

A simple vector like this will do, but you can also use the factor object – R's categorical data type. Factors are vectors of integers under the hood but they have associated name labels called levels. These are used instead of the numbers to give you a prettier read out of the factor. The factor object retains all levels it knows about, even when a subset is taken without all levels, which sometimes results in empty levels.

Step 4 creates a subset of the `count_matrix` object called `counts_of_interest` that includes only the columns specified by the `columns_of_interest` object.

Step 5 loads the `edgeR` library and then creates a `DGEList` object called `count_dge` using the `DGEList()` function. The `counts_of_interest` object and the grouping factor are passed as arguments to `DGEList()`.

Step 6 performs differential expression analysis on the `count_dge` object using a series of functions from the `edgeR` package. First, we create the experimental design descriptor object with the `model.matrix()` function using the grouping variable we created. The `estimateDisp()` function is used to estimate the dispersion parameter of the count data, the `glmQLFit()` function is used to fit a generalized linear model to the data, and the `glmQLFTest()` function is used to perform a likelihood ratio test to identify differentially expressed genes. The resulting object is stored in an object called `result`. Finally, the `topTags()` function is used to display the top differentially expressed genes. The columns show the gene name, the F value, the P value, and the **false detection rate** (**FDR**), which is usually the column from which we want to make statistical conclusions.

Using edgeR from an ExpressionSet object

Step 1 displays the first few rows of data stored in an `ExpressionSet` object called `modencodefly.eset` using the `head()` function. This can be useful for inspecting the data to ensure it has been correctly loaded and to get a sense of the structure of the data.

Step 2 defines an object called `experiments_of_interest` that contains the `L1Larvae` and `L2Larvae` character strings. Another object called `columns_of_interest` is created by using the `which()` function to identify the indices of the columns in `phenoData()` of `modencodefly.eset`, where the `stage` column is equal to one of the experiments of interest. This step is used to specify which experiments to include in the differential expression analysis and to identify the columns of the data that correspond to these experiments.

Step 3 creates a grouping factor called `grouping` by extracting the `stage` column using the `phenoData()` function, which extracts phenodata from `modencodefly.eset` and then removes any unused levels of the factor using the `droplevels()` function. The grouping factor is used to specify which samples belong to each experimental group and will be used in the differential expression analysis.

Step 4 creates a subset of the data from `modencodefly.eset` called `counts_of_interest` that includes only the columns specified by the `columns_of_interest` object. As we had for `phenodata`, we have a dedicated function for `ExpressionSets` that extract the expression values – `exprs()`. This step is used to extract only the data that corresponds to the experiments of interest.

Step 5 creates a `DGEList` object called `eset_dge` using the `DGEList()` function from the `edgeR` package. The `counts_of_interest` object and the grouping factor are passed as arguments to `DGEList()`. A `DGEList` object is a special type of object that's used by the `edgeR` package to store count data for differential expression analysis.

Step 6 performs differential expression analysis on the `eset_dge` object using a series of functions from the `edgeR` package. The `estimateDisp()` function is used to estimate the dispersion parameter of the count data, the `glmQLFit()` function is used to fit a generalized linear model to the data, and the `glmQLFTest()` function is used to perform a likelihood ratio test to identify differentially expressed genes. The resulting object is stored in an object called `result`. Finally, the `topTags()` function is used to display the top differentially expressed genes. This step is used to identify which genes are significantly differentially expressed between the two experimental groups.

Estimating differential expression with DESeq2

The `DEseq2` package is a popular tool for performing differential analysis of count data, so it is ideal for expression analysis of RNA-Seq data in R and other count data such as ChIPSeq.

`DEseq2` performs normalization using a method called **variance stabilizing transformation** (VST), which is a type of transformation that aims to stabilize the variance of the data across the range of counts. This is in contrast to other normalization methods that aim to bring the mean of the data to a specific value, such as the mean of all the samples or the median of all the samples. The VST method is effective at reducing the variance of the data estimating with and improving the statistical power of differential expression analyses. This allows us to focus on improving gene ranking in results tables.

`DEseq2` uses a negative binomial model to fit the count data and estimate the dispersion parameter. This model is commonly used for RNA-Seq data because it can accommodate the overdispersion that's often observed in such data. For differential expression, `DEseq2` uses a likelihood ratio test to compare the negative binomial models fit to the data for each experimental group. This test is based on the ratio of the maximum likelihoods of the full and reduced models, with the full model being the model that includes all the parameters and the reduced model being the model that constrains some of the parameters to be equal across groups. Other packages, such as `edgeR` and `limma`, use different statistical tests for differential expression. For example, `edgeR` uses a likelihood ratio test similar to `DEseq2`, while `limma` uses an empirical Bayes method to estimate fold changes and test for differential expression.

The process we'll look at in this recipe is similar to that for `edgeR` in the preceding recipe. We will use a count table and `ExpressionSet` objects as input and then use DESeq2's specific data structures and functions.

Getting ready

As in the previous recipe, the data is provided as a count DataFrame, similar to what we might load in from a text file, and an `ExpressionSet` object. A Bioconductor `ExpressionSet` object is a data structure that's used to store and manipulate gene expression data in R. It is a list-like object that contains the raw expression data and associated metadata, such as sample annotations and feature annotations.

How to do it...

As with `edgeR`, we're going to look at how to do this from two different starting points – first with a count table/matrix and then with an `ExpressionSet` object.

Using DESeq2 from a count matrix

Estimating differential expression with `DESeq2` from a count table is done as follows:

1. Load the count data and convert it into a matrix:

```
library(rbioinfcookbook)
genes <- count_dataframe[['gene']]
count_dataframe[['gene']] <- NULL
count_matrix <- as.matrix(count_dataframe)
rownames(count_matrix) <- genes
```

2. Specify experiments of interest:

```
experiments_of_interest <- c("L1Larvae", "L2Larvae")
columns_of_interest <- which(
  pheno_data[['stage']] %in%
    experiments_of_interest
)
```

3. Form the grouping factor:

```
stages <- pheno_data[['stage']][columns_of_interest] |>
  forcats::as_factor()
grouping <- data.frame(
  stage = stages
)
```

4. Form the subset of count data:

```
counts_of_interest <- count_matrix[,columns_of_interest]
```

5. Build the `DESeq` object:

```
library(DESeq2)
dds <- DESeqDataSetFromMatrix(
  countData = counts_of_interest,
  colData = grouping,
  design = ~ stage
)
```

6. Carry out the analysis:

```
dds <- DESeq(dds)
```

7. Extract the results:

```
res <- results(dds,
             contrast=c("stage", "L2Larvae", "L1Larvae")
             )
res
log2 fold change (MLE): stage L2Larvae vs L1Larvae
Wald test p-value: stage L2Larvae vs L1Larvae
DataFrame with 14869 rows and 6 columns
        baseMean log2FoldChange      lfcSE       stat      pvalue
        padj
       <numeric>      <numeric> <numeric> <numeric>   <numeric>
       <numeric>
1        0.000           NA         NA        NA
         NA           NA
2      562.467    -0.0567898 0.0553041  -1.02686 3.04484e-
01 3.87814e-01
3      894.891    -0.7973532 0.0456110 -17.48159 1.97888e-
68 1.54274e-67
4      323.316    -0.8454425 0.0745500 -11.34061 8.25709e-
30 3.64326e-29
5      862.122    -0.2538090 0.0480525  -5.28191 1.27845e-
07 2.92354e-07
...      ...            ...        ...       ...
...      ...
14865    0.0000          NA         NA        NA
NA         NA
14866   71.9698    -2.201803 0.1546498 -14.23735 5.37280e-
46 3.11925e-45
14867  311.1002    -0.311300 0.0686318  -4.53580 5.73868e-
06 1.19200e-05
14868 1477.7729    -0.557711 0.0446208 -12.49888 7.57122e-36
3.70604e-35
14869 1214.1409     0.346754 0.0481392   7.20316 5.88342e-13
1.67726e-12
```

That is how we do it with a standard count table that could have come from many upstream sources. Now, let's look at the next input type.

Using DESeq2 from an ExpressionSet object

To estimate differential expression with DESeq2 from an ExpressionSet object, we must perform the following steps:

1. Load the eset data and convert it into a DESeqDataSet():

```
library(SummarizedExperiment)
summ_exp <-
makeSummarizedExperimentFromExpressionSet(modencodefly.eset)
ddsSE <- DESeqDataSet(summ_exp, design = ~ stage)
```

2. Carry out analysis and extract the results:

```
ddsSE <- DESeq(ddsSE)
resSE <- results(ddsSE, contrast=
                    c("stage", "L2Larvae", "L1Larvae"))
resSE
log2 fold change (MLE): stage L2Larvae vs L1Larvae
Wald test p-value: stage L2Larvae vs L1Larvae
DataFrame with 14869 rows and 6 columns
              baseMean log2FoldChange      lfcSE        stat
      pvalue
             <numeric>      <numeric> <numeric> <numeric>
       <numeric>
FBgn0000003     0.000            NA        NA        NA
          NA
FBgn0000008   918.783     -0.115736 0.0522570  -2.21474
    2.67780e-02
FBgn0000014   867.608     -0.856229 0.0379936 -22.53616
    1.83576e-112
FBgn0000015   306.805     -0.904863 0.0760892 -11.89213
    1.30043e-32
FBgn0000017  1755.817     -0.313555 0.0522008  -6.00671
    1.89325e-09
...             ...           ...       ...       ...
      ...
FBgn0261571   51.2588      0.000000 1.3585552   0.00000
    1.00000e+00
FBgn0261572   44.6647     -2.260062 0.1546197 -14.61691
    2.19130e-48
FBgn0261573  563.7577     -0.369160 0.0844196  -4.37292
    1.22596e-05
FBgn0261574 2091.9427     -0.617805 0.0838364  -7.36918
    1.71682e-13
```

```
FBgn0261575   599.6725        0.292291 0.0399686     7.31301
    2.61228e-13
                        padj
                    <numeric>
FBgn0000003            NA
FBgn0000008   4.16746e-02
FBgn0000014 2.21580e-111
FBgn0000015   5.99754e-32
FBgn0000017   4.79873e-09
...                    ...
FBgn0261571   1.00000e+00
FBgn0261572   1.29821e-47
FBgn0261573   2.53877e-05
FBgn0261574   5.04156e-13
FBgn0261575   7.62380e-13
```

With that, we've learned how to work through DESeq2 using multiple initial data inputs.

How it works...

Similar to what we covered edgeR earlier, we'll go through how to do this from a count matrix, then an ExpressionSet object.

Using DESeq2 from a count matrix

In *step 1*, the count_dataframe DataFrame is loaded and a matrix called count_matrix is created by converting count_dataframe and setting the row names to the gene column from count_dataframe. The gene column is then removed from count_dataframe.

In *step 2*, a character vector called experiments_of_interest is created that contains the L1Larvae and L2Larvae elements. Then, a numeric vector called columns_of_interest is created by finding the indices in the stage column of pheno_data that are elements of experiments_of_interest.

In *step 3*, a character vector called stages is created by subsetting the stage column of pheno_data using columns_of_interest and then converted into a factor using the as_factor() function from the forcats package. A DataFrame called grouping is then created with a single column called stage containing the stages vector.

In *step 4*, a matrix called counts_of_interest is created by subsetting count_matrix using columns_of_interest.

In *step 5*, the DESeq2 package is loaded and a DESeq object called dds is created using the DESeqDataSetFromMatrix() function. counts_of_interest and grouping are passed to the countData and colData arguments, respectively. The design argument is set to a formula specifying that the stage column of grouping should be used as a predictor.

In *step 6*, the dds object is passed to the DESeq() function to carry out the analysis.

In *step 7*, a res object is created by calling the results() function on the dds object and setting the contrast argument to a contrast comparing the L2Larvae and L1Larvae levels of the stage factor. The res object is a DataFrame that contains several columns that summarize the results of a differential expression analysis carried out using the DESeq2 package. The headings of the DataFrame and the column's contents are as follows:

- 'baseMean': The mean of the normalized counts across all samples.
- 'log2FoldChange': The log2-fold change in expression between the levels of the factor being compared in the contrast argument.
- 'lfcSE': The standard error of the 'log2FoldChange' value.
- 'stat': The test statistic for the hypothesis test for differential expression.
- 'pvalue': The p-value for the hypothesis test for differential expression.
- 'padj': The adjusted p-value, which takes into account the multiple hypothesis testing problem. Genes with a small 'padj' value are considered differentially expressed.

Using DESeq2 from an ExpressionSet object

This part of the recipe is short – it takes only two small steps to do the same procedure from an ExpressionSet object ebecause DESeq2 is set up nicely to work with Bioconductor.

In *step 1*, the SummarizedExperiment package is loaded and a SummarizedExperiment object called summ_exp is created using the makeSummarizedExperimentFromExpressionSet() function, where it is then passed the modencodefly.eset object. Then, a DESeq object called ddsSE is created using the DESeqDataSet() function and is passed summ_exp as the first argument. A formula is used to specify that the stage column should be used as a predictor.

In *step 2*, the ddsSE object is passed to the DESeq() function to carry out the analysis. Then, a resSE object is created by calling the results() function on the ddsSE object and setting the contrast argument to a contrast argument that compares the L2Larvae and L1Larvae levels of the stage factor. Finally, the resSE object is printed to the console.

There's more...

If you wish to cluster experiments to assess the variability between samples, as is often done with PCA, please see the recipe *Clustering with k-means and hierarchical clustering* in *Chapter 11, Machine Learning with mlr3*, where a general technique for that is discussed. Note the danger of evaluating **outliers** this way. Be careful not to cherry-pick data inadvertently by throwing away real, but variable, data points.

Estimating differential expression with Kallisto and Sleuth

Kallisto is an RNA-Seq read aligner that uses a pseudoalignment algorithm, which allows it to map reads to a reference transcriptome without using traditional alignment methods such as Smith-Waterman or Needleman-Wunsch. Instead, it uses a k-mer index of the reference transcriptome to quickly and accurately quantify expression levels of transcripts. This allows Kallisto to run much faster than traditional aligners, making it a popular choice for large-scale RNA-Seq experiments.

The companion R package called Sleuth is a tool for analyzing the output from Kallisto. It allows users to perform differential expression analysis and identify transcripts that are differentially expressed between different samples or conditions. Sleuth uses a Bayesian framework to model the expression levels of transcripts and take into account technical variability in the data, such as sequencing depth and batch effects. The package also provides several visualization tools to help users explore the results of their analysis.

Sleuth uses a statistical model called the **hierarchical beta-binomial model** to quantify the expression levels of transcripts. This model takes into account the variability of the sequencing data, such as the number of reads mapped to each transcript, to estimate the expression levels with greater precision. Additionally, Sleuth can consider any known covariates, such as treatment conditions, to help control for any potential confounding effects. In this recipe, we'll learn how to use Kallisto and Sleuth to do differential gene expression.

Getting ready

For this recipe, we'll need to have Kallisto installed, which we can do with `bioconda`. Assuming `bioconda` is set up, you can run this in your terminal to install Kallisto:

```
conda install -c bioconda kallisto
```

You'll need Sleuth, too.

We'll be using human RNA-Seq reads from the `https://doi.org/10.5281/zenodo.1294051` example dataset. We will have three replicates from a male human sample and three replicates from a female human sample. The experiment used paired-end Illumina reads, so there will be two files per sample and a reference FASTA file of transcripts.

The data we need has been downsampled so that it can be used in a short period but is still quite numerous and too large to distribute within an R package. I have created a function in the `rbioinfcookbook` package that will automatically download the files to your current working directory. To get the files, run this in your R console:

```
rbioinfcookbook::chapter_6_recipe_3()
```

This should automatically put the files in your current working directory as needed.

How to do it...

The first step is to create the index for Kallisto. It might take 10 minutes to run:

1. We do this in the terminal, not in R:

    ```
    kallisto index -i gc38 gc38_transcripts.fa
    ```

2. Run `kallisto` on each replicate. We have a short bash command to do that for us – do this in the terminal, not in R. Again, this can take 10 minutes or so:

    ```
    for sample in 245 428 337 401 257 383
    do
       kallisto  quant -i gc38 \
       -t 1 -b 42 -o quantifications_${sample} \
       ERR188${sample}_1.fq.gz ERR188${sample}_2.fq.gz
    done
    ```

3. Back in R, we can start to use `sleuth`. As preparation, we need to make a sample condition file mapping:

    ```
    base <- c("245", "428", "337", "401", "257", "383")

    s2c <- data.frame(
       sample = paste0("ERR188", base),
       condition = c( rep("F", 3), rep("M",3) ),
       path =  paste0("quantifications_", base)
    )
    ```

4. Now, set up the `sleuth` object:

    ```
    library(sleuth)
    so <- sleuth_prep(s2c, extra_bootstrap_summary = TRUE)
    ```

5. Carry out a fit to a full and a null (reduced) model:

```
so <- sleuth_fit(so, ~condition, 'full',
                 transformation_function = function(x) log2(x +
0.5))
so <- sleuth_fit(so, ~1, 'reduced')
```

6. Carry out tests:

```
so <- sleuth_wt(so, "conditionM")
results <- sleuth_results(so, "conditionM")
```

7. Arrange and examine the results:

```
dplyr::arrange(results, desc(b) )
```

And that is all we need to do to get results from Kallisto and Sleuth.

How it works...

In *step 1*, the bash command creates an index for the kallisto program by using the gc38_ transcripts.fa file as input and saving the index as gc38.

In *step 2*, the code runs the kallisto quantification command for each of the six replicates specified in the base variable using the previously created index, gc38. The quantification results for each replicate are output to a directory called quantifications_${sample}, where ${sample} is the specific replicate being run.

In *step 3*, the R code creates a DataFrame called s2c that maps the samples to the conditions they belong to and the path of their quantification results. The base variable is used to create the sample column, and the condition column is created by repeating F for the first three samples and M for the last three. The path column is created by concatenating quantifications_ with the elements of the base variable.

In *step 4*, the R code loads the sleuth library and creates a sleuth object called so using the s2c DataFrame while setting the extra_bootstrap_summary option to TRUE. so is a container for all of the data and information necessary for running differential expression analysis using the sleuth package. It includes information about the samples, conditions, and quantification results, as well as any models and test results that have been run. The extra_bootstrap_summary option provides additional information about the bootstrap samples, which can be useful for interpreting results.

In *step 5*, the code fits so to a full model, which is specified as ~condition, and a null (reduced) model, which is specified as ~1. The full model is also using a transformation function that takes log2 of the input plus 0.5. The full model design in this case is ~condition, which means that the effects of the condition variable will be included in the model. The null or reduced model is specified as ~1, which means that no variables are included in the model. The transformation function is used to normalize the data before the analysis.

In `sleuth`, the full model is typically used to test for the effects of specific variables of interest, such as the `condition` variable in this case. The null or reduced model is used as a baseline for comparison and tests whether there is any significant difference in expression between the samples. The transformation function is used to account for the technical variability in the data and thus the results of the analysis are more robust.

In *step 6*, the code carries out tests on the `conditionM` level and creates a new object called `results` that contains the results of the tests. The test that's carried out is a *Wald Test*, a statistical test that's used to test the null hypothesis that the parameters of a linear model are equal to zero – in other words, the test checks if there is any significant difference in expression between `conditionM` and the other condition. The Wald Test is based on the ratio of the estimated parameter to its standard error. It calculates a test statistic, which is then compared to a critical value from a chi-squared distribution to determine the p-value. The Wald Test is commonly used in the `sleuth` package and it is useful for testing the significance of individual coefficients in a linear model.

In *step 7*, the R code uses the `dplyr` library to arrange the rows of the `results` object in descending order based on the `b` column. The resulting DataFrame can then be examined to see the results of the tests. The columns of most interest are the `b` column, which contains the `log2` ratio between the conditions, and the `qval` column, which contains the adjusted p-value for each target/transcript.

Using Sleuth to analyze time course experiments

Multiple-condition, multiple-level experiments, such as timecourse experiments, are more difficult to analyze than simple comparisons because they involve a greater amount of data and complexity. In a timecourse experiment, for example, the goal is to understand how a biological system changes over time in response to a particular treatment or condition. This requires analyzing data from multiple timepoints and conditions, which can make the data more complex and harder to interpret.

One aspect that makes timecourse experiments more difficult is the filter function in the `sleuth_prep()` filter argument. This function is used to filter out low-quality or non-informative data from the analysis. The filter function works by excluding targets that are not present in a minimum percentage of samples. In a simple comparison, the filter function is relatively straightforward to apply as it is only necessary to compare two conditions and identify any samples or transcripts that do not meet the desired count in most samples. However, in a timecourse experiment, there are multiple conditions and multiple timepoints, and genes important in one sample could easily be absent from many others, which means that the filter function must be applied separately to each condition and timepoint. This can make the filtering process more time-consuming and complicated.

To overcome this limitation, the filter function in the `sleuth_prep()` filter argument can be overridden with a custom filter function that is tailored to the specific needs of the experiment. In this recipe, we'll look at how to compose a custom filter function for per-condition filtering.

Getting ready

This recipe will not use any data. Instead, we will consider a single custom function that is designed to work on a multi-factor experiment. In Sleuth terms, this means the condition mapping will have more columns than the *Estimating differential expression with Kallisto and Sleuth* recipe. It may look like this:

```
data.frame(
    sample = c(paste0("WT_mock_", 1:3), paste0("WT_infect_", 1:3),
paste0("MUT_mock_", 1:3), paste0("MUT_infect_", 1:3)),
    condition = c(rep("WT", 6), rep("MUT", 6)),
    treatment = c(rep("mock", 3), rep("infect", 3), rep("mock",3),
rep("infect",3)),
    path = paste0(c(paste0("WT_mock_", 1:3), paste0("WT_infect",
1:3), paste0("MUT_mock", 1:3), paste0("MUT_infect", 1:3)), "_kallisto_
results")
)
```

Of course, this is a code representation of a DataFrame. Entering this into R will give you the actual DataFrame and provide an example of what the data would look like if you needed to create it in a spreadsheet.

How to do it...

Let's create the function that will allow us to work on a multi-factor experiment:

1. Create a custom filter function:

```
custom_filter <- function(design,
                          row,
                          min_reads = 5,
                          min_prop = 0.47) {
  sum(apply(design, 2, function(x) {
    y <- as.factor(x)
    return(max(tapply(row, y, function(f) {
      sum(f >= min_reads)
    }) /
      tapply(row, y, length)) == 1
    || basic_filter(row, min_reads, min_prop))
  })) > 0
}
```

2. Use it in the `sleuth_prep` stage:

```
so <- sleuth_prep(s2c, ~treatment*condition,
                    filter_fun=function(x){custom_
filter(so$design,x)})
```

Those two steps show how to create, then use, the function.

How it works...

In *step 1*, a custom filter function called `custom_filter` is created in R. The function takes in four parameters: `design` is a matrix describing the design of the experiment, `row` is a vector of counts for a given gene, `min_reads` is the minimum number of reads required for a gene to be considered, and `min_prop` is the minimum proportion of samples in which a gene must be present to be considered. The function applies a logical test to the design matrix that tests if, for each column, the maximum proportion of samples in which a gene is present is equal to `1` or if the basic filter function, which takes in the row, `min_reads`, and `min_prop` returns true. If either of the two conditions is true, the function returns true and the gene will be considered.

The custom filter function is used to filter out genes that do not meet the specified criteria. The function first checks if the maximum proportion of samples in which a gene is present is equal to `1` across all columns of the design matrix. If this is true, the gene is considered to be present in all samples and is kept. If this is not the case, the basic filter function is applied to the gene, which checks if the gene is present in at least the minimum proportion of samples and if it has at least the minimum number of reads. If these criteria are met, the gene is kept; otherwise, it is removed. This function allows us to filter the genes in a way that is tailored to the specific needs of the experiment, rather than using the default filter function in the `sleuth` package.

In *step 2*, the custom filter function is used in the `sleuth_prep()` function to prepare the data for analysis. The `sleuth_prep()` function takes in the `s2c` DataFrame, a formula describing the design of the experiment, and a `filter_fun` argument, which is used to specify the custom filter function. The custom filter function is passed the `so$design` matrix and the `x` vector of counts for a given gene as input. The default values of the function are set to match those in Sleuth, but they can be changed, depending on the specific needs of the experiment.

Analyzing splice variants with SGSeq

Alternative splicing is a process by which different variants of a gene are produced from a single primary transcript. This process allows you to generate multiple different proteins from a single gene, increasing the functional diversity of the genome. Alternative splicing can be regulated by different mechanisms, including cis-acting elements in the primary transcript and trans-acting factors that bind to these elements.

Analyzing alternative splicing in genomics can be beneficial in several ways, including allowing you to understand the genetic basis of disease. Many diseases are caused by mutations in genes that lead to changes in protein function. Alternative splicing can create different variants of a protein with different functions, and understanding how these variants are regulated can provide insights into disease mechanisms. The SGSeq R Bioconductor package can be used to help us analyze alternatively spliced transcripts. This package is a flexible tool for analyzing RNA-Seq data as it can detect alternative splicing events, quantify gene expression, and identify differentially expressed genes. The package uses a splice graph so that we can identify differentially spliced exons. It also allows you to integrate multiple datasets so that you can detect alternative splicing events across different conditions or samples. The package also provides visualization tools that allow you to easily interpret results and identify biologically relevant events. In this recipe, we'll look at how to find different splice variants from RNA-Seq data using SGSeq.

Getting ready

For an analysis like this, we need alignments of sequence reads from a splice-aware aligner and annotation information for the genome. The Bioconductor `RNAseqData.HNRNPC.bam.chr14` package provides 8 BAM files from a TopHat2 alignment of paired-end Illumina read data against the human genome (hg19), while `TxDb.Hsapiens.UCSC.hg19.knownGene` Bioconductor package carries transcript annotations for the correct version of the genome. Analysis and plotting will be done with the `SGSeq` package and `DEXSeq`, also from Bioconductor.

Beware of *step 4* – it takes a long time to run; about 1.5 hours per BAM file on my laptop (an M1 Mac). There are options to parallelize this in the package but the code we'll be using here uses defaults. If this takes too long for you, there is a precomputed version of this step's output in the `rbioinfcookbook` package called `package_sgfc`.

How to do it...

The following steps will walk us through the process of finding splice variants:

1. Load the libraries and prepare a sample information `data.frame`:

```
library(RNAseqData.HNRNPC.bam.chr14)
library(TxDb.Hsapiens.UCSC.hg19.knownGene)
library(SGSeq)

si <- data.frame(
    sample_name = RNAseqData.HNRNPC.bam.chr14_RUNNAMES,
    file_bam = RNAseqData.HNRNPC.bam.chr14_BAMFILES
    )

si <- getBamInfo(si)
```

2. Get the transcript annotation:

```
txdb <- TxDb.Hsapiens.UCSC.hg19.knownGene
txdb <- keepSeqlevels(txdb, "chr14")
seqlevelsStyle(txdb) <- "NCBI"
```

3. Convert into features:

```
txf_ucsc <- convertToTxFeatures(txdb)
seqlevels(txf_ucsc) <- "chr14"
sgf_ucsc <- convertToSGFeatures(txf_ucsc)
```

4. Analyze the features:

```
sgfc <- analyzeFeatures(si, txf_ucsc)
#or use package_sgfc from the package rbioinfcookbook
```

5. Plot a gene:

```
df <- plotFeatures(sgfc, geneID = 1)
```

6. Predict the variants:

```
sgvc_pred <- analyzeVariants(sgfc)
```

7. Prepare the data from SGSeq to DEXSeq for differential analysis:

```
sag <- rowRanges(sgvc_pred)
sgvc <- getSGVariantCounts(sgv, sample_info = si)
counts <- counts(sgvc)
exon_id <- variantID(sgvc)
group_id <- eventID(sgvc)

sample_info <- data.frame(
  sample = colnames(counts),
  condition = c(rep("Test", 4), rep("Control",4))
)

library(DEXSeq)
dx <- DEXSeqDataSet(
  counts,
  sample_info,
  design = ~ sample + exon + condition:exon,
  as.character(exon_id),
  as.character(group_id)

)
```

8. Test for differential exon usage:

```
dx <- estimateSizeFactors(dx)
dx <- estimateDispersions(dx)
dx <- testForDEU(dx)
```

```
dx <- estimateExonFoldChanges(dx, fitExpToVar="condition")

results <- DEXSeqResults(dx)
```

And with that, the `results` object should contain our different splice variant information.

How it works...

In *step 1*, the `RNAseqData.HNRNPC.bam.chr14`, `TxDb.Hsapiens.UCSC.hg19.knownGene` and `SGSeq` libraries are loaded. The `RNAseqData.HNRNPC.bam.chr14` library contains the BAM files of alignments we will need, whereas `TxDb.Hsapiens.UCSC.hg19.knownGene` contains the annotations.

A DataFrame is created from the list of BAM files and the samples contained in the `RNAseqData.HNRNPC.bam.chr14` packages and saved in the `si` variable. The `getBamInfo()` function is then used on the `si` variable to add the sample information needed by `SGSeq` into the DataFrame.

The `TxDb.Hsapiens.UCSC.hg19.knownGene` library is a Bioconductor annotation library that provides transcript annotation for the human genome (hg19). It is used to locate, extract, and manipulate information about transcriptional features from a specific genome build.

In *step 2*, a new variable called `txdb` is created, which is a `TxDb` object that contains the transcript annotation for the human genome hg19. The `keepSeqlevels()` function is then used on the `txdb` variable to keep only the sequence levels for chromosome 14; it filters out all other chromosomes. The `seqlevelsStyle()` function is then used to set the style of the sequence levels to NCBI.

In *step 3*, the `txdb` variable is passed to the `convertToTxFeatures()` function to coerce the object into a feature representation and save it in a new variable called `txf_ucsc`, which contains the transcript features. The `seqlevels()` function is then used to rename the sequence levels so that they match the convention in the input BAM files, which is `chr14`. The `convertToSGFeatures()` function is then used on `txf_ucsc` to create a new variable called `sgf_ucsc` that contains the spliced gene features needed by `SGSeq`. The analysis can take a long time in this step, perhaps an hour.

In *step 4*, the `analyzeFeatures` function is used to analyze the transcript features using the sample information DataFrame and the transcript feature data. It processes the input data, aligns the reads in the BAM files to the transcript features, and calculates expression values for each feature in each sample. The expression values are calculated as the total number of reads that align with the feature, normalized by the length of the feature and the total number of reads in the sample. The resulting expression values are then used as input for downstream analysis, such as visualization and variant analysis. The function returns a `SGFeatureCollection` object, which is a data structure that contains the expression values as well as additional information about the features, such as gene IDs and exon IDs.

The output of the `analyzeFeatures` function is assigned to the `sgfc` variable, which can then be used for further analysis and visualization.

In *step 5*, the `plotFeatures()` function is used on the calculated splice data in the `'sgf_ucsc'` variable, and the geneID argument is set to 1 to create a plot of the expression values for the gene ID 1. The plot, which is a heatmap of exon coverage, is not saved to a variable; instead, it is plotted directly to the screen, but a DataFrame of intron/exon junctions is saved to the `df` variable. The resulting heatmap plot looks like this:

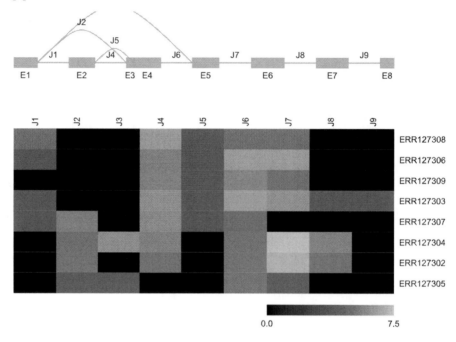

Figure 6.1 – Predicted exon heatmap

In *step 6*, the `analyzeVariants` function is used to predict variants using the `sgfc` variable we created in *step 4*. The output is assigned to the `sgvc_pred` variable.

In *step 7*, the `SGSeq` data is prepared for differential analysis using the DEXSeq package. The `rowRanges` function is used to extract the exon information from the `sgvc_pred` variable. The `getSGVariantCounts` function is used to extract the counts of the variants for each exon in each sample. The counts, exon ID, and group ID are assigned to variables. A typical `sample_information` DataFrame containing the sample names and conditions is created and assigned to the `sample_info` variable. For this experiment, we assign the first four BAM files to a TEST condition and the rest to a CONTROL condition. Lastly, the `DEXSeqDataSet` function is used to create a DEXSeq dataset from the counts, sample information, and exon and group IDs. The design parameter is the simple test versus control by exon design that we expect for a straightforward one-sample analysis. The R formula here expresses that. These are the preliminary objects that we need for a differential analysis in DEXSeq.

In *step 8*, the DEXSeq package is used for differential analysis. We move through the typical workflow using the estimateSizeFactors, estimateDispersions, testForDEU, and estimateExonFoldChanges functions, which are used together to test for differential exon usage. The output is assigned to the dx variable and the final results are obtained from that object using the DEXSeqResults function. The results object lists the gene and exon IDs, as given by SGSeq. The padj and log2fc objects of the read counts expressed as **Fragments Per Kilobase per Million mapped fragments (FPKM)** can be found in that table.

Performing power analysis with powsimR

Statistical power analysis is used to determine the sample size needed to detect an effect of a certain size with a certain level of statistical significance. This is important because it allows researchers to ensure that their studies are adequately powered (that is, enough replicates have been sampled) to detect the effects that they are interested in. Without sufficient power, there is a higher risk of failing to reject the null hypothesis when it is false – that is, to miss important differentially expressed genes. In this recipe, we'll use the powsimR package (which is not in Bioconductor) to perform two types of power analysis. Both of these will be performed with a small real dataset. First, we shall do power analysis with two treatments, test and control, and then with just one. With each, we shall estimate the replicates that are needed to spot differences in gene expression of a particular magnitude – if they're present. powsimR takes a simulation-based approach in that it generates many datasets and evaluates the detection power in each to create a distribution of detection power. The first step is to estimate some parameters for these simulations for which we'll need sample or preliminary data. With that, we can simulate and assess power.

Getting ready

powsimR has a lot of dependencies, some of which are a bit fiddly to install. I recommend manual installation, but often, that isn't necessary. Try installing the Python magic-impute dependency first and then install the Rmagic package from GitHub before installing the powsimR package itself. The following steps outline the procedure:

1. In a terminal, run the following command to install the Python magic-impute dependency:

    ```
    pip install —user magic-impute
    ```

2. Then, we can install the R packages as usual:

    ```
    renv::install("cran/Rmagic)
    renv::install("bvieth/powsimR")
    ```

The package should be installed. If it raises any errors, please see the complete documentation for this package on its GitHub page: https://github.com/bvieth/powsimR.

One tip I do have when installing this fiddly package is that it sometimes tells you lots of dependencies that you are certain were installed are not. If this happens, try restarting R and it should straighten things out.

The data we will use for this recipe will be from a set of test Arabidopsis thaliana plant samples infected with Pseudomonas syringae hrcC mutant (hrcc) versus a set of control mock infection samples (mock). There are three replicates in each sample type. These are available in the `rbioinfcookbook` data package as a single matrix with six columns called `arab_infection`.

How to do it...

Let's do the power analysis by performing the following steps:

1. Estimate the simulation parameter values:

```
library(rbioinfcookbook)

means_mock <- rowMeans(arab_infection[, c("mock1", "mock2",
"mock3")])
means_hrcc <- rowMeans(arab_infection[, c("hrcc1", "hrcc2",
"hrcc3")])

log2fc <- log2(means_hrcc / means_mock)
prop_de <- sum(abs(log2fc) > 2) / length(log2fc)
```

2. Examine the distribution of the log2 fold change ratios:

```
finite_log2fc <- log2fc[is.finite(log2fc)]
plot(density(finite_log2fc))
extRemes::qqnorm(finite_log2fc)
```

3. Set up parameter values for the simulation run:

```
library(powsimR)
params <- estimateParam(
    countData = arab_infection,
    Distribution = "NB",
    RNAseq = "bulk",
    Normalisation = "TMM"
)

de_opts <- Setup(
    ngenes = 1000,
    nsims = 25,

    p.DE = prop_de,
    pLFC = finite_log2fc,
```

```
    estParamRes = params
)


num_replicates <- c(3,6,12,18)
```

4. Run the simulation:

```
simDE <- simulateDE(de_opts,
   DEmethod = "edgeR-LRT",
   Normalisation = "TMM",
   verbose = FALSE
)
```

5. Run an evaluation of the simulation:

```
evalDE <- evaluateDE(simDE,
   alpha.type = "adjusted",
   MTC = "BH",
   alpha.nominal = 0.1,
   stratify.by = "mean",
   filter.by = "none",
   strata.filtered = 1,
   target.by = 'lfc',
   delta = 0
)
```

6. Plot the evaluation:

```
plotEvalDE(evalDE,
         rate = "marginal",
         quick = FALSE,
         Annot = TRUE
         )
```

And that gives us the power analysis we need.

How it works...

In *step 1*, the rbioinfcookbook library is loaded. Then, the rowMeans() function is used to calculate the mean of the values in each row for the mock1, mock2, and mock3 columns and assign the result to means_mock; the same is done for the hrcc1, hrcc2, and hrcc3 columns, whose result is assigned to means_hrcc. The log2() function is then used to calculate the log base 2 of the ratio of means_hrcc to means_mock and assign the result to log2fc. Finally, prop_de is calculated as the ratio of the number of elements in `log2fc` with an absolute value greater than 2 to the length of `log2fc`. This gives us an estimate of the proportion of genes that are differentially expressed. Inspecting it gives us the following output:

```
prop_de
## [1] 0.2001754
```

This shows that about 20% of the features have counts changing by `log2` 2-fold or more.

In *step 2*, the `is.finite()` function is used to select only the finite elements of `log2fc` and assign the result to `finite_log2fc`. This is done to ensure that any potentially infinite ratios caused by a zero count in the mock sample are removed safely. The `plot()` function is then used to create a density plot of `finite_log2fc`, and the `qqnorm()` function from the `extRemes` library is used to create a quantile-quantile plot of `finite_log2fc`.

In *step 3*, the `estimateParam()` function from the `powsimR` library is used to estimate the parameters needed to run a simulation based on the data in `arab_infection`. The distribution of the data is specified as a negative binomial distribution, the type of RNA sequencing is specified as `bulk` (as ours is – which just means all the sampled RNA), and the normalization method is specified as TMM. The result is assigned to `params`.

Then, the `Setup()` function from `powsimR` is used to set up the options for the simulation run. The number of genes is set to `1000`, the number of simulations is set to `25`, the proportion of differentially expressed genes is set to `prop_de`, the log fold change ratios are set to `finite_log2fc`, and the estimated parameter values are set to `params`. The result is assigned to `de_opts`.

`num_replicates` is then defined as a vector with values of `3`, `6`, `12`, and `18`.

In *step 4*, the `simulateDE()` function from `powsimR` is used to run the simulation with the options specified in `de_opts`. The method for identifying differentially expressed genes is specified as `edgeR-LRT`, the normalization method is specified as TMM, and verbosity is turned off. The result is assigned to `simDE`.

In *step 5*, the `evaluateDE()` function from `powsimR` is used to evaluate the results of the simulation stored in `simDE`. The type of alpha adjustment is specified as `adjusted`, the multiple test correction method is specified as the Benjamini-Hochberg procedure, the nominal alpha level is set to `0.1`, the data is stratified by mean expression level, no filtering is applied, the first stratum is used for filtering, the target for evaluation is log fold change, and the delta value is set to `0`. The result is assigned to `evalDE`.

In *step 6*, the `plotEvalDE()` function from `powsimR` is used to plot the evaluation stored in `evalDE`. The rate is specified as `marginal`, quick plotting is turned off, and annotation is turned on.

The final plot is created with the final call. We can't show it here as it's a dense multi-faceted plot with axes that don't render legibly in print format. You should be able to see it well on your screen, though. Once you've got it, you should be able to see the different powers at different replicate numbers. Note that the *X*-axis indicates the number of replicate RNA samples used and the metrics include **False Detection Rate (FDR)**, **False Negative/Positive Rate (FNR/FPR)**, and **True Negative/Positive Rate (TNR/TPR)**.

There's more...

When we have only one sample (or maybe just one replicate), we have difficulty estimating the `log2` fold change distribution and the number of differentially expressed genes. In place of estimates, we can use a function that generates numbers for us. The body of the function needs to generate numbers as needed. An example that generates normally distributed numbers with a mean of 0 and a standard deviation of 2 is as follows:

```
log2fc_func <- function(x){ rnorm(x, 0, 2) }
```

This can then be used in place of the estimate in the `pLFC` slot of the `Setup()` function.

Finding unannotated transcribed regions

Finding unannotated transcribed regions can be useful in several different genomics applications. One of the main use cases is identifying novel genes. Unannotated transcribed regions may represent novel genes that have not been previously identified.

By identifying these regions, researchers can gain a better understanding of the genome and potentially discover new biological pathways or proteins. Another use case is identifying alternative splicing events, where different exons are used to create different protein products. Identifying these events can provide insight into how the genome is regulated and how different proteins are produced from the same gene. Additionally, unannotated transcribed regions may include **untranslated RNAs (UTRs)**, lncRNAs, miRNAs, and other types of non-coding RNAs, which can provide a more complete understanding of the functional elements in the genome and characterize the non-coding genome. Lastly, unannotated transcribed regions may also be specific to certain tissues, which can provide insight into tissue-specific functions and pathways. In this recipe, we'll learn how to find regions in a genome that have sequence reads that can be mapped to them but that are not currently covered by our available annotation.

Getting ready

Conceptually, unannotated regions look like what's shown in *Figure 6.2*, with the annotated genes having reads aligned to them (known as coverage) and a third peak of reads in between:

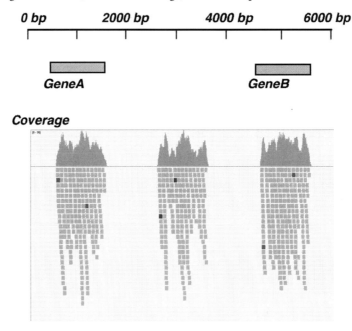

Figure 6.2 – Example coverage diagram of our reads

We wish to find this unannotated region from the alignment directly. We'll need the Bioconductor csaw, IRanges, SummarizedExperiment, and rtracklayer packages to do so.

Our dataset will be a synthetic one that has a small 6 kb genome region and two gene features. Aligned reads will be in a BAM file and the gene annotations will be in a GFF file. The data can be found in this book's data package and the recipe explicitly shows how to get it.

How to do it...

Here is how we can find unannotated regions:

1. Set up a loading function:

```
library(rtracklayer)
get_annotated_regions_from_gff <- function(file_name) {
  gff <- rtracklayer::import.gff(file_name)
  as(gff, "GRanges")
}
```

2. Get counts in windows across the whole genome:

```
library(csaw)
library(rbioinfcookbook)

bam_path <- fs::path_package("extdata",
                             "windows.bam",
                             package="rbioinfcookbook"
                             )

gff_path <- fs::path_package("extdata",
                             "genes.gff",
                             package="rbioinfcookbook"
                             )

whole_genome <- csaw::windowCounts(
  bam_path,
  bin = TRUE,
  filter = 0,
  width = 500,
  param = csaw::readParam(minq = 20,
                          dedup = TRUE,
                          pe = "both")
)

colnames(whole_genome) <- c("small_data")
annotated_regions <-
  get_annotated_regions_from_gff(gff_path)
```

3. Find overlaps between annotations and our windows, and subset the windows:

```
library(IRanges)
library(SummarizedExperiment)

windows_in_genes <- IRanges::overlapsAny(
  SummarizedExperiment::rowRanges(whole_genome),
  annotated_regions
)
```

4. Subset the windows into those in annotated and non-annotated regions:

```
annotated_window_counts <- whole_genome[windows_in_genes, ]

non_annotated_window_counts <- whole_genome[!windows_in_genes, ]
```

5. Put the data in a DataFrame:

```
window_counts <- data.frame(assay(non_annotated_window_counts))
window_ranges <- data.frame(ranges(non_annotated_window_counts))
results <- cbind(window_ranges, window_counts)
results
```

These five steps are what we need to do to find unannotated transcribed regions.

How it works...

In *step 1*, a loading function is set up to import a GFF file into R using the rtracklayer package. Specifically, the function takes in a filename and reads it into a variable, gff. Then, the function converts the gff object into a GRanges object and returns it.

In *step 2*, the csaw and rbioinfcookbook packages are loaded and the paths of two files are specified – that is, bam_path and gff_path. The bam_path variable holds the path of the windows.bam file, which is an indexed binary alignment file that contains the reads for a dataset, while the gff_path variable holds the path of the genes.gff file, which contains the annotated regions for the genome. The windowCounts() function from the csaw package is used to count reads in windows of width 500 base pairs across the entire genome. The resulting matrix is stored in the whole_genome variable. In the next line, the columns are given the name small_data. Then, the get_annotated_regions_from_gff function is called on gff_path and the resulting GRanges object is stored in annotated_regions

In *step 3*, the IRanges and SummarizedExperiment packages are loaded and the IRanges function, overlapsAny(), is used to identify which of the windows in the whole_genome object overlap with regions in the annotated_regions object. The result is a logical vector indicating whether each window overlaps with an annotated region, and it is stored in the windows_in_genes variable.

In *step 4*, two subsets of the whole_genome object are created based on the logical windows_in_genes vector. The annotated_window_counts variable holds the windows that overlapped with the annotated regions and the non_annotated_window_counts variable holds the windows that did not overlap with annotated regions.

In *step 5*, the assay() function is used to extract the count data from the non_annotated_window_counts object and returns it as a matrix. This matrix contains the count data for all the windows that did not overlap with annotated regions and is converted into a more friendly DataFrame. Similarly, the ranges() function is used to output the window extents that were used. The cbind function is used to join the DataFrames together into one results DataFrame. The output DataFrame contains the counts of reads in windows of width 500 base pairs across the entire genome that did not overlap with any of the annotated regions – in this case, the genes. It looks like this:

```
##    start   end width small_data
## 1   1501  2000   500          0
## 2   2001  2500   500          0
## 3   2501  3000   500         24
## 4   3001  3500   500         25
## 5   3501  4000   500          0
## 6   5501  6000   500          0
```

This is the minimal amount of information we need to spot the regions.

There's more...

We may need to get annotated regions from file formats other than GFF. rtracklayer supports various formats – here's a function for working with BED files:

```
get_annotated_regions_from_bed <- function(file_name) {
  bed <- rtracklayer::import.bed(file_name)
  as(bed, "GRanges")
}
```

This works as a standalone function, so call it when you need to load a BED file.

Finding regions showing high expression ab initio using bumphunter

The bumphunter package in R's Bioconductor ecosystem is a tool for identifying genomic regions that exhibit *bumps* of enrichment in high-throughput sequencing data. These bumps may represent functional regions, such as enhancers or transcription factor binding sites, and the package can be used to identify both known and novel regions of interest.

The bumphunter package works by scanning a given genomic region to enrich a particular feature of interest, such as the presence of certain transcription factor binding sites, or the level of histone modifications. It does this by dividing the region into non-overlapping windows and comparing the mean signal within each window to the overall mean signal across the entire region. The package then employs a statistical model to determine whether any particular window is significantly enriched for the feature of interest.

bumphunter can be used to identify novel enhancer regions in ChIP-Seq data, characterize the distribution of transcription factor binding sites, identify Histone modification peaks, and identify *open chromatin* regions in ATAC-Seq data.

The workflow typically begins with preprocessing the high-throughput sequencing data, which may involve quality control, aligning a reference genome, and converting the alignment data so that it's in a format that can be used with the package. The package will then scan genomic regions and output a list of significantly enriched windows, along with the mean signal level within each window. This recipe will teach you how to use high-throughput alignment and a set of thresholds defining a peak region with the `bumphunter` package to discover regions of alignment containing bumps.

Getting ready

We'll use the same windows data that we used in the previous recipe. We'll need the `Rsamtools` and `bumphunter` libraries to do so.

How to do it...

We will start by loading the data from a BAM file:

1. Load the data and get per-position coverage:

```
library(rbioinfcookbook)
library(Rsamtools)

bam_path <- fs::path_package("extdata",
                             "windows.bam",
                             package="rbioinfcookbook"
                             )
pileup_df <- Rsamtools::pileup(bam_path)
```

2. Find the preliminary clusters:

```
library(bumphunter)
clusters <- bumphunter::clusterMaker(pileup_df$seqnames,
                                     pileup_df$pos,
                                     maxGap = 100
                                     )
```

3. Find the bumps with a minimum cutoff:

```
final_bumps <- bumphunter::regionFinder(pileup_df$count,
                     pileup_df$seqnames,
                     pileup_df$pos,
                     clusters,
                     cutoff = 1
                     )
```

And this short recipe is all we need.

How it works...

In *step 1*, the rbioinfcookbook and Rsamtools packages are loaded, both of which provide several functionalities, such as reading BAM/SAM/CRAM files and BED files, handling BAM indices, and retrieving data from BAM files. Then, the path_package function from the fs package is used to get the path of the windows.bam file, which is a BAM file containing aligned sequencing reads. This file is part of the data that comes with the rbioinfcookbook package, and it will be used in the following steps of the analysis.

In *step 2*, the clusterMaker function from the bumphunter package is used to find preliminary clusters in the data. The clusterMaker function expects a vector of chromosome names (pileup_df$pos) and a maxGap parameter that defines the maximum allowed distance between two positions in the same cluster. Here, the maximum distance allowed is 100 bp. The clusterMaker function returns a vector of cluster IDs, where positions that belong to the same cluster have the same ID. Refer to the following code:

```
## clusters
##    1    2    3
## 1486 1552 1520
```

This gives us the clusters that were obtained in *step 2*, represented as a table showing the number of positions that belong to each cluster.

In *step 3*, the regionFinder function is used to find the actual *bumps* of enrichment in the data, based on the preliminary clusters obtained in the previous step. The regionFinder function expects a vector of counts (pileup_df$counts), a vector of positions (pileup_df$pos), the clusters obtained from the previous *tep 2*, and a cutoff parameter that defines the minimum allowed count for a position to be considered part of a bump. Here, the minimum count is set to 1.

The regionFinder function returns a DataFrame with cluster positions and metrics on the bump sizes:

Hopefully, this has outlined how to find peaks or bumps with expression data alone.

There's more...

If you have multiple experiments to analyze, try the bumphunter function. This will operate over multiple data columns in a matrix and perform linear modeling to assess uncertainty about the position and existence of the replicates. It is very similar to regionFinder() in operation.

Differential peak analysis

Identifying differentially expressed peaks in genomics data is a key task in bioinformatics and has many uses. One of the most common applications is the analysis of ChIP-Seq data, where the technique is used to identify binding sites of transcription factors and other DNA-binding proteins. By comparing ChIP-Seq data between different samples or conditions, researchers can identify peaks of enrichment that are differentially expressed and gain insight into how the protein in question regulates the expression of different genes. Another example is RNA-Seq data – by comparing RNA-Seq data between different samples or conditions, researchers can identify peaks of expression that are differentially expressed and gain insight into how different samples or conditions affect the expression of different genes.

Other use cases include Histone modification and ATAC-Seq data analysis to study the regulation of gene expression through chromatin accessibility or modifications. We've already looked at how we can analyze differentially expressed annotated regions, and the same principles hold here – we just need to come up with names for the unannotated regions – usually, we can use the coordinates – and then analyze as before. One problem that we have is to go from the bump/peak data, which is usually in an object such as a Bioconductor `SummarizedExperiment/Ranged SummarizedExperiment` object, to the count matrix or `DESeq2` objects. In this recipe, we'll look at how to do that.

Getting ready

In this recipe, we'll need a `RangedSummarizedExperiment` version of RNAseq data. The data we will use for this recipe will be from a set of test Arabidopsis thaliana plant samples infected with Pseudomonas syringae hrcC mutant (hrcc) versus a set of control mock infection samples (mock). There are three replicates in each sample type. The data is provided in the `rbionfcookbook` R package as `arab_infection.rse`. We'll also need the Bioconductor `SummarizedExperiment` package.

How to do it...

We can do the peak comparison as follows:

1. Load the data and set up a function that creates tags:

```
library(rbioinfcookbook)
library(SummarizedExperiment)

make_tag <- function(grange_obj) {
  paste0(
    grange_obj@seqnames,
    ":",
    grange_obj@ranges@start,
    "-",
    (grange_obj@ranges@start + grange_obj@ranges@width)
```

```
    )
  }
```

2. Extract the data and annotate the rows:

```
counts <- assay(arab_infection.rse)

if ( ! is.null(names(rowRanges(arab_infection.rse))) ){
    rownames(counts) <- names(rowRanges(arab_se))
} else {
    rownames(counts) <- make_tag(rowRanges(arab_infection.rse))
}
```

Only two steps are needed here, but they're very powerful.

How it works...

In *step 1*, two R libraries, rbioinfcookbook and SummarizedExperiment, are loaded. The rbioinfcookbook package provides the dataset we need, while the SummarizedExperiment package provides a container for storing the results of an experiment, such as the reads that align to a genome.

Additionally, a function named make_tag is defined. This function takes in an object of the Granges class, which is a container for genomic ranges and annotations, and creates a tag by concatenating the sequence name, the start position, and the end position of the range. This function will be used later to create tags for the rows of a DataFrame.

In *step 2*, the assay() function is used to extract the data of the arab_infection.rse object, which is saved to the variable counts. The if statement checks if rowRanges of the arab_infection. rse object contains names. If true, it assigns names to the rows of the counts DataFrame using names(rowRanges(arab_infection.rse)); otherwise, it assigns row names to the counts DataFrame by using the make_tag function on rowRanges(arab_infection.rse).

The output is a count matrix, as shown here:

```
## head(counts)
##              mock1 mock2 mock3 hrcc1 hrcc2 hrcc3
## Chr1:3631-5900    35    77    40    46    64    60
## Chr1:5928-8738    43    45    32    43    39    49
## Chr1:11649-13715  16    24    26    27    35    20
## Chr1:23146-31228  72    43    64    66    25    90
## Chr1:31170-33154  49    78    90    67    45    60
## Chr1:33379-37872   0    15     2     0    21     8
```

This contains the genomic regions and the counts.

Estimating batch effects with SVA

Batch effects occur in scientific experiments when there are systematic differences in the measurements that are made between different groups of samples, even though the samples themselves are biologically the same. These differences can be caused by various factors, such as differences in the lab conditions, the equipment used, or the time of the experiment. In RNA-Seq experiments, batch effects can occur when samples are run on different sequencing platforms or at different times, leading to differences in the read counts between samples. This can affect the statistical power of the experiment, as well as introduce bias into the analysis.

One common approach to address batch effects in RNA-Seq experiments is to use the **surrogate variable analysis** (**SVA**) Bioconductor package. The SVA package uses a statistical method to identify and correct the batch effects by identifying sources of variation in the data that are likely to be caused by technical factors. The package works by first finding a set of *surrogate variables* that are strongly correlated with the technical factors causing the batch effects. Then, it uses these surrogate variables as covariates in a linear model to correct for the batch effects. This allows the experimenter to remove any bias introduced by the technical factors and improve the statistical power of the experiment.

The package uses principal component analysis to identify a set of principal components that explain most of the variability in the data. It also has a built-in method to identify which of these principal components are correlated with known technical factors, such as batch, plate, or chip number. Then, it uses these correlated principal components as covariates in the statistical model to adjust for the batch effects.

It's important to note that any adjustment made by the package is not based on the underlying biology of the samples but rather on the association between the technical factors and the data. The package allows you to better control the batch effect by removing any systematic error caused by these technical factors and improving the power of downstream statistical analysis. In this recipe, we'll learn how to develop a model that can be used to better statistically correct our data to account for batch effects.

Getting ready

For this recipe, we'll need the SVA package from Bioconductor. Once again, the data we will use will be from a set of test Arabidopsis thaliana plant samples infected with Pseudomonas syringae hrcC mutant (hrcc) versus a set of control mock infection samples (mock). There are three replicates in each sample type. The data is provided in the `rbionfcookbook` R package as a count matrix in the `arab_infection` object.

How to do it...

To estimate batch effects using SVA, follow these steps:

1. Load the necessary libraries and data:

    ```
    library(sva)
    library(rbioinfcookbook)
    ```

2. Filter out the rows with too few counts in some experiments:

    ```
    keep <- apply(arab_infection, 1, function(x) {length(x[x>3])}>=2
    } )
    arab_filtered <- arab_infection[keep,]
    ```

3. Create the initial design:

    ```
    groups <- as.factor(rep(c("mock", "hrcc"), each=3))
    ```

4. Set up the test and null models and run SVA:

    ```
    test_model <- model.matrix(~groups)
    null_model <- test_model[,1]
    svar <- svaseq(arab_filtered, test_model, null_model, n.sv=1)
    ```

5. Extract the surrogate variables to a new design for downstream use:

    ```
    design <- cbind(test_model, svar$v)
    ```

And that's all we need to do to generate a new model design for statistical analyses.

How it works...

In *step 1*, the sva and rbioinfcookbook libraries are loaded. These libraries provide functions for performing SVA and the data needed for this book, respectively.

In *step 2*, the arab_infection data is filtered to only keep the rows that have at least two counts greater than 3 using the apply function. The apply function is used to apply a function to each row of arab_infection. The function that is being applied checks the number of counts in the row that are greater than 3 and only keeps the row if this number is greater than or equal to 2. The filtered data is then stored in the arab_filtered variable.

In *step 3*, the groups variable is set as a factor, which is a categorical variable that can take on one of two values, mock or hrcc, which are repeated three times each.

In *step 4*, the `test_model` variable is defined as a matrix that is created using the `model.matrix` function. This function provides a matrix of predictors that is used as a design matrix for a linear model. This `test_model` variable is defined as a linear combination of the `groups` variable, which is a categorical variable. The `null_model` variable is defined as the first column of the `test_model` matrix. The `svaseq` function is then used to perform the surrogate variable analysis on the filtered data, `arab_filtered`, with the `test_model` and `null_model` matrices as input, and the number of surrogate variables set to 1. The output of this function is stored in the `svar` variable.

In *step 5*, the `design` variable is created by combining the `test_model` variable and the `svarv` variable by using the `cbind` function. The `svar` variable contains the surrogate variables that were generated in *step 4*, and it is added as additional columns to the `test_model` matrix, creating the final `design` variable. This variable can be used in downstream analysis, such as a linear model used in packages such as `edgeR` and `DESeq2`, to incorporate the information from the surrogate variables.

Finding allele-specific expression with AllelicImbalance

Allele-specific expression (ASE) refers to the differential expression of alleles (different versions of a gene) in a diploid organism. It occurs when one allele is expressed more or less than the other allele, resulting in an imbalance of expression. ASE can occur in both coding and non-coding regions of the genome and can have a significant impact on the phenotype of an organism. Analyzing ASE can help with identifying genetic variations that contribute to the development of diseases such as cancer and inherited disorders.

The R Bioconductor `AllelicImbalance` package can be used to analyze ASE data. This package provides a set of tools for identifying, quantifying, and visualizing ASE in high-throughput sequencing data. The package can be used to quantify ASE at both the gene and transcript level and to identify differentially expressed alleles. Additionally, `AllelicImbalance` can help identify the genomic regions that are likely to be associated with ASE. The package can read in various sequencing file formats, process the data, and generate a set of ASE-related metrics, such as ASE p-value, ASE fold-change, and others.

It can also plot various ASE-related visualizations to help in data exploration and interpretation, such as ASE plots, allele imbalance plots, box plots, and more. These visualizations can be very useful for identifying potential ASE events or even potential allelic imbalance events. These events could be further analyzed to explore the underlying biological mechanisms that lead to ASE. This package is widely used in genetics, genomics, and functional genomics research and has been applied to study many different organisms and biological systems.

In this recipe, we'll take a look at a method for determining which of the variants of a transcript may have preferential expression in different samples. The reads will come from different BAM files and the variants must already be known. This implies that you have already carried out a read alignment and a variant call step and have per sample BAM and VCF files.

Getting ready

We'll need the `AllelicImbalance` and `VariantAnnotation` packages from Bioconductor for this recipe. The `AllelicImbalance` package provides a small but informative dataset of three SNPs on Chromosome 17 of the hg19 build of the human genome. The files have been saved in the `rbioinfcookbook` data package.

How to do it...

Start looking at allele-specific expression, as follows:

1. Load the necessary libraries and set up an `import` folder:

```
library(AllelicImbalance)
library(VariantAnnotation)
library(rbioinfcookbook)

region_of_interest <- GRanges(seqnames = c("17"),
                              ranges =
                                IRanges(79478301, 79478361))
bam_folder <- fs::path_package("extdata", "allele_expression",
                               package="rbioinfcookbook")
```

2. Load the reads and variants in regions of interest:

```
reads <- impBamGAL(bam_folder, region_of_interest,
                   verbose = FALSE)

vcf_file <- fs::path_package("extdata","allele_expression",
                             "ERP000101.vcf",
package="rbioinfcookbook")

variant_positions <- granges(VariantAnnotation::readVcf(vcf_
file), "hg19")
allele_counts <- getAlleleCounts(reads, variant_positions,
                   verbose = FALSE)
```

3. Build the `ASEset` object:

```
ase.vcf <- ASEsetFromCountList(rowRanges = variant_positions,
                               allele_counts)

reference_sequence <- fs::path_package("extdata","allele_
expression",
                             "hg19.chr17.subset.fa",
                             package="rbioinfcookbook")
```

```
ref(ase.vcf) <- refAllele(ase.vcf, fasta = reference_sequence)
alt(ase.vcf) <- inferAltAllele(ase.vcf)
```

4. Run the test on all variants:

```
binom.test(ase.vcf, n="*")
```

And that's what we need to do for allele-specific expression analysis.

How it works...

In *step 1*, the `AllelicImbalance`, `VariantAnnotation`, and `rbioinfcookbook` libraries are loaded. The `AllelicImbalance` package provides a set of tools for identifying, quantifying, and visualizing ASE in high-throughput sequencing data. The `VariantAnnotation` package is used for reading variant data in VCF format and `rbioinfcookbook` contains the data we need. The `region_of_interest` variable is defined as a GRanges object containing the coordinates of a region on chromosome 17, in this case between 79478301 and 79478361. The `bam_folder` variable is defined as the path to the folder containing the `allele_expression` data, as provided by the `rbioinfcookbook` package.

In *step 2*, the `reads` variable is defined as the reads in the region of interest using the `impBamGAL` function from the `AllelicImbalance` package, by specifying the BAM folder and the region of interest, with `verbose` set to `false`. The `vcf_file` variable is defined as the path to the VCF file containing the variants, and the `variant_positions` variable is defined as the positions of the variants in the form of a GRanges object. The `allele_counts` variable is defined by passing `reads` and `variant_positions` to the `getAlleleCounts` function, which counts the number of alleles at each variant position and stores them in the `allele_counts` variable.

In *step 3*, the `ase.vcf` variable is created by passing `variant_positions` and `allele_counts` to the `ASEsetFromCountList` function, creating an `ASEset` object that contains information about the allele-specific expression for each variant. The `reference_sequence` variable is defined as the path to a reference sequence FASTA file that is passed to the `refAllele` function. This function sets the reference allele for each variant in the `ASEset` object. The `inferAltAllele` function is used to infer the alternate alleles for each variant in the `ASEset` object.

In *step 4*, the `binom.test` function is applied to the `ASEset` object, `ase.vcf`. It performs a binomial test on the counts of each allele in each sample for each variant in the object to determine whether the ratio of alternate allele to reference allele is different from 0.5. It will output a table that contains the statistics of the test, including p-values, confidence intervals, and odds ratios. This final output table allows us to identify alleles that are differentially expressed and therefore could be associated with specific biological mechanisms:

```
##               chr17_79478287 chr17_79478331 chr17_79478334
## ERR009113.bam        0.500   1.000000e+00   1.000000e+00
## ERR009115.bam        0.125   6.103516e-05   3.051758e-05
```

Note that the table has one region per coordinate.

There's more...

The preceding analysis can be extended to carry out per-strand and phenotype tests if required. The code would need amending to introduce strand information in the `ASEset` object construction step. Doing so usually requires that the RNA-Seq experiment and alignment steps were performed with strandedness in mind and the bioinformatics pipeline configured accordingly. Phenotype information can be added to the construction step using the `colData` parameter and a vector of phenotype or sample types for columns in the `ASEset` object.

Presenting RNA-Seq data using ComplexHeatmap

A heatmap plot is a graphical representation of data where values are represented by colors, typically with a color scale. In bioinformatics, heatmap plots are often used to visualize large datasets and identify patterns in genomics data, such as variations in gene expression or mutation rates. They can be used to display data from a wide range of sources, such as microarray, RNA-Seq, and ChIP-Seq. Heatmap plots are particularly useful for visualizing data in large matrices, such as gene expression data, where the rows represent the genes and the columns represent the samples.

When creating heatmap plots, it is important to use accessible color schemes that can be easily interpreted by a wide range of users. This includes using a color scale that is easily distinguished by individuals with color vision deficiencies and using a consistent color scheme across different plots. Using a legend to indicate the values represented by different colors is crucial. A perceptually uniform color scheme is a color map where the difference in color between two adjacent color stops is perceived as being the same across the entire color range. It allows accurate data interpretation, which is particularly useful in scientific data plots, where the goal is to accurately convey information about the data. The `viridis` package in R provides a set of color maps designed to be perceptually uniform. These color maps are widely used in bioinformatics and are popular due to their simplicity of use and accessibility. Similarly, the `ColorBrewer` maps are useful for distinct categorical or diverging palettes.

The R Bioconductor `ComplexHeatmap` package is an advanced tool for creating heatmap plots that can handle large datasets. It provides a wide range of functionalities for creating, customizing, and annotating heatmaps, including the ability to layer multiple heatmaps on top of each other and add annotations such as gene ontology terms. Additionally, the package can also be used to create heatmaps of other types of data, such as chromatin accessibility data.

This package can be used to create a heatmap of gene expression data, for example, where each row represents a gene, and each column represents a sample. The package can also provide a range of customizations, such as changing the color scale and color legend, adding annotations to the heatmap, or even creating a combination of heatmaps by combining multiple data sources. This is particularly useful for combining different types of data in a single plot, such as combining the expression data with the annotation data, and helps with interpreting the data.

In this recipe, we'll take some matrices of data representing RNA-Seq expression in log-fold change format and create multipanel annotated heatmaps using `ComplexHeatmap`.

Getting ready

This visualization recipe needs a few packages, including `ComplexHeatmap` for our main plot. We'll use `stringr` so that we can work with strings with ease and sort labels and the data from our `rbioinfcookbook` package. The rest – `viridisLite`, `RColorBrewer`, and `circlize` – are all for creating usable color schemes.

How to do it...

This fun task can be accomplished as follows:

1. Load the data and divide the columns by data type:

```
library(ComplexHeatmap)
library(viridisLite)
library(stringr)
library(RColorBrewer)
library(circlize)
library(rbioinfcookbook)


mat <- log(as.matrix(at_tf_gex[, 5:55]))
ecotype <- stringr::str_split(colnames(mat), ",", simplify=TRUE)
[,1]
part <- stringr::str_split(colnames(mat), ", ", simplify=TRUE)
[,2]
```

2. Set up the color palettes for the different datasets:

```
data_col_func <- circlize::colorRamp2(seq(0, max(mat), length.
out = 6), viridisLite::magma(6))

ecotype_colors <- c(RColorBrewer::brewer.pal(12, "Set3"),
                    RColorBrewer::brewer.pal(5, "Set1"))
names(ecotype_colors) <- unique(ecotype)

part_colors <- RColorBrewer::brewer.pal(3, "Accent")
names(part_colors) <- unique(part)
```

3. Create the `Annotation` objects that will sit alongside the main heatmap:

```
top_annot <- HeatmapAnnotation("Ecotype" = ecotype,
                               "Plant Part" = part,
                               col = list("Ecotype" = ecotype_
colors,
                                          "Plant Part" = part_
colors),
                               annotation_name_side = "left")

side_annot <- rowAnnotation(length = anno_points(at_tf_
gex$Length, pch = 16, size = unit(1, "mm"),
     axis_param = list(at = seq(1, max(at_tf_gex$Length), length.
out=4)
         ),
      ))
```

4. Create the first heatmap:

```
ht_1 <- Heatmap(mat, name="log(TPM)", row_km = 6,
                col = data_col_func,
                top_annotation = top_annot,
                right_annotation = side_annot,
                cluster_columns = TRUE,
                column_split = ecotype,
                show_column_names = FALSE,
                column_title = " "
                )
```

5. Manipulate the TF family data into a simpler version and select colors to display it:

```
of_interest <- c("bHLH", "WRKY", "bZIP")
short_family <- at_tf_gex$Family
short_family[! short_family %in% of_interest] <- "other"
```

```
fam_colors <- RColorBrewer::brewer.pal(4, "Set1")
names(fam_colors) <- unique(short_family)
```

6. Create the second heatmap of TF information:

```
ht_2 <- Heatmap(short_family, name = "TF Family",
                top_annotation =
                  HeatmapAnnotation(
                    summary = anno_summary(which= "row",
                                           height = unit(2,
"cm")

                                          )

                  ),
                col = fam_colors,
                width = unit(0.75, "cm")

      )
```

7. Combine and draw the final heatmap from the two smaller ones:

```
ht <- ht_1 + ht_2
ComplexHeatmap::draw(ht)
```

And that is all the code we need to create a very pretty and informationally rich plot.

How it works...

In *step 1*, we load the necessary libraries. The `ComplexHeatmap` library is used to generate complex heatmaps, `viridisLite` is used for color scales, `stringr` is used for text manipulation, `RColorBrewer` is used for generating palettes of colors for the heatmaps, `circlize` is used for circular data visualization, and `rbioinfcookbook` is this book's package for the data we need.

The `at_tf_gex` dataset is a DataFrame and `mat` is created from it by log-transforming a subset of that dataset – specifically, the columns 5 to 55 – with `as.matrix(at_tf_gex[, 5:55])`. This step is done to scale the data and make it more visually interpretable.

Then, the ecotype and part of the samples are extracted by splitting the column names of the matrix using the `stringr::str_split` function, where in `ecotype`, the split is by , and in `part`, the split is by `', '` (note the space in the pattern in the second one – this is a quick way of removing that fiddly leading space in the match). The `str_split()` function takes three arguments: the string you want to split, the delimiter on which you want to split the string, and whether you want the output to be simplified or not. The `simplify=TRUE` argument tells the function to return a vector, where the string is split at every occurrence of the specified delimiter, rather than returning a list of vectors.

In *step 2*, the code creates color palettes for the different types of data in the heatmap. `Data_col_func` is a function that's created using the `circlize::colorRamp2` function, which maps the values in `mat` to the range of colors provided by the `viridisLite::magma` function, with a total of 6 colors. `data_col_func` will be called later to generate colors dynamically across a range. The `colorRamp2()` function takes two arguments, the first being a vector of numerical values, and the second being the color scale to derive color values from.

`ecotype_colors` is an `RColorBrewer`-derived palette of 12 colors from the `Set3` palette and five from the `Set1` palette (we have 17 ecotypes and `RcolorBrewer` has a maximum of 12 colors in its biggest palette, so we must borrow further colors from the complementary palette). `part_colors` is an `RColorBrewer` palette consisting of three colors for highlighting the plant part information. The `RColorBrewer::brewer.pal()` function provides predefined color palettes. It takes two arguments – the first one is the number of colors and the second one is the name of the palette.

The names of `ecotype_colors` and `part_colors` are assigned to the unique elements in `ecotype` and `part`, respectively, so that the resulting annotation will be color-coded based on these unique elements.

In *step 3*, the code creates two annotation objects that will be displayed alongside the main heatmap. `top_annot` is created using the `HeatmapAnnotation()` function and will display the ecotype and plant part information. The `annotation_name_side` argument is set to `left` so that the column titles are shown to the left of the annotation.

The `side_annot` object is created using the `rowAnnotation()` function. This function is used to add an annotation to the rows of the heatmap – in this case, it is used to display the length information of the samples. The length argument is used to specify the length of the annotation – in this case, the lengths of the samples. The `anno_points()` function is used to specify the positions of the points; it takes `at_tf_gex$Length` as input, and the `pch` argument is used to specify the shape of the points. The `size` argument is used to specify the size of the points and the `axis_param` argument is used to specify the locations of the ticks on the *X*-axis.

In *step 4*, the first heatmap is created using the `Heatmap()` function. `mat` is used as the input data. The `row_km` option is used to set the number of clusters for the rows – in this case, 6. The `col` option is set to `data_col_func` so that it can use the color palette that was created in *step 2*. `top_annot` and `side_annot` are used as annotations to display the ecotype, plant part, and length information. The `cluster_columns = TRUE` option causes the columns to be clustered based on their similarity. The `column_split = ecotype` option groups the columns by ecotype. The `show_column_names = FALSE` option is used to hide the column names and the `column_title = " "` option sets the title of the columns as empty. On its own, this heatmap looks as follows:

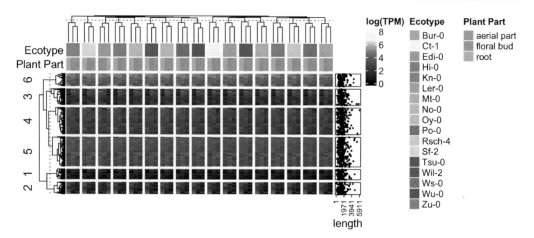

Figure 6.3 – The first section of the heatmap

In *step 5*, the code picks the TF families of interest from the dataset and renames the rest as other. The of_interest variable is defined to hold the families of interest, which is an array of bHLH, WRKY, and bZIP TFs. Then, short_family is created by the subsetting at_tf_gex$Family variable and short_family, where short_family is not one of the of_interest and is set to other. Then, a color palette is created with the RcolorBrewer::brewer.pal() function and is assigned the unique elements in short_family.

In *step 6*, a second heatmap is created using the Heatmap() function. Short_family is used as the input data. The HeatmapAnnotation() function is used to display the summary of TF family information (note that this time, we didn't use an intermediate variable, we just set the function in the Heatmap() call). Though this part looks like an annotation, it's coded as a second single-column heatmap. The col option is set to fam_colors and the width is set to unit(2, "cm") (this can be varied, depending on the size of the graphics output device). The HeatmapAnnotation() function can be used to add various annotation elements to the heatmap – in this case, it's used to add a summary of the row. The anno_summary() function is used to display the summary, the which parameter is used to specify whether it's for the rows or columns, and the height parameter is used to specify the height of the summary. This section looks as follows:

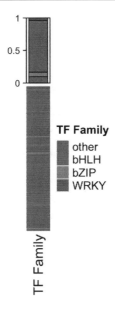

Figure 6.4 – The second section of the heatmap

In *step 7*, the two heatmaps are combined using the + operator, and the final heatmap is rendered with the `ComplexHeatmap::draw()` function. The `draw()` function is used to render the final heatmap, which is created by combining the two heatmaps, `ht_1` and `ht_2`. The resulting heatmap is a combination of the two heatmaps and will show the data on `mat`, the ecotype and part information, the length information, and the TF family data on the right-hand side of the heatmap. The final combined complex heatmap looks as follows:

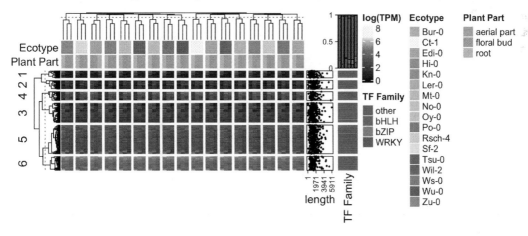

Figure 6.5 – The final combined heatmap

This shows us an information-rich, multi-dimensional heatmap of publication quality.

7
Finding Genetic Variants with HTS Data

High-throughput sequencing (HTS) has made it possible to discover genetic variants and carry out genome-wide genotyping and haplotyping in many samples in a short space of time. The deluge of data that this technology has released has created some unique opportunities for bioinformaticians and computer scientists, and some really innovative new data storage and data analysis pipelines have been created. The fundamental pipeline in variant calling starts with the quality control of HTS reads and aligning those reads to a reference genome. These steps invariably take place before analysis in R and typically result in a BAM file of read alignments or a **variant call file** (**VCF**) of variant positions that we'll want to process in our R code.

As variant calling and analysis is such a fundamental technique in bioinformatics, Bioconductor is well-equipped with the tools we need to construct our software and perform our analysis. The key questions researchers will want to ask will range from *Where are the genetic variants in my genome?* to *How many are there?* to *How can I classify them?* In this chapter, we'll take a look at some recipes that address these questions and also look at other important general techniques that allow us to visualize variants and markers on a genome and assess associations of variants with genotypes. We'll also look at other definitions of the term **genetic variant** and see how we can assess the copy number of individual loci.

In this chapter, we will cover the following recipes:

- Finding SNPs and INDELs in sequence data using `VariantTools`
- Predicting open reading frames in long reference sequences
- Plotting features on genetic maps with `karyoploteR`
- Selecting and classifying variants with `VariantAnnotation`
- Extracting information in genomic regions of interest

- Finding phenotype and genotype associations with GWAS
- Estimating the copy number at a locus of interest

Technical requirements

We will use `renv` to manage packages in a project-specific way. To use `renv` to install packages, you will first need to install the `renv` package. You can do this by running the following commands in your R console:

1. Install `renv`:

```
install.packages("renv")
```

2. Create a new `renv` environment:

```
renv::init()
```

This will create a new directory called `.renv` in your current project directory.

3. You can then install packages with the following command:

```
renv::install_packages()
```

4. You can also use the `renv` package manager to install Bioconductor packages by running the following command:

```
renv::install("bioc::package name")
```

5. For example, to install the `Biobase` package, you would run the following:

```
renv::install("bioc::Biobase")
```

6. You can use `renv` to install development packages from GitHub, like this:

```
renv::install("user name/repo name")
```

7. For example, to install the `danmaclean` user's `rbioinfcookbook` package, you would run the following:

```
renv::install("danmaclean/rbioinfcookbook")
```

You can also install multiple packages at once by separating the package names with a comma. `renv` will automatically handle installing any required dependencies for the packages you install.

With `renv`, all packages will be installed in the local project directory and not the main central library, meaning you can have multiple versions of the same package, one specific one for each project.

All the sample data you need for this package is in the specially created data package on GitHub called `danmaclean/rbioinfcookbook`. The data will become available in your project once you've installed it.

For this chapter, we'll need the following packages:

- Regular packages:

  - `fs`

  - `readr`

  - `systemPipeR`

- Bioconductor packages:

  - `Biostrings`

  - `csaw`

  - `GenomicRanges`

  - `gmapR`

  - `karyoploteR`

  - `rrBLUP`

  - `rtracklayer`

  - `SummarizedExperiment`

  - `VariantAnnotation`

  - `VariantTools`

- GitHub:

  - `danmaclean/rbioinfcookbook`

Further information

Not all the recipes in this chapter run in R – some are command-line-based setups. I generally use a bash terminal for these bits. Most macOS and Linux machines will have these available in a **Terminal** application. Windows users will likely not need these specific steps, though various packages for running a Linux subsystem on Windows exist if you wish to search them out.

In R, it is normal practice to load a library and use functions directly by name. Although this is great in short interactive sessions, it can cause confusion when many packages are loaded at once and share function names. To clarify which package and function I am using at a given moment, I will occasionally use the `packageName::functionName()` convention.

Sometimes, in the middle of a recipe, I'll interrupt the code to dive into some intermediate output or to look at the structure of an object. When that happens, you'll see a code block where each line begins with ## (double hash symbols). Consider the following command:

```
letters[1:5]
```

This will give us the following output:

```
## a b c d e
```

Note that the output lines are prefixed with ##.

Finding SNPs and INDELs from sequence data using VariantTools

A key bioinformatics task is to take an alignment of high-throughput sequence reads, typically stored in a BAM file, and compute a list of variant positions. Of course, this is ably handled by many external command-line programs and tools and usually results in a VCF file of variants, but some really powerful packages in Bioconductor can do the whole thing, quickly and efficiently, by taking advantage of BiocParallel's facilities for parallel evaluation, a set of tools designed to speed up work with large datasets in Bioconductor objects. Using Bioconductor tools allows us to keep all of our processing steps within R, and in this recipe, we'll go through a whole pipeline – from reads to lists of genes carrying variants – using purely R code and several Bioconductor packages.

Getting ready

In this recipe, we'll use a set of synthetic reads on the first 83 KB or so of the human genome chromosome 17. The reads were generated using the wgsim tool in samtools, an external command-line program. They have 64 **single nucleotide polymorphisms** (**SNPs**) introduced by wgsim, which can be seen in the snp_positions DataFrame that comes in rbioinfcookbook. We'll use BAM and reference genome files that are stored in that package too, so we'll need to install that along with the GenomicRanges, gmapR, rtracklayer, VariantAnnotation, and VariantTools Bioconductor packages, as well as the fs CRAN package.

How to do it...

Finding SNPs and **insertions/deletions** (**INDELs**) from sequence data using VariantTools can be done by performing the following steps:

1. Import the required libraries:

```
library(GenomicRanges)
library(gmapR)
library(rtracklayer)
library(VariantAnnotation)
library(VariantTools)
```

2. Then, load the datasets:

```
bam_file <- fs::path_package("extdata",
                             "hg17_snps.bam",
                             package="rbioinfcookbook"
                             )


fasta_file <- fs::path_package("extdata",
                               "chr17.83k.fa",
                               package="rbioinfcookbook"
                               )
```

3. Set up the genome object and the parameter objects:

```
fa <- rtracklayer::FastaFile(fasta_file)

genome <- gmapR::GmapGenome(fa, create=TRUE)


qual_params <- TallyVariantsParam(
  genome = genome,
  minimum_mapq = 20)


var_params <- VariantCallingFilters(read.count = 19,
                                    p.lower = 0.01
)
```

4. Call the variants:

```
called_variants <- callVariants(bam_file,
                                qual_params,
                                calling.filters = var_params
)

head(called_variants)
```

5. Now, we can move on to annotation and load in the feature position information from a `.gff` or `.bed` file:

```
VariantAnnotation::sampleNames(called_variants) <- "sample_name"
vcf <- VariantAnnotation::asVCF(called_variants)
VariantAnnotation::writeVcf(vcf, "hg17.vcf")

get_annotated_regions_from_gff <- function(file_name) {
  gff <- rtracklayer::import.gff(file_name)
  as(gff, "GRanges")
}

get_annotated_regions_from_bed <- function(file_name){
  bed <- rtracklayer::import.bed(file_name)
  as(bed, "GRanges")
}

genes <- get_annotated_regions_from_gff(fs::path_
package("extdata",
                              "chr17.83k.gff3",
                              package="rbioinfcookbook"
                              ))
```

6. Now, we can calculate which variants overlap which genes:

```
overlaps <- GenomicRanges::findOverlaps(called_variants, genes)
overlaps
```

7. Finally, we can subset the genes with the list of overlaps:

```
genes[subjectHits(overlaps)]
```

This gives us the regions with polymorphisms.

How it works...

This is a long and involved pipeline with a few complicated steps. After loading the libraries, the next two lines set up the files we're going to need from the data package. Note that we need a `.bam` file and a `.fasta` file. Next, we create a GmapGenome object using the `gmapR::GmapGenome()` function with the `fasta` object – this describes the genome to the later variant calling function. The next two functions we use, `TallyVariantParams()` and `VariantCallingFilters()`, are vital for correctly calling and filtering candidate SNPs. These are the functions in which you can set the parameters that define an SNP or INDEL. The options here are deliberately very poor. As shown here, 6 were called when we created 64.

Once the parameters have been defined, we use the `callVariants()` function with all of the information we set up to get a `vranges` object of variant:

```
## VRanges object with 6 ranges and 17 metadata columns:
##              seqnames     ranges
strand            ref                  alt      totalDepth
##                <Rle> <IRanges>  <Rle> <character> <characterOrRle>
<integerOrRle>
## [1] NC_000017.10        64                     G
T              759
## [2] NC_000017.10        69                     G
T              812
## [3] NC_000017.10        70                     G
T              818
## [4] NC_000017.10        73                     T
A              814
## [5] NC_000017.10        77                     T
A              802
## [6] NC_000017.10        78                     G
T              798
```

We can then set up the `GRanges` object of the GFF file of annotations (I also provided a function for getting annotation from BED files), resulting in the following output (truncated here):

```
## Hits object with 12684 hits and 0 metadata columns:
##          queryHits subjectHits
##          <integer>   <integer>
##    [1]       35176           1
##    [2]       35176           2
##    [3]       35176           3
##    [4]       35177           1
```

The final step is to use the powerful overlapping and subsetting capability of the `XRanges` objects. We use `GenomicRanges::findOverlaps()` to find the actual overlap – the returned `overlap` object contains the indices in each input object of the overlapped object:

```
## GRanges object with 12684 ranges and 20 metadata columns:
##                 seqnames       ranges strand |   source        type
     score
##                    <Rle>    <IRanges>  <Rle> | <factor>    <factor>
  <numeric>
##       [1] NC_000017.10 64099-76866        - |   havana ncRNA_gen
e          NA
##       [2] NC_000017.10 64099-76866        - |   havana lnc_RNA
           NA
```

```
##        [3] NC_000017.10 64099-65736        - |    havana exon
                 NA
```

Hence, we can use `subjectHits(overlaps)` to directly subset the genes with SNPs inside and get a non-redundant list.

There's more...

Once we're happy with the filters and the set of variants we called, we can save a VCF file of the variants using the following code:

```
VariantAnnotation::sampleNames(called_variants) <- "sample_name"
vcf <- VariantAnnotation::asVCF(called_variants)
VariantAnnotation::writeVcf(vcf, "hg17.vcf")
```

The results go into the `"hg.17.vcf"` file. You can change the name as you see fit.

See also

Although this recipe makes the steps and code clear, the actual parameters and values we need to change can't be decided so easily – the value will be very data-dependent. The `VariantTools` documentation contains a good discussion of how to work out and set parameters properly.

Predicting open reading frames in long reference sequences

A draft genome assembly of a previously unsequenced genome can be a rich source of biological knowledge, but when genomics resources such as gene annotations aren't available, it can be tricky to proceed. In this recipe, we'll look at a first-stage pipeline for finding potential genes and genomic loci of interest absolutely *de novo* and without information beyond the sequence. We'll use a very simple set of rules to find **open reading frames (ORFs)** – sequences that begin with a start codon and end with a stop codon. The tools for doing this are encapsulated within a single function in the `systemPipeR` Bioconductor package. We'll end up with yet another `GRanges` object that we can integrate into processes downstream that allow us to cross-reference other data, such as *RNA-Seq*. As a final step, we'll look at how we can use a genome simulation to assess which of the open reading frames are likely to be real and not just occurring by chance.

Getting ready

In this recipe, we'll use the short DAN sequence of the Arabidopsis chloroplast genome as input; it is provided with the `rbioinfcookbook` package, so we'll get the file out of that with the `fs` package and the `Biostrings` and `systemPipeR` Bioconductor packages.

How to do it...

Predicting open reading frames in long reference sequences can be done by performing the following steps:

1. Load the libraries and input the genome:

```
library(Biostrings)
library(systemPipeR)

dna_object <- readDNAStringSet(
  fs::path_package("extdata",
                   "arabidopsis_chloroplast.fa",
                   package="rbioinfcookbook"
                   )

  )
```

2. Predict the ORFs:

```
predicted_orfs <- predORF(dna_object, n = 'all', type = 'gr',
mode='ORF', strand = 'both', longest_disjoint = TRUE)
predicted_orfs
```

3. Calculate the properties of the reference genome:

```
bases <- c("A", "C", "T", "G")
raw_seq_string <- strsplit(as.character(dna_object), "")

seq_length <- width(dna_object[1])
counts <- lapply(bases, function(x) {sum(grepl(x, raw_seq_
string))} )
probs <- unlist(lapply(counts, function(base_count){signif(base_
count / seq_length, 2) }))
```

4. Create a function that finds the longest ORF in the simulated genome:

```
get_longest_orf_in_random_genome <- function(x,
                                             length = 1000,
                                             probs = c(0.25,
0.25, 0.25, 0.25),
                                             bases =
c("A","C","T","G")){

  random_genome <- paste0(sample(bases, size = length, replace =
TRUE, prob = probs), collapse = "")
  random_dna_object <- DNAStringSet(random_genome)
  names(random_dna_object) <- c("random_dna_string")
  orfs <- predORF(random_dna_object, n = 1, type = 'gr',
mode='ORF', strand = 'both', longest_disjoint = TRUE)
```

```
        return(max(width(orfs)))
}
```

5. Run the function on 10 simulated genomes:

```
random_lengths <- unlist(lapply(1:10, get_longest_orf_in_random_
genome, length = seq_length, probs = probs, bases = bases))
```

6. Get the length of the longest random ORF:

```
longest_random_orf <- max(random_lengths)
```

7. Keep only predicted ORFs longer than the longest random ORF:

```
keep <- width(predicted_orfs) > longest_random_orf
orfs_to_keep <- predicted_orfs[keep]
orfs_to_keep
```

And with that, we've predicted ORFs from long reference sequences.

How it works...

The first part of this recipe is where we predict ORFs. Initially, we load the DNA sequence as a DNAStringSet object using readDNAStringSet() from Biostrings. The predORF() function from systemPipeR uses this object as input and predicts ORFs according to the options set. In the following command block, we're returning all ORFs on both strands.

This will result in the following output:

```
## GRanges object with 2501 ranges and 2 metadata columns:
##          seqnames      ranges strand | subject_id inframe2end
##             <Rle>   <IRanges>  <Rle> |  <integer>   <numeric>
##     1 chloroplast 86762-93358      + |          1           2
##  1162 chloroplast   2056-2532      - |          1           3
##     2 chloroplast 72371-73897      + |          2           2
##  1163 chloroplast 77901-78362      - |          2           1
##     3 chloroplast 54937-56397      + |          3           3
```

We have received a GRanges object in return, with 2,501 ORFs described. This is far too many, so we need to filter them; in particular, we can work out which are ORFs that occurred by chance from the sequence. To do this, we need to do a little simulation; that's what happens in the next section of code. To estimate the length that random ORFs can reach, we're going to create a series of random genomes of a length equal to our input sequence and with the same base proportion and see what the longest ORF that can be predicted is. We do a few iterations of this and we get an idea of what the longest ORF occurring by chance could be. This length serves as a cut-off we can use to reject the predicted ORFs in the real sequence.

Achieving this needs a bit of setup and custom functions. First, we define the bases we will use as a simple character vector. Then, we get a character vector of the original DNA sequence by splitting the `as.character` version of `dna_object`. We use this information to work out the proportions of each base in the input sequence by first counting the number of each base (resulting in `counts`), then dividing it by the sequence length, resulting in `probs`. In both these steps, we use `lapply()` to loop over the vector `bases` and the list `counts` and apply an anonymous function that uses these two variables to give lists of results. `unlist` is used on our final list to reduce it to a simple vector.

Once we have the setup done, we can build our `get_longest_orf_in_random_genome()` simulation function. This generates a random genome by sampling length characters from the selection in `bases` with probabilities given in `probs`. We use `paste0()` to make the vector into a single string and then converted into a `DNAStringSet` object for the `predORF()` function. This time, we ask for only the longest ORF using `N = 1` and return the length of that.

This will result in the following output:

```
## GRanges object with 11 ranges and 2 metadata columns:
##           seqnames        ranges strand | subject_id inframe2end
##              <Rle>     <IRanges>  <Rle> |  <integer>   <numeric>
##   1 chloroplast   86762-93358      + |          1           2
##   2 chloroplast   72371-73897      + |          2           2
##   3 chloroplast   54937-56397      + |          3           3
##   4 chloroplast   57147-58541      + |          4           1
```

Now, we can run the function, which we do 10 times using `lapply()` and the `length`, `probs`, and `bases` information we calculated previously. `unlist()` turns the result into a simple vector and we extract the longest of the runs with `max()`. We can use subsetting on our original `predicted_orfs` object to keep the ORFs longer than the ones generated by chance.

There's more...

Once you've got a set of ORFs you're happy with, you'll likely want to save them to a file. You can do that using the `getSeq()` function in the `BSgenome` package, passing it the original sequence object and the ranges, and then giving the result the same names before saving them to a file with `writeXStringSet()`. The following code does this:

```
extracted_orfs <- BSgenome::getSeq(dna_object, orfs_to_keep)
names(extracted_orfs) <- paste0("orf_", 1:length(orfs_to_keep))
writeXStringSet(extracted_orfs, "saved_orfs.fa")
```

The results go into the `saved_orfs.fa` file, but you can change that as you wish.

Plotting features on genetic maps with karyoploteR

One of the most rewarding and insightful things we can do is visualize data. Very often, we want to see where some features lie concerning others on a chromosome or genetic map. These are sometimes called chromosome plots or ideograms. In this recipe, we'll learn how to create one of these using the karyoploteR package. This package takes the familiar GRanges objects as input and creates detailed plots from the configuration. We'll take a quick look at some different plot styles and configuration options for ironing out the bumps in your plots when labels spill off the page or overlap each other.

Getting ready

For this recipe, you'll need karyoploteR installed. All of the data we'll use will be generated within the recipe itself.

How to do it...

Plotting features on genetic maps with karyoploteR can be done by performing the following steps:

1. First, load the necessary libraries:

    ```
    library(karyoploteR)
    library(GenomicRanges)
    ```

2. Then, set up the genome object that will be the base for our karyotype:

    ```
    genome_df <- data.frame(
      chr = paste0("chr", 1:5),
      start = rep(1, 5),
      end = c(34964571, 22037565, 25499034, 20862711, 31270811)
    )
    genome_gr <- makeGRangesFromDataFrame(genome_df)
    ```

3. Set up the SNP positions we will draw on as markers:

    ```
    snp_pos <- sample(1:1e7, 25)
    snps <- data.frame(
      chr = paste0("chr", sample(1:5,25, replace=TRUE)),
      start = snp_pos,
      end = snp_pos
    )
    snps_gr <- makeGRangesFromDataFrame(snps)
    ```

4. Create some labels for the markers:

    ```
    snp_labels <- paste0("snp_", 1:25)
    ```

5. Set the plot margins:

```
plot.params <- getDefaultPlotParams(plot.type=1)
plot.params$data1outmargin <- 600
```

6. Create the base plot and add tracks:

```
kp <- plotKaryotype(genome=genome_gr, plot.type = 1, plot.params
= plot.params)
kpPlotMarkers(kp, snps_gr, labels = snp_labels)
```

This gives us a nice plot of the markers in context on a map.

How it works...

First, the code loads the libraries we'll need, after which we construct a data.frame object describing the genome we want to draw with names and lengths set accordingly. data.frame is then converted into genome_gr, a GRanges object with the makeGrangesFromDataFrame() conversion function. Next, we create a data.frame objects of 25 random SNPs using the sample() function to choose a position and chromosome. Again, this is converted into GRanges. Now, we can set up our plot. First, we get the default plot parameter object from inside the package using getDefaultPlotParams(). We can modify this object to make any changes to the default settings in our plot. Note that we have selected plot.type = 1, which is a simple plot with one data track directly above each chromosome region. We'll need to change the margin height of the data track to stop our marker labels from pouring out over the top with plot.params$data1outmargin. Finally, we can draw our plot; we create the base plot, kp, by calling plotKaryotype() and passing in the genome_gr object, plot.type, and the parameters in the modified plot.params object. The resulting plot looks like what's shown in *Figure 7.1*:

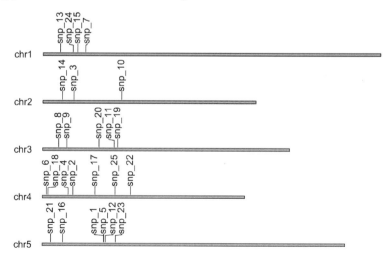

Figure 7.1 – An ideogram/karyoplot

This is a clear plot of markers on a simple genetic map.

There's more...

We can add numeric data of many different types into data tracks with `karyoploteR`. The following example shows how to draw some numeric data onto a plot as a simple line. The first step is to prepare our data. We create a `data.frame` object that has 100 random numbers that are put in 100 windows of chromosome 4 and, as before, create a `GRanges` object. This time, we'll have a data track above and below our chromosome – one for SNP markers and the other for the new data (note that this is `plot-type=2`). Then, we need to set the parameters for the plot – in particular, the margins – to stop labels and data overlapping; after that, it's the same plot calls adding a `kplines()` call. The key parameter here is `y`, which describes the y value of the data at each plotting point:

1. Create some numeric data:

    ```
    numeric_data <- data.frame(
        y = rnorm(100,mean = 1,sd = 0.5  ),
        chr = rep("chr4", 100),
        start = seq(1,20862711, 20862711/100),
        end = seq(1,20862711, 20862711/100)
    )

    numeric_data_gr <- makeGRangesFromDataFrame(numeric_data)
    ```

2. Set up plot margins:

    ```
    plot.params <- getDefaultPlotParams(plot.type=2)
    plot.params$data1outmargin <- 800
    plot.params$data2outmargin <- 800
    plot.params$topmargin <- 800
    ```

3. Create a plot and add tracks:

    ```
    kp <- plotKaryotype(genome=genome_gr, plot.type = 2, plot.params
    = plot.params)
    kpPlotMarkers(kp, snps_gr, labels = snp_labels)
    kpLines(kp, numeric_data_gr, y = numeric_data$y, data.panel=2)
    ```

We now have a plot with a numeric data track along chromosome 4, as shown in *Figure 7.2*:

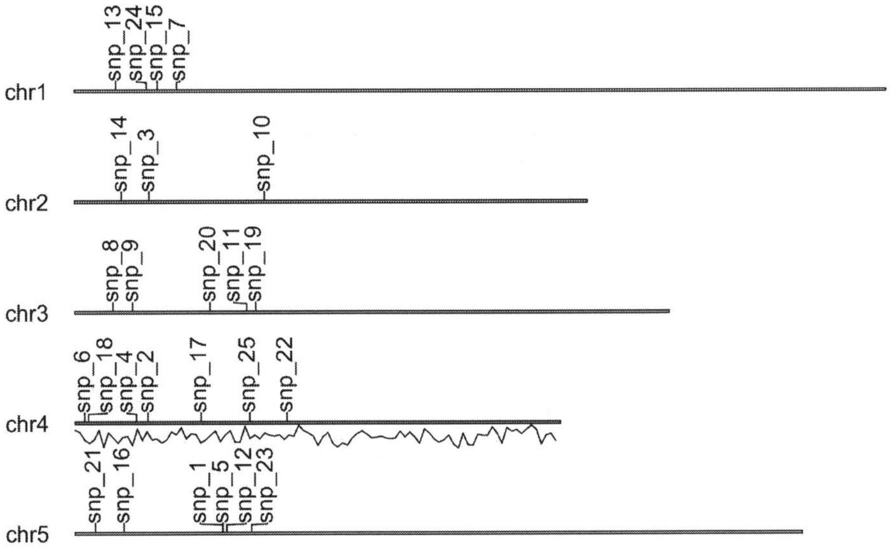

Figure 7.2 – Another ideogram with a data track

Note the wiggly line that was added to **chr4**.

See also

There are many more types of tracks and plot layouts that haven't been covered here. Try the `karyoploteR` vignette for a definitive list (type `vignette("karyoploteR")`).

One quirk of `karyoploteR` is that it only draws chromosomes horizontally. For vertical maps, there is also the `chromPlot` package in Bioconductor.

Selecting and classifying variants with VariantAnnotation

In variant calling pipelines, we'll often want to do subsequent analysis steps that need further filtering or classification based on the features of the individual variants, such as the depth of coverage in the alternative allele. This is best done from a VCF file, and a common protocol is to save a VCF of all variants found and experiment with filtering that. In this recipe, we'll look at taking an input VCF and filtering it to retain variants in which the alternative allele is the major allele in the sample.

Getting ready

We'll need a tabix index VCF file; one is provided in the `rbioinfcookbook` package. To extract it, we'll use the `fs` package. For analysis, we shall use the `VariantAnnotation` Bioconductor package.

How to do it...

Selecting and classifying variants with `VariantAnnotation` can be done as follows:

1. Create a prefilter function:

```
library(VariantAnnotation)
is_not_microsat <- function(x){ !grepl("microsat", x, fixed =
TRUE) }
```

2. Load the prefilter function:

```
prefilters <- FilterRules(list(microsat = is_not_microsat) )
```

3. Create a filter function to keep variants where the reference allele is represented in less than half the reads:

```
major_alt <- function(x){
   af <- info(x)$AF ## also geno() fixed()
   result <- unlist(lapply(af, function(x){x[1] < 0.5}))
   return(result)
}
```

4. Load the filter function into a `FilterRules` object:

```
filters <- FilterRules(list(alt_is_major = major_alt))
```

5. Load the input VCF and apply filters:

```
vcf_file <- fs::path_package("extdata",
                             "sample.vcf.gz",
                             package="rbioinfcookbook"
                             )
filterVcf(vcf_file, "hg17", "filtered.vcf", prefilters =
prefilters, filters = filters)
```

This is all we need to do to filter our variants.

How it works...

There is a surprisingly large amount of stuff going on in this very short recipe. The general outline is that we need to define two sets of filtering rules (prefilter and filter). This is achieved by defining functions that take the parsed VCF record and return TRUE if the record passes. Prefilters are generally text-based filters on the raw text of the record – the is_not_microsat() function does that by using grepl to spot the word *microsat* in the record. The function is bundled into a FilterRules object called prefilters.

The filters are more complex. These take the parsed VCF records and operate on those. Our major_alt() function uses the info() VCF accessor function to extract data in the record. It returns a DataFrame in which each column is a separate part of the info section. We extract the AF column, returning a list with an element for each VCF. To iterate over those elements, we use the lapply() function to apply an anonymous function that returns TRUE if the reference allele has a proportion lower than 0.5. We unlist() that to get a vector. We bundle the function into a FilterRules object called filters.

With all the setup done, we load the VCF file and run filtering with filterVCF(), after which we write the results to the output file, filtered.vcf.

See also

When using the filter function, we can take advantage of other accessor functions to get at different parts of the VCF record. There are geno() and fixed() functions that return data structures describing these parts of the VCF. You can use these to create filters in the way we did with info().

Extracting information in genomic regions of interest

Often, you'll want to look in more detail at data that falls into a particular genomic region of interest, whether that be the SNPs and variants in a gene or the genes at a particular locus. This common task is handled extremely well by the powerful GRanges and SummarizedExperiment objects. They are a little fiddly to set up but have very flexible subsetting operations that make the effort well worth it. In this recipe, we'll look at a few ways to set up these objects and a few ways we can manipulate them to get interesting information.

Getting ready

For this recipe, we'll need the GenomicRanges, SummarizedExperiment, and rtracklayer Bioconductor packages. We will also use a GFF file of features of the Arabidopsis chromosome 4 and a smaller text version of gene features only. These are both in the rbioinfcookbook package, so we'll extract them from that.

How to do it...

Extracting information in genomic regions of interest can be done by performing the following steps:

1. Load in the packages and define some custom functions that create GRanges from common files:

```r
library(GenomicRanges)
library(rtracklayer)
library(SummarizedExperiment)


get_granges_from_gff <- function(file_name) {
  gff <- rtracklayer::import.gff(file_name)
  as(gff, "GRanges")
}


get_granges_from_bed <- function(file_name){
  bed <- rtracklayer::import.bed(file_name)
  as(bed, "GRanges")
}


get_granges_from_text <- function(file_name){
  df <- readr::read_tsv(file_name, col_names = TRUE )
  GenomicRanges::makeGRangesFromDataFrame(df, keep.extra.columns
= TRUE)
}


get_annotated_regions_from_gff <- function(file_name) {
  gff <- rtracklayer::import.gff(file_name)
  as(gff, "GRanges")
}
```

2. Create GRanges using those functions:

```r
library(rbioinfcookbook)
gff_file <- fs::path_package(
  "extdata",
  "arabidopsis_chr4.gff",
  package="rbioinfcookbook"
)


txt_file <- fs::path_package(
  "extdata",
  "arabidopsis_chr4.txt",
  package="rbioinfcookbook"
```

```
    )

    gr_from_gff <- get_annotated_regions_from_gff(gff_file)
    gr_from_txt <- get_granges_from_text(txt_file)
```

3. Extract a region by filtering on attributes:

```
    genes_on_chr4 <- gr_from_gff[ gr_from_gff$type == "gene" &
    seqnames(gr_from_gff) %in% c("Chr4") ]
```

4. Manually create a region of interest:

```
    region_of_interest_gr <- GRanges(
      seqnames = c("Chr4"),
      IRanges(c(10000), width= c(1000))
    )
```

5. Use the region of interest to subset the larger object:

```
    overlap_hits <- findOverlaps(region_of_interest_gr, genes_on_
    chr4)
    features_in_region <- genes_on_chr4[subjectHits(overlap_hits) ]
    features_in_region
```

And with that, we have features in a particular region.

How it works...

In *step 1*, we create a GRanges object that describes the features of the genome you're interested in. The three functions we create all load in information from different file types and return the necessary GRanges object. In *step 2*, we make use of the GFF and text functions to create two GRanges: gr_from_gff and gr_from_txt. These are then used in the subsetting. In *step 3*, we subset on feature attributes. The code finds features of the gene type. Note the difference in syntax between finding genes and features. The base columns in the GRanges object – namely seqnames, width, and start – all have accessor functions that return vectors. Hence, we use that in the second part of the condition. All other columns – called metadata in GRanges parlance – can be accessed with the standard $ syntax, so we use that in the first part of the condition.

In *step 4*, we create a specific region in a custom minimal GRanges object. This contains only one region but more could be added just by putting more values for regions in the manually specified vectors. Finally, in *step 5*, we use the findOverlaps() function to get the indices of features in the gr_from_gff object that overlap the manually created regions_of_interest_gr and use those to subset the large gr_from_gff object.

The output looks like this:

```
## GRanges object with 1 range and 10 metadata columns:
##         seqnames       ranges strand
|     source       type      score      phase          ID          Name
                   Note                Parent          Index Derives_from
##            <Rle>  <IRanges>   <Rle> | <factor> <factor> <numeric>
<integer> <character> <character>       <CharacterList> <CharacterList>
<character>   <character>
##    [1]       Chr4 2895-10455      -
|    TAIR10       gene          NA        <NA>   AT4G00020    AT4G00020
protein_coding_gene                      <NA>          <NA>
##    -------
##    seqinfo: 1 sequence from an unspecified genome; no seqlengths
```

This is a summary object full of different features in our original region of interest.

There's more...

It's also possible to extract the subsets of DataFrames or matrices in the same way by taking advantage of GRanges that are part of other objects. In the following example, we're creating a matrix of random data and using that to build a SummarizedExperiment object that uses a GRanges object to describe its rows:

```
set.seed(4321)
experiment_counts <- matrix( runif(4308 * 6, 1, 100), 4308)
sample_names <- c(rep("ctrl",3), rep("test",3) )
se <- SummarizedExperiment::SummarizedExperiment(rowRanges = gr_from_
txt, assays = list(experiment_counts), colData = sample_names)
overlap_hits <- findOverlaps(region_of_interest_gr, se)
data_in_region <- se[subjectHits(overlap_hits) ]
assay(data_in_region)
```

This will give us the following output:

```
##           [,1]     [,2]     [,3]     [,4]     [,5]     [,6]
## [1,]  91.00481 34.41582 42.7602 36.13053 47.6775 19.21672
```

This shows the summary of the data in that region of interest from a different type of input object.

Finding phenotype and genotype associations with GWAS

A powerful application of a variant calling many thousands of SNPs with high-throughput sequencing is **genome-wide association studies** (**GWAS**) of genotype and phenotype. GWAS is a genomic analysis of variants in different individuals or genetic lines to see whether any particular variant is associated with a trait. There are numerous techniques for doing this, but all of them rely on gathering data on variants in particular samples and working out each sample's genotype before cross-referencing with the phenotype in some way. In this recipe, we'll look at the sophisticated mixed linear model described by *Yu et al.* in 2006 (*Nature Genetics*, 38:203-208). Describing the workings of the unified mixed linear model is beyond the scope of this recipe, but it is a suitable model for use in data with large samples and broad allelic diversity and can be used on plant and animal data.

Getting ready

In this recipe, we'll look at constructing the structures we need to run the analysis from input VCF files. We'll use the `GWAS()` function in the `rrBLUP` package to do so. Our sample data contains just three SNPs – for didactic purposes, this will aid our programming task but for a GWAS study, the number is laughably small. Although the code will work, the results will not be biologically meaningful. We'll need the `rrBLUP` and `VariantAnnotation` Bioconductor packages, as well as a data file called `small_sample.vcf`, which is provided in the `rbioinfcookbook` packages.

How to do it...

Finding phenotype and genotype associations with GWAS can be done by performing the following steps:

1. Load in the libraries and get the VCF file:

```
library(VariantAnnotation)
library(rrBLUP)
library(rbioinfcookbook)
set.seed(1234)

vcf_file <- fs::path_package(
  "extdata",
  "small_sample.vcf",
  package="rbioinfcookbook"
)

vcf <- readVcf(vcf_file, "hg19")
```

2. Extract the genotype, sample, and marker position information:

```
gts <- geno(vcf)$GT
samples <- samples(header(vcf))
markers <- rownames(gts)
chrom <- as.character(seqnames(rowRanges(vcf)))
pos <- as.numeric(start(rowRanges(vcf)))
```

3. Create a custom function to convert VCF genotypes into the convention used by the GWAS function:

```
convert <- function(v){
   v <- gsub("0/0", 1, v)
   v <- gsub("0/1", 0, v)
   v <- gsub("1/0", 0, v)
   v <- gsub("1/1",-1, v)
   return(v)
}
```

4. Call the function and convert the results into a numeric matrix:

```
gt_char<- apply(gts, convert, MARGIN = 2)
genotype_matrix <- matrix(as.numeric(gt_char), nrow(gt_char) )
colnames(genotype_matrix)<- samples
```

5. Build a DataFrame describing the variant:

```
variant_info <- data.frame(marker = markers,
                    chrom = chrom,
                    pos = pos)
```

6. Build a genotype/variant DataFrame:

```
genotypes <-  cbind(variant_info, as.data.frame(genotype_
matrix))
genotypes
```

7. Build a phenotype DataFrame:

```
phenotypes <- data.frame(
   line = samples,
   score = rnorm(length(samples))
)

phenotypes
```

8. Run GWAS:

```
GWAS(phenotypes, genotypes,plot=FALSE)
```

This gives us a full GWAS. Note that the example data is small and that a real dataset would take a long time to run.

How it works...

Most of the code in this recipe is setup code. After loading the libraries and fixing the random number generator for reproducibility (set.seed()) in *step 1*, we get the VCF file of useful variants loaded. In *step 2*, we extract useful information: we get a matrix of genotypes with the geno(vcf)$GT call in which the row is a variant, a column is a sample, and the genotype is recorded at the intersection. Next, we use some accessor functions to pull sample and marker names and the reference sequence (chrom) and position (pos) for each variant. In *step 3*, we define a translation function called convert() to map VCF-style heterozygous and homozygous annotations to those used in GWAS. Briefly, in VCF, "0/0" means *AA* (homozygous), which is encoded as 1 in GWAS(); "0/1" and "1/0" are heterozygous *Aa* or 0 in GWAS(), and "1/1" is homozygous *aa* or -1 in GWAS().

In *step 4*, we apply convert() to the gts matrix and convert it back into a numeric matrix. In *step 5*, we build a DataFrame describing the variant from the sample, marker, and sequence information we created before and in *step 6*, we combine the variant information with the genotype encodings to get the following result:

```
##              marker chrom      pos NA00001 NA00002 NA00003
## 1          rs6054257    20    14370       1       0      -1
## 2     20:17330_T/A    20    17330       1       0       1
## 3 20:1230237_T/G    20  1230237       1       1       0
```

Note that the order of the columns is important. The GWAS() function expects us to have this information in the order specified here.

In *step 7*, we build the phenotype information. The first column must be called line but contain the sample names in the same order as the columns of the genotype matrix. The rest of the columns can be phenotype scores and have fixed effects.

This results in the following command block (the actual numbers may vary if you omit the set. seed() call):

```
##      line       score
## 1 NA00001 -1.2070657
## 2 NA00002  0.2774292
## 3 NA00003  1.0844412
```

Finally, we run the GWAS() function in *step 8*. The following output is generated – note that the function tries to generate a plot, but there are too few points for that to work in this example, so we turn it off with plot = FALSE:

```
## [1] "GWAS for trait: score"
## [1] "Variance components estimated. Testing markers."
##           marker chrom     pos      score
## 1      rs6054257    20   14370 0.3010543
## 2    20:17330_T/A    20   17330 0.3010057
## 3 20:1230237_T/G    20 1230237 0.1655498
```

If you want to see the plot, simply remove plot = FALSE.

Estimating the copy number at a locus of interest

We will often want to know how often a sequence occurs in a sample of interest – that is, to estimate whether in a given sample, a locus has been duplicated or its copy number has increased. The locus could be anything from a gene at a Kbp scale or a large section of DNA at a Mbp scale. Our approach in this recipe will be to use HTS read coverage after alignment to estimate a background level of coverage and then compare it to the coverage in a region of interest. The ratio will give us an estimate of the copy number of our region of interest. The recipe here is the first step. The background model we'll use is very simple – we'll only calculate a global mean, but we'll discuss some alternatives later. This recipe does not cover ploidy – the number of genomes present in the whole cell. It is possible to estimate ploidy from similar data but it is a more involved pipeline. Take a look at the *See also* section for recommendations on packages to use for that analysis.

Getting ready

For this recipe, we need the csaw Bioconductor package and the hg17_snps.bam dataset from the rbioinfcookbook package.

How to do it...

Estimating the copy number of a locus of interest can be done by performing the following steps:

1. Load the library and get counts in windows across the genome:

    ```
    library(csaw)
    library(rbioinfcookbook)
    bam_file <- fs::path_package(
      "extdata",
      "hg17_snps.bam",
      package="rbioinfcookbook"
    )
    ```

```
whole_genome <- csaw::windowCounts(
  bam_file,
  bin = TRUE,
  filter = 0,
  width = 100,
  param = csaw::readParam(
    minq = 20,
    dedup = TRUE,
    pe = "both"
  )
)
colnames(whole_genome) <- c("h17")
```

2. Extract needed data from `SummarizeExperiment`:

```
counts <- assay(whole_genome)[,1]
```

3. Work out a low count threshold and set windows with lower counts to NA:

```
min_count <- quantile(counts, 0.1)[[1]]
counts[counts < min_count] <- NA
```

4. Double the counts of a set of windows in the middle – our high copy region:

```
n <- length(counts)
doubled_windows <- 10
left_pad <- floor( (n/2) - doubled_windows )
right_pad <- n - left_pad -doubled_windows
multiplier <- c(rep(1, left_pad ), rep(2,doubled_windows),
rep(1, right_pad) )
counts <- counts * multiplier
```

5. Calculate the mean coverage and ratio to the mean in each window, then plot it:

```
mean_cov <- mean(counts, na.rm=TRUE)
ratio <- matrix(log2(counts / mean_cov), ncol = 1)
plot(ratio)
```

6. Build `SummarizedExperiment` with the new data and the row data of the old one:

```
se <- SummarizedExperiment(assays=list(ratio), rowRanges=
rowRanges(whole_genome), colData = c("CoverageRatio"))
```

7. Create a region of interest and extract coverage data:

```
region_of_interest <- GRanges(
  seqnames = c("NC_000017.10"),
```

```
    IRanges(c(40700), width = c(1500) )
)


overlap_hits <- findOverlaps(region_of_interest, se)
data_in_region <- se[subjectHits(overlap_hits)]
assay(data_in_region)
```

This is all we need to do to estimate the copy number.

How it works...

In *step 1*, we use the `csaw` package to get read counts in 100 bp windows over our small section of human chromosome 17. The read filtering options are set in the `param` argument. In *step 2*, we extract the first and only column of data to give us a simple vector of the counts using the `assay()` function and subsetting. Next, in *step 3*, we use the `quantile()` function to get the `min_count` value in the lower 10th percentile of the `counts` vector. The double-bracket subsetting is needed to get a single number from the named vector that the `quantile()` function returns. The `min_count` value is a cut-off. All values in the `counts` vector lower than this are set to NA to remove them from the analysis – this acts as a low coverage threshold and the percentile used can be modified in your adaptations of the recipe as needed.

In *step 4*, we add some regions with doubled coverage so that we can detect them. We select several windows to double and then create a multiplier vector of equal length that contains *1* where we don't wish to change counts and *2* where we want to double them. We apply the multiplication. *Step 4* will not likely be in your analysis as it is a synthetic data generation step.

In *step 5*, we compute the background coverage level. Our function here is a simple global mean that's saved in `mean_cov`, but you can use many other summary statistic functions. We also calculate the `log2()` of the ratio of each window count to the global `mean_cov` and save it in a one-column matrix object called `ratio` since we need the result to be a matrix in our final `SummarizedExperiment` object. We quickly use `plot` and can see the count of doubled windows in the middle of the data *Figure 7.3*:

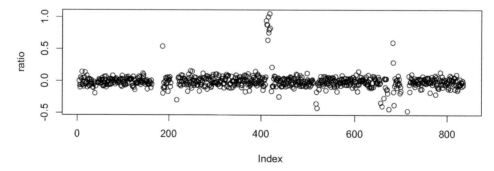

Figure 7.3 – A window count plot

In *step 6*, we build a new SummarizedExperiment object called se to hold the window ranges and the new ratio data. We take the GRanges and colData objects from window_counts and add our new ratio matrix. We can now subset this and see what coverage is in our region of interest. This generates the following output:

```
##                 [,1]
##  [1,]    0.01725283
##  [2,]    0.03128239
##  [3,]  -0.05748994
##  [4,]    0.05893873
##  [5,]    0.94251006
##  [6,]    0.88186246
##  [7,]    0.87927929
##  [8,]    0.63780103
##  [9,]    1.00308550
## [10,]    0.75515798
## [11,]    0.80228189
## [12,]    1.05207419
## [13,]    0.82393626
## [14,]            NA
## [15,]            NA
## [16,]  -0.16269298
```

We can see that the region has a log2 ratio of 1 (twofold) coverage relative to the background, which we can interpret as a copy number of two.

See also

The calculation for the background level in this recipe is really simple – which is great for learning the recipe, but it might be quickly underpowered in your real data. There are numerous options you could take to modify the way you calculate the background level for your data. Check out the rollmeans() and rollmedians() functions in the zoo package. These can give you the mean or median in rolling windows of arbitrary step length and give you a moving window background average that may be more appropriate. A related analysis to copy number is the estimation of ploidy from SNP allele frequencies. You can check out the vcfR package's freq_peaks() function as a starting point to estimate ploidy from variant information in BAM files.

8
Searching Gene and Protein Sequences for Domains and Motifs

The sequences of genes, proteins, and entire genomes hold clues to their function. Repeated subsequences or sequences with strong similarities to each other can be clues to things such as evolutionary conservation or functional relatedness. Sequence analysis for motifs and domains is a core technique in bioinformatics. Bioconductor contains many useful packages for analyzing genes, proteins, and genomes. In this chapter, you will learn how to use Bioconductor to analyze sequences for features of functional interest, such as *de novo* DNA motifs and known domains from widely used databases. You'll learn about some packages for kernel-based machine learning to find protein sequence features. You will also learn about some large-scale alignment techniques for many sequences or very long sequences. You will use Bioconductor and other statistical learning packages.

In this chapter, we will cover the following recipes:

- Finding DNA motifs with `universalmotif`
- Finding protein domains with `PFAM` and `bio3d`
- Finding InterPro domains
- Finding transmembrane domains with `tmhmm` and `pureseqTM`
- Creating figures of protein domains using `drawProteins`
- Performing multiple alignments of proteins or genes
- Aligning genomic length sequences with `DECIPHER`
- Novel feature detection in proteins
- 3D structure protein alignment in `bio3d`

Technical requirements

We will use `renv` to manage packages in a project-specific way. To use `renv` to install packages, you will first need to install the `renv` package. You can do this by running the following commands in your R console:

1. Install `renv`:

   ```
   install.packages("renv")
   ```

2. Create a new `renv` environment:

   ```
   renv::init()
   ```

   This will create a new directory called `.renv` in your current project directory.

3. You can then install packages with the following command:

   ```
   renv::install_packages()
   ```

4. You can also use the `renv` package manager to install Bioconductor packages by running the following command:

   ```
   renv::install("bioc::package name")
   ```

5. For example, to install the `Biobase` package, you would run the following:

   ```
   renv::install("bioc::Biobase")
   ```

6. You can use `renv` to install development packages from GitHub like this:

   ```
   renv::install("user name/repo name")
   ```

7. For example, to install the `danmaclean` user's `rbioinfcookbook` package, you would run the following:

   ```
   renv::install("danmaclean/rbioinfcookbook")
   ```

You can also install multiple packages at once by separating the package names with a comma. `renv` will automatically handle installing any required dependencies for the packages you install.

Under `renv`, all packages will be installed in the local project directory and not the main central library, meaning you can have multiple versions of the same package, one specific one for each project.

All the sample data you need for this package is in the specially created data package on GitHub called `danmaclean/rbioinfcookbook`. The data will become available in your project once you've installed it.

For this chapter, we'll need the following packages:

- Regular packages:

    - `ape`

    - `bio3d`

    - `dplyr`

    - `fs`

    - `ggplot2`

    - `knitr`

    - `readr`

    - `reticulate`

    - `seqinr`

    - `tibble`

- GitHub:

    - `danmaclean/rbioinfcookbook`

    - `richelbilderbeek/pureseqtmr`

    - `richelbilderbeek/tmhmm`

- Bioconductor:

    - `biomaRt`

    - `Biostrings`

    - `DECIPHER`

    - `drawProteins`

    - `EnsDb.Rnorvegicus.v79`

    - `ensembldb`

    - `kebabs`

    - `msa`

    - `org.At.tair.db`

    - `org.Hs.eg.db`

- `PFAM.db`

- `seqinr`

- `universalmotif`

In addition to these packages, we will also need some R tools such as *conda*; all these will be described when needed.

Further information

Not all the recipes in this chapter run in R – some are command-line-based setups. I generally use a bash terminal for these bits. Most macOS and Linux machines will have these available in a **Terminal** application. Windows users will likely not need these specific steps, though various packages for running a Linux subsystem on Windows exist if you wish to search them out.

In R, it is normal practice to load a library and use functions directly by name. Although this is great in short interactive sessions, it can cause confusion when many packages are loaded at once and share function names. To clarify which package and function I am using at a given moment, I will occasionally use the `packageName::functionName()` convention.

Sometimes, in the middle of a recipe, I'll interrupt the code to dive into some intermediate output or look at the structure of an object. When that happens, you'll see a code block where each line begins with ## (double hash symbols). Consider the following command:

```
letters[1:5]
```

This will give us the following output:

```
## a b c d e
```

Note that the output lines are prefixed with ##.

Any other information will be given when required.

Finding DNA motifs with universalmotif

A very common task when working with DNA sequences is finding instances of **motifs** – a short-defined sequence – within a longer sequence. These could represent protein-DNA binding sites such as transcription factor binding sites in a gene promoter or enhancer region. There are two starting points for this analysis – you either have a database of motifs that you want to use to scan target DNA sequences and extract wherever the motif occurs or you have just the sequences of interest and you want to find out whether there are any repeating motifs in there. We'll look at ways of doing both of these things in this recipe.

Getting ready

For this recipe, we need a matrix describing the motif (a **position-specific weight matrix** or **PWSM**) and a set of sequences from upstream of transcriptional start sites. These are provided in the rbioinfcookbok package. We'll use the universalmotif package to work with motifs and the reticulate package to help us find paths to external tools. We will need to install the meme external tool before we begin. This can be done through bioconda, as described in *Chapter 1, Setting Up Your R Bioinformatics Working Environment*, in the *Use bioconda to install external tools* recipe. The package can be found at https://anaconda.org/bioconda/meme.

Now, we're ready to go.

How to do it...

Finding DNA motifs with universalmotif can be done as follows:

1. Create a function that will find the path to meme:

```
env_path <- function(env, program = ""){

  df <- reticulate::conda_list()
  b <- df$python[which(df$name == env)]

  if (length(b) == 0) {
    stop("no environment with that name found")
  }

  file.path(dirname(b), program)
}

meme_path <-  env_path("bioinformatics_project", "meme")
```

2. Load the necessary libraries and the motif of interest:

```
library(universalmotif)
library(Biostrings)

motif_file <- fs::path_package("extdata",
                                              "simple_motif.txt",

package="rbioinfcookbook")
motif <- read_matrix(motif_file)
promoter_file <- fs::path_package(
  "extdata",
  "promoters.fa",
```

```
    package = "rbioinfcookbook"
)
sequences <- readDNAStringSet(promoter_file)
```

3. Scan the sequences:

```
motif_hits <- scan_sequences(motif, sequences = sequences)
head(motif_hits)
```

4. Calculate whether the motif is enriched in the sequences:

```
motif_info <- enrich_motifs(motif,
                                        sequences,
                                        shuffle.k = 3,
                                        verbose = 0, RC = TRUE)
motif_info
```

5. Run MEME to find novel motifs:

```
meme_run <- run_meme(sequences, bin = meme_path, output = "meme_
out", overwrite.dir = TRUE)
motifs <- read_meme("meme_out/meme.txt")
view_motifs(motifs)
```

And that's all we need to do to see the results of the motif searches.

How it works...

This is efficient code! In just a few lines, we were able to complete a whole analysis. In *step 1*, we created a function that would find the path to the external meme program. Then, in *step 2*, we loaded in a matrix description of a motif and some sequences we hope to use to find the promoter. In *step 3*, we scanned the sequences and got back a universalmotif object and a DNAStringSet object to work with. The scan_sequences() function searches each of the sequences and reports where it finds motifs – check out the motif_hits object to see where they are. The object prints like this:

```
## motif   motif.i sequence sequence.i start  stop  score
## 1 YTTTYTTTTTYTTTY  1 AT1G05670 47      62     76   9.402
## 2 YTTTYTTTTTYTTTY  1 AT1G05670 47      65     79    10.290
```

When it comes to working out whether a motif is significant, enrich_motifs() does this work for us in *step 4* and reports where it finds significant motifs. It searches the sequences to find likely instances of motifs and uses *Fisher's exact test* to compare the frequencies of motifs in our set of sequences with their frequencies in an automatically generated background set. The final motif_info output contains a report of the *p*-value. To find novel motifs, we ran the external software called MEME in *step 5*. The run_meme() function needs to know where the MEME package is on your system, so we defined that in the meme_path variable that we generated from our function in *step 1*.

We passed that information to `run_meme()`, along with the `DNAStringSet()` object containing the sequences. The function also needed an output directory to write results to as it doesn't return anything useful to R. The `run_meme()` function executes *MEME* in the background and once the run is finished, we can load in results from the `meme.txt` file using `read_meme()`. It returns a `universalmotif` object. Finally, we can inspect the motifs found with the `view_motifs()` function – which looks like what's shown in *Figure 8.1*:

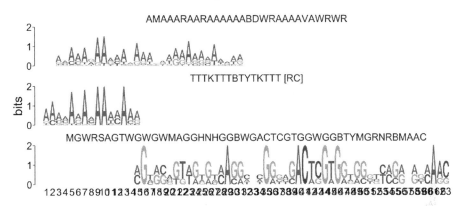

Figure 8.1 – Motifs found in sequences

The plot is a standard Logo-style plot in which the contribution of each base in the motif is represented by its size in the Logo.

There's more...

Loading in motifs from databases such as `JASPAR` and `TRANSFAC` is very easy with `universlamotif` as there are straightforward replacements for the `read_matrix()` function. To load motifs in various formats, we can use the `read_cisbp()`, `read_homer()`, `read_jaspar()`, `read_matrix()`, `read_meme()`, `read_motifs()`, and `read_uniprobe()` functions.

Finding protein domains with PFAM and bio3d

Discovering the function of a protein sequence is a key task. We can do this in many ways, including by conducting whole sequence similarity searches against databases of known proteins using tools such as BLAST. If we want more informative and granular information, we can instead look for individual functional domains within a sequence. Databases such as `PFAM` and tools such as `hmmer` make this possible. `PFAM` encodes protein domains as *Hidden Markov Models*, which `hmmer` uses to scan sequences and report any likely occurrences of the domains. Often, genome annotation projects will carry out the searches for us, meaning that finding the `PFAM` domains in our sequence is a question of searching a database. Bioconductor does a great job of packaging up the data in these databases in particular packages, usually with names ending in `.db`. In this recipe, we'll look at how to work out whether a package contains PFAM domain information, how to extract it for specific genes of interest, and an alternative method for running a PFAM search yourself if there isn't any pre-existing information.

Getting ready

For this example, we'll need the `org.Hs.eg.db` Bioconductor annotation package and a FASTA sequence file, which can be found in the `rbioinfcookbook` package. To connect remotely to the `hmmer` service, we'll need the `bio3d` package. We will coincidentally use the `fs` and `dplyr` packages.

How to do it...

Finding proteins with a PFAM database can be done by performing the following steps:

1. Load the database package and inspect the types of keys in the database:

```
library(org.Hs.eg.db)
keytypes(org.Hs.eg.db)
```

2. Get a vector of keys:

```
k <- head(keys(org.Hs.eg.db, keytype = "ENSEMBL"), n = 3 )
```

3. Query the database:

```
result <- select(org.Hs.eg.db, keys = k, keytype="ENSEMBL",
columns = c("PFAM"))
result
```

4. Load the PFAM database to extract descriptions:

```
library(PFAM.db)
descriptions <- PFAMDE
```

5. Get all the keys from the database:

```
all_ids <- mappedkeys(descriptions)
```

6. Get all the descriptions from the IDs:

```
id_description_mapping <- as.data.frame(descriptions[all_ids])
```

7. Join the descriptions to PFAM:

```
dplyr::left_join(result, id_description_mapping, by = c("PFAM" =
"ac") )
```

Here, we added the necessary PFAM descriptions.

How it works...

The key to this approach is finding out whether the database we're trying to use carries the domain information. That's what happens in *step 1* – we use the keytypes() function to list the search keys available and we can see PFAM in the results. Once we've verified that we can use this database for the information we want, we can follow a fairly standard procedure from *step 2* on. In *step 2*, we get a list of keys to query with – like gene names. We pull them from the database directly, but they could come from anywhere. In *step 3*, we query the database with the select() function to pull data for the given keys. The columns argument tells it which data to pull. In *step 4*, we make a list of all PFAM IDs and descriptions. We load the PFAM.db package and use the PFAMDE object it provides to get a mapping between IDs and descriptions. This will result in the following output:

```
##              ENSEMBL      PFAM
## 1 ENSG00000121410 PF13895
## 2 ENSG00000175899 PF00207
## 3 ENSG00000175899 PF17789
## 4 ENSG00000175899 PF07677
## 5 ENSG00000175899 PF17791
## 6 ENSG00000175899 PF01835
## 7 ENSG00000175899 PF07703
## 8 ENSG00000175899 PF07678
```

We can then get the actual descriptions with mappedkeys() in *step 5*, and then extract and convert the descriptions of all the IDs into a DataFrame in *step 6*. Finally, we join the descriptions of the domains to the IDs by using the columns that contain common data (PFAM and ac), resulting in the following output:

```
##                  ENSEMBL      PFAM
                                  de
## 1 ENSG00000121410
   PF13895                              Immunoglobulin domain
## 2 ENSG00000175899 PF00207                   Alpha-2-macroglobulin
   family
## 3 ENSG00000175899 PF17789                         Macroglobulin
   domain MG4
## 4 ENSG00000175899 PF07677  A-macroglobulin receptor binding domain
## 5 ENSG00000175899 PF17791
   Macroglobulin domain MG3
```

This is a DataFrame with the gene ID and the PFAM attached.

There's more...

I mentioned that the key to this recipe was to make sure that the database contained the right keys (here, PFAM). Depending on the organism and database, the key you want may not exist. You can check for the right keys with the columns() function, as we do here for the Arabidopsis package:

```
library(org.At.tair.db)
columns(org.At.tair.db)
```

If PFAM doesn't appear in the list, it is possible to run PFAM remotely on the server at the **European Bioinformatics Institute** (**EBI**) using the hmmer() function in bio3d:

```
library(bio3d)
seq_file <- fs::path_package("extdata",
                                    "ecoli_hsp.fa",

package="rbioinfcookbook")

sequence <- read.fasta(seq_file)
result <- hmmer(sequence, type="hmmscan", db="pfam")
result$hit.tbl
```

This will give us the following output:

```
##    name           acc bias desc  evalue flags hindex ndom nincluded
nregions nreported   pvalue score
## 1 GrpE PF01025.22 3.2 GrpE 1.3e-46       3  10091      1
1          1              1 -115.541 158.4
##          taxid       pdb.id bitscore mlog.evalue
## 1 PF01025.22 PF01025.22     158.4     105.6566
```

Note that the server has limits on the number of sequences and rate of submissions. For very large numbers of sequences, you will want to look at running PFAM and so on locally.

With that, we've performed PFAM domain finding.

Finding InterPro domains

InterPro is a database of predictive models, or signatures, provided by multiple protein databases. InterPro aggregates information from multiple sources to reduce redundancy in annotations and aid with interoperability. In this recipe, we'll extend the approach we used for PFAM domains in the previous recipe and look at getting annotations of InterPro domains on sequences of interest. We'll start this recipe with something similar for Ensembl core databases.

Getting ready

We'll need the `ensembldb`, `EnsDb.Rnorvegicus.v79`, and `biomaRt` packages from Bioconductor.

How to do it...

Finding InterPro domains can be done by performing the following steps:

1. Load the necessary libraries and check for protein data in the database:

```
library(ensembldb)
library(EnsDb.Rnorvegicus.v79)
hasProteinData(EnsDb.Rnorvegicus.v79)
```

2. Build a list of genes to query with:

```
listTables(EnsDb.Rnorvegicus.v79) e <- EnsDb.Rnorvegicus.v79
k <- head(keys(e, keytype = "GENEID"), n = 3 )
```

3. Pull out the relevant data:

```
select(e, keys = GeneIdFilter(k),
        columns = c("TXBIOTYPE", "UNIPROTID",
"PROTEINID","INTERPROACCESSION"))
```

This is all the code we need.

How it works...

The code is a database lookup on the *Rattus norvegicus* Ensembl database that's performed through the relevant package. In *step 1*, we use the `hasProteinData()` function to check whether the database has what we need. If it returns TRUE, we're good.

In *step 2*, we load the database into the e object and pull out three IDs from the database using `keytype` of GENEID. In *step 3*, we search the database with GENEID as the key. Note that we need the `GeneIdFilter()` function wrapper and the `columns` argument to select which data we want to return. This will result in a DataFrame with the InterPro accession.

There's more...

The approach we used in this recipe works well for Ensembl core databases, but there are other non-core databases that we could search and for that, there is `biomaRt`. The `biomaRt` package allows us to define connections to other databases that have a `biomaRt` interface for querying. To do this, we must load the package and use the `useMart()` function to define a connection to the appropriate host and dataset. Then, we must use the `getBM()` function with the columns and gene IDs to query with. You'll get the search results for InterPro back if your query is `interpro`. The following example searches for two Arabidopsis genes at `plants.ensembl.org`:

```
library(biomaRt)

biomart_athal <- useMart(biomart = "plants_mart",
                                     host = "plants.ensembl.org",
                                     dataset = "athaliana_eg_gene")

getBM( c("tair_locus", "interpro"),
        filters=c("tair_locus"),
        values = c("AT5G40950", "AT2G40510"), mart = biomart_athal)
```

This generates the following output:

```
##   tair_locus  interpro
## 1   AT2G40510  IPR000892
## 2   AT2G40510  IPR038551
## 3   AT5G40950  IPR001684
## 4   AT5G40950  IPR018261
```

This is a DataFrame of loci and domain IDs that we can use in downstream analyses.

See also...

If you're having trouble working out the names of marts and columns, try using the `listMarts()` and `listDatasets()` functions from `biomaRt`, which will provide lists of currently available marts and the data they contain.

Finding transmembrane domains with tmhmm and pureseqTM

Protein transmembrane domains are the parts of a protein that pass through the lipid bilayer of a cell membrane. These domains are typically composed of hydrophobic amino acids that allow the protein to interact with the nonpolar interior of the membrane. Transmembrane domains play an important role in many cellular processes, including cell signaling, transporting molecules, and cell adhesion. One important application of bioinformatics is identifying protein transmembrane domains from amino acid sequences. Several methods are used to identify transmembrane domains bioinformatically, including hydrophobicity analysis, in which we identify regions of a protein sequence that have a high degree of hydrophobicity and are likely to be transmembrane domains. There are also hidden Markov models that are trained to identify transmembrane domains based on a set of known transmembrane proteins. We can also use machine learning algorithms trained to identify transmembrane domains based on a set of features derived from the amino acid sequence, such as hydrophobicity, charge, and secondary structure.

In this recipe, we'll use the external **tmhmm** and **pureseqTM** programs to find transmembrane domain candidates.

Getting ready

We'll be using the `"richelbilderbeek/tmhmm"` and `"richelbilderbeek/pureseqtmr"` GitHub hosted packages. These have some custom install steps, so we'll do the installation as part of this recipe. These programs will currently only work on a Linux machine. Linux machines are common in bioinformatics but you may not be working on one as your primary computer. If you don't have easy access to a Linux machine, then you can use a Google Colab notebook as an alternative. Look at the *See also* section of this recipe to learn how to do that.

The `tmhmm` program has a specialist license. You can only get that by applying by going to the software authors at `https://services.healthtech.dtu.dk/service.php?TMHMM-2.0`. They'll send you a URL from which to download the software. You can use that in this recipe to let the package download and install the actual tool.

The example data for this recipe comes from a file of **Receptor-like Kinase** (**RLK**) proteins in a file provided in the `rbioinfcookbook` package.

How to do it...

We can find transmembrane domains with `tmhmm` and `pureseqTM` as follows:

1. Install `tmhmm`:

    ```
    my_url <- "whatever_the_url_you_get_is"
    library(tmhmm)
    install_tmhmm(my_url)
    ```

2. Run a protein FASTA file through `tmhmm`:

    ```
    fasta_file <- fs::path_package(
      "extdata"
      "rlk_proteins.fa",
      package = "rbioinfcookbook"
    )

    tmhmm_predictions <- tmhmm::predict_topology(fasta_filename)
    ```

3. Install `pureseqTM`:

```
library(pureseqtmrinstall)
install_pureseqtm()
```

4. Run a protein FASTA file through `pureseqTM`:

```
pureseq_tm_predictions <- pureseqtmrinstall::predict_
topology(fasta_filename)
```

That should install the programs that we need.

How it works...

This recipe is fiddly to set up but brief in its execution, so it should be simpler on runs after the first. In *step 1*, we use the URL from the email sent by the software authors to download and install `tmhmm`. In *step 2*, we get the input data file of RLK proteins and pass that to the `tmhmm::predict_topology()` function to receive a DataFrame of topology predictions.

In *step 3*, we start to use the `pursetTM` tool, which can be installed via the `pureseqtminstall` package without any further information. The package also contains the code for running the tool. Note that the primary function is the same in *step 4* as it is in *step 2*, but they come from different packages. If you're running both, it's safest to use the fully resolved `packagename::function` syntax to prevent name masking from becoming a problem. Again, we get a DataFrame of topology predictions, which is the final output and what we wanted to get from this recipe.

There's more...

Both packages have a `plot_topology()` function that will draw the proteins for you.

See also

If you don't have access to a Linux machine, you can access a free tier of Google Colab at `https://colab.research.google.com/`. The tutorial should get you started. Although it's Python-based, you can start a notebook in R by going to `https://colab.research.google.com/notebook#create=true&language=r`. Then, you can type R code into each cell and press the *play* button to execute it. You'll need to install the `devtools` package to install the GitHub packages we need:

```
install.packages("devtools")
devtools::install_github("richelbilderbeek/tmhmm")
devtools::install_github("richelbilderbeek/pureseqtmrinstall")
```

When that has been executed, you should be good to go in the Colab Jupyter Notebook, as per the code in this recipe.

Creating figures of protein domains using drawProteins

Protein visualization is a powerful tool in bioinformatics that allows researchers to explore the structure and function of proteins. Visualizing proteins in two dimensions can help researchers understand and compare the domain structures of different proteins, which can reveal similarities and differences that may be important for understanding their function. This can be particularly useful in the study of evolutionary relationships between proteins.

In this recipe, we'll look at a package called `drawProteins` that can create two-dimensional renders of proteins and their domains. The package seems to have been designed to work best with Uniprot data as input, but we'll look at setting up data so that you can use protein and domain information from any source.

Getting ready

To complete this recipe, you will need the `drawProteins` Bioconductor package. We'll generate the sample data in the code as understanding it is the key part of this recipe.

How to do it...

Rendering some proteins into a two-dimensional structure begins by defining the DataFrames of the elements to be plotted:

1. Define a DataFrame of chain information:

    ```
    chain_df <- tibble::tibble(
      "type" = "CHAIN",
      "description" = c("example protein", "different protein"),
      "begin" = c(1,1),
      "end" = c(300, 450),
      "length" = c(300, 450),
      "accesion" =  c("AB1", "AB2"),
      "entryName" = c("protein_1", "protein_2"),
      "taxid" = c(2712, 2712),
      "order" = c(1,2)
    )
    ```

2. Define a DataFrame of domain information:

    ```
    domain_df <- tibble::tibble(
      "type" = "DOMAIN",
      "description" = c("dom1", "dom1", "dom2"),
      "begin" = c(100, 150, 350),
      "end" = c(200, 250, 420),
      "length" = c(100, 100, 70),
    ```

```
    "entryName" = c("protein_1", "protein_2", "protein_2"),
    "taxid" = c(2712,2712,2712),
    "order" = c(1,2,2)
)
```

3.   Render the plot in drawProteins:

```
library(drawProteins)
protein_df <- dplyr::bind_rows(chain_df, domain_df)

draw_canvas(protein_df) |>
  draw_chains(protein_df) |>
  draw_domains(protein_df, label_domains = TRUE)
```

With that, we have a nice plot of the protein and its domains.

How it works...

The key to using drawProteins is to get the DataFrame format right. The structure is shallow but hierarchical within a single DataFrame. Each protein is referenced as a *chain* defined in rows; this is what we did in *step 1*. Consider this to be the *backbone* that defines the extent of the whole protein. The type column must be CHAIN. For all *backbones*, then, the begin column must contain *1*, and the end and length columns must contain the length of the sequence in amino acids. accession should contain an accession if one is available, and entryName should contain the key that identifies this protein – so, a unique protein name. The taxid column is a little irrelevant most of the time and I usually just put the **National Center for Biotechnology Information (NCBI)** taxonomy identifier for Arabidopsis (2712). The order column determines the position the protein will be drawn on the *Y* axis, so each row should be unique.

In *step 2*, we set up the next layer of structure, defining the domains that will be plotted onto the backbones. Here, type must be "DOMAIN". description gives us the domain name. This doesn't need to be unique – the same sort of domain can appear on multiple proteins. In this DataFrame, begin, end, and length refer to the values for the individual domain on the particular protein. The crucial column, entryName, defines which protein the domain belongs to. Again, taxid is largely irrelevant. order is the position on the *Y* axis that the domain should render, so it should match the order of the protein it belongs to.

By *step 3*, we can combine the DataFrames into one and then pass that to the drawProteins functions to draw the things. The output looks like what's shown in *Figure 8.2*:

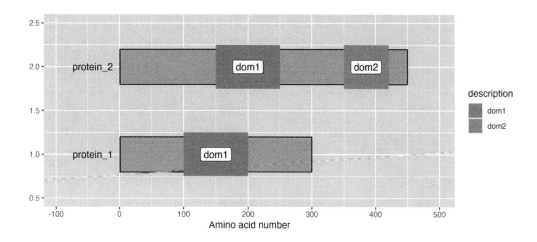

Figure 8.2 – A drawProteins protein plot

This is an accurate, if basic, representation of our proteins.

There's more...

The returned object from `drawProteins` is a `ggplot2` object, so it can be themed using the `theme_*` package. *Figure 8.3* shows what a cleaned-up version of *Figure 8.2* would look like if `theme_minimal()` were to be applied:

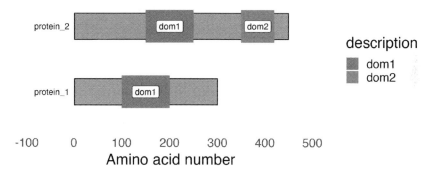

Figure 8.3 – A nicer themed protein plot

As we can see, adding `theme_minimal()` gives us a nicer background.

Performing multiple alignments of proteins or genes

Aligning sequences as a task before building phylogenetic trees or as an end in itself to determine conserved and divergent regions is a mainstay in bioinformatics analysis and is amply covered in R with ape and in Bioconductor with the msa and DECIPHER packages. We'll look at the extremely straightforward procedures for going from sequence to alignment in this recipe.

There are different techniques for different sequence length categories. In the first part of this recipe, we'll look at sequences on the order of a couple of thousand residues or smaller, such as those that represent genes and proteins.

Getting ready

For this recipe, you'll need the msa package. This is a pretty hefty package and includes external software: *Clustal*, *Clustal Omega*, and *Muscle*. The ape and seqinR packages are also needed. As a test dataset, we'll use some hemoglobin protein sequences stored in the rbioinfcookbook package. You'll need a version of LaTeX on your system too – if you have already installed quarto or rmarkdown on your system, you should be good, though you can get it from https://anaconda. org/conda-forge/texlive-core.

How to do it...

Performing multiple alignments of genes or proteins can be done by performing the following steps:

1. Load in the necessary libraries and sequences:

```
library(msa)

seq_file <- fs::path_package(
    "extdata",
    "hglobin.fa",
    package="rbioinfcookbook"
)
seqs <- readAAStringSet(seq_file)
```

2. Perform the multiple sequence alignments:

```
alignment <- msa(seqs, method = "ClustalOmega")
```

3. Render a view of the result:

```
msaPrettyPrint(alignment, output="pdf", showNames="left",
               showLogo="none", verbose=FALSE,
               file="whole_align.pdf")
```

4. View a zoomed-in region:

```
msaPrettyPrint(alignment, c(10,30),
                    output="pdf", showNames="left",
                    file = "zoomed_align.pdf",
                    showLogo="top", askForOverwrite=FALSE,
verbose=FALSE)
```

This is all the code we need to do the alignment and render the output.

How it works...

This brief recipe gets us a good-looking alignment quickly. Performing MSA with msa is easy; let's take a look at the steps involved. In *step 1*, we load the packages and sequences with the common readAAStringSet() function to give us seqs and an AAStringSet object. In *step 2*, we give that object to the msa() function and the name of an alignment method. We use ClustalOmega (you can choose ClustalOmega, ClustalW, or Muscle), which specifies the program to use to do the alignment. The aligner runs and you get back an MsaMultipleAlignment object, which is a container for the aligned sequences. It looks like this:

```
## ClustalOmega 1.2.0
##
## Call:
##      msa(seqs, method = "ClustalOmega")
##
## MsaAAMultipleAlignment with 3 rows and 142 columns
##       aln
                              names
## [1] MVLSPADKTNVKAAWGKVGAHAGEYGA...AEFTPAVHASLDKFLASVSTVLTSKYR HBA_
HUMAN
## [2] MVLSGEDKSNIKAAWGKIGGHGAEYGA...ADFTPAVHASLDKFLASVSTVLTSKYR HBA_
MOUSE
## [3] MSLTRTERTIILSLWSKISTQADVIGT...ADFTADAHAAWDKFLSIVSGVLTEKYR HBAZ_
CAPHI
## Con MVLS??DKTNIKAAWGKIG?HA?EYGA...ADFTPAVHASLDKFLASVSTVLTSKYR
Consensus
```

In *step 3*, we write a visualization of the alignment to a PDF file using the msaPrettyPrint() function. This function takes many arguments that describe the layout. The visualization must be written to a file. It can't be sent to a window like a normal plot. *Figure 8.4* shows the alignment visualization we just created:

Figure 8.4 – A full-length alignment

In *step 4*, we use the second positional argument of `msaPrettyPrint()` to restrict the view between positions 10 and 30, which results in the output shown in *Figure 8.5*:

Figure 8.5 – A zoomed-in alignment

The alignment shown here is more than what can be rendered in this book, but these figures should have given you an idea. You should see more when you run the code on your computer.

There's more...

A tree visualization of sequence similarity is often useful at this stage. We can generate one of these with the `ape` and `seqinr` packages. We can convert our alignment object into a `seqinr distance` object that describes the sequence distances, and from that, use `ape` to create a simple neighbor-joining tree that we can plot. This looks as follows:

Phylogenetic Tree of HBA Sequences

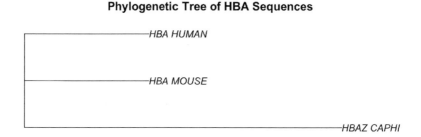

Figure 8.6 – A tree of the alignment

The code for this is as follows:

```
alignment_seqinr <- msaConvert(alignment, type="seqinr::alignment")
distances <- seqinr::dist.alignment(alignment_seqinr, "identity")
tree <- ape::nj(distances)
plot(tree, main="Phylogenetic Tree of HBA Sequences")
```

That is all we need for a quick tree visualization.

Aligning genomic length sequences with DECIPHER

Aligning sequences longer than genes and proteins, such as contigs from assembly projects, chromosomes, or whole genomes is a tricky task. For such tasks, we need different techniques than those for short sequences. The longer sequences get, the harder they are to align. Long alignments are especially costly in terms of the computational time taken. The algorithms that are effective on short sequences take up exponentially more time with increasing sequence length. Performing longer alignments generally starts with finding short anchor alignments and working the long alignment out from there. We typically end up with blocks of synteny regions that match well between the different sequences.

In this recipe, we'll look at the DECIPHER package for genome length alignments. We'll use some **chloroplast genomes** – small organelle genomes of about 150 Kbp that are pretty well conserved as our sequences of interest.

Getting ready

For this recipe, we'll need the DECIPHER Bioconductor package and the plastid_genomes.fa file, which can be found in the rbioinfcookbook package.

How to do it...

Aligning genomic length sequences with DECIPHER can be done by performing the following steps:

1. Load in the necessary libraries and genome sequences:

```
library(DECIPHER)
genomes_file <- fs::path_package(
  "extdata",
  "plastid_genomes.fa",
  package = "rbioinfcookbook"
)
long_seqs <- readDNAStringSet(genomes_file)
long_seqs
```

2. Prepare the sequences in a local database:

```
Seqs2DB(long_seqs, "XStringSet", "long_db", names(long_seqs))
```

3. Find the blocks of synteny:

```
synteny <- FindSynteny("long_db", verbose=FALSE)
pairs(synteny)
```

4. Plot the syntenic blocks:

```
plot(synteny)
```

5. Complete the alignment:

```
alignment <- AlignSynteny(synteny, "long_db", verbose=FALSE)
```

6. Save pairwise alignments:

```
blocks <- unlist(alignment[[1]])
writeXStringSet(blocks, "genome_blocks_out.fa")
```

That is all we need to do for a genome length alignment.

How it works...

The DECIPHER package is very powerful, so there is a little bit of setup to do before we can do the alignments. In *step 1*, we load the necessary libraries and sequence data into long_seqs, a DNAStringSet object; in *step 2*, we build an on-disk SQLite database for the subsequent steps. This is done with the Seqs2DB() function, which takes long_seqs, an input type (here, XStringSet, which is the parent class of DNAStringSet), a name for the database, and a vector of sequence names. Once we've got the database built, in *step 3*, we find syntenic blocks in the sequence database with FindSynteny(), which results in the following output:

```
## DNAStringSet object of length 5:
     width seq
                                       names
## [1] 130584 GGCATAAGCTATCTTCCC...CTATGATTCAAACATAAAAGTCCT
NC_018523.1 Sacch...
## [2] 161592 ATGGGCGAACGACGGGAA...AAAAAGAAAAAAAAATAGGAGTAA
NC_022431.1 Ascle...
## [3] 117672 ATGAGTACAACTCGAAAG...TTTTGATTTCATCCACAAACGAAC
NC_022259.1 Nanno...
## [4] 154731 TTATCCATTTGTAGATGG...TTCATATACACTAAGACAAAAGTC
NC_022417.1 Cocos...
## [5] 156618 GGGCGAACGACGGGAATT...ACCCTTTTGTAGCGAATCCGTTAT
NC_022459.1 Camel...
```

We can view a pairs-style visualization of the syntenic blocks with the `pairs(synteny)` call:

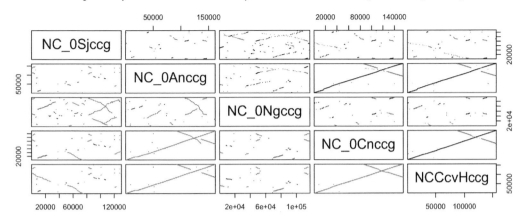

Figure 8.7 – Syntenic pairs plot

The heatmap style visualization with `plot(synteny)` is depicted in *Figure 8.8*:

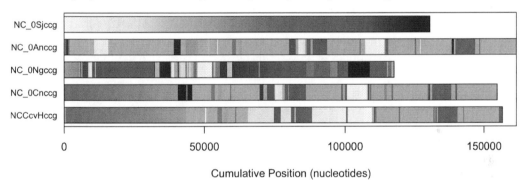

Figure 8.8 – A heatmap of the syntenic regions

Then, we use those syntenic blocks to do the alignment in *step 5* using the `AlignSynteny()` function and save the alignment to disk in *step 6*. This is slightly fiddly as the `alignment` object is an R list in which each member represents an alignment – itself a list data structure object. You can extract each element in turn using `unlist` but you'll need to iterate through all the elements to save all the pairwise alignments.

Novel feature detection in proteins

Sometimes, we'll have a list of protein sequences that have come from some analysis or experiment that are in some way biologically related. We might wish to determine the parts of those proteins that are responsible for the action. Domain and motif finding, as we've done in the preceding recipes, can only be helpful if we've seen the domains before or the sequence is well conserved or statistically over-represented. A different approach is to try machine learning, in which we build a model that can classify our proteins accurately and use the properties of that mode to show us which parts of the proteins result in the classification. We'll take that approach in this recipe by training and analyzing a **support vector machine (SVM)**.

Getting ready

For this recipe, we'll need the `kebabs` and `Biostrings` Bioconductor packages, as well as the `e1071` and `readr` packages. We'll also need two input data files that are provided in the `rbioinfcookbook` package and will be extracted using the `fs` package. The data files represent *170 Escherichia coli* proteins, for which the `STRING` database (`https://string-db.org`) provides evidence that these proteins interact with the protein pfo. These are all positive training examples. 170 E. coli proteins have been randomly selected but have no evidence of interaction with pfo. All the proteins are in the `ecoli_proteins.fa` file. The second file, `ecoli_protein_classes.txt`, is a single-column text file that describes the class of each protein, using a *1* for a pfo interactor and a *-1* otherwise. Note that the row index of the *class* file matches the protein index in the *sequence* file.

How to do it...

We can use machine learning for novel feature detection in proteins by performing the following steps:

1. Load the necessary libraries and input files:

```
library(kebabs)
library(Biostrings)
sequence_file <- fs::path_package(
  "extdata",
  "ecoli_proteins.fa",
  package = "rbioinfcookbook"
)
seqs <- readAAStringSet(sequence_file)

class_file <-  fs::path_package(
  "extdata",
  "ecoli_protein_classes.txt",
  package = "rbioinfcookbook"
)
```

```
classes <- readr::read_csv(class_file, col_names = TRUE)
classes <- classes$class
```

2. Divide the data into training and test sets:

```
num_seqs <- length(seqs)
training_proportion <- 0.75
training_set_indices <- sample(1:num_seqs, training_proportion *
num_seqs)
test_set_indices <- c(1:num_seqs)[-training_set_indices]
```

3. Build the model with the training set:

```
kernel <- gappyPairKernel(k=1, m=3)

model <- kbsvm(x=seqs[training_set_indices],
               y=classes[training_set_indices],
               kernel=kernel,
               pkg="e1071",
               svm="C-svc", cost=15)
```

4. Use the model to predict the classes of the test set:

```
predictions <- predict(model, seqs[test_set_indices])
evaluatePrediction(predictions, classes[test_set_indices],
allLabels=c(1,-1) )
```

5. Examine the prediction profile of a sequence:

```
seq_to_test <- seqs[[1]][1:10]
prediction_profile <-getPredictionProfile(seq_to_test, kernel,
featureWeights(model), modelOffset(model) )
```

6. Plot the prediction profile:

```
plot(prediction_profile)
```

This code should give us a nice prediction profile.

How it works...

Step 1 is straightforward – we load in sequences we're working with and the classes they belong to. As we need just a simple vector of classes for that data, we extract that from the DataFrame using the $ operator. Then, we get on to the main workflow. In *step 2*, we decide how much of the data we use for training and how much should be tested. We set 75% of the training data when we create the `training_proportion` variable. This is used in conjunction with num_seqs in the `sample()` function to randomly choose indices of the sequences to put into the training set. The `training_set_indices` variable contains integers that we will use to subset data later. Then, we make a vector of complementary indices for the test set in `test_set_indices` by using the square bracket notation and the negation operator (`-`). In essence, this construct is an idiomatic way of creating a vector that contains every index *not* in `training_set_indices`.

In *step 3*, we construct and train the SVM model, and we start by choosing a kernel to map the input data into a matrix space that the SVM can learn from. Here, it's from the `gappyPairKernel()` function. Note that there are lots of kernel types; this one is pretty well suited to sequence data. We pass `kernel` to the `kbsvm()` function, along with the `training_set_indices` subset of sequences as the `x` parameter and the same subset of classes as the `y` parameter. Other arguments in this function determine the exact model type and package and they can have a strong effect on the quality of the final model. It is well worth reading up and doing some scientific experimentation on what works best for your particular data. The final model is saved in the `model` variable.

By *step 4*, although our model is constructed, we must now test its accuracy. To do this, we run it with the unseen data from earlier, indexed by `test_set_indices`, and compare its predictions with real labels. Again, we use the `prediction()` function to do this and `evaluatePrediction()`, along with the real class labels from the `classes` vector and also a vector of all possible class labels. Using the `allLabels` argument returns a summary of the accuracy and other metrics of the model, as shown here:

```
##        1 -1
## 1   25 13
## -1 14 36
##
## Accuracy:              69.318% (61 of 88)
## Balanced accuracy:     68.786% (25 of 39 and 36 of 49)
## Matthews CC:            0.377
##
## Sensitivity:           64.103% (25 of 39)
## Specificity:           73.469% (36 of 49)
## Precision:             65.789% (25 of 38)
```

We have an accuracy of 69% in the model here, which is okay; it is better than random. We do have a rather small dataset and the model isn't optimized; with more work, it could be better. Note that if you run the code, you may get different answers. Since the selection of training set sequences is random, the models might do slightly worse or better, depending on the exact input data.

In *step 5*, we estimate the prediction profile of a sequence. To find the regions that are important in classification, and presumably in the function of the protein, we use the `getPredictionProfile()` function on a sequence. We do this on a small 10 AA fragment extracted from the first sequence using list-double-bracket indexing to get the first sequence and single-bracket indexing to get a range – for example, `seqs[[1]][1:10]`. We do this just to clarify the explanation and visualization in the last step. You can use the whole sequence as well. The `getPredictionProfile()` function needs the `kernel` and `model` objects to work.

In *step 6*, we `plot()` the prediction profile. This profile shows the contribution of each amino acid to the overall decision made and adds to the interpretability of the learning results. Here, the fourth residue, *D*, makes a strong contribution to the decision made for this protein. By examining this across many sequences, the patterns contributing to the decision can be elucidated. It's worth noting that you may get a slightly different picture to that in *Figure 8.9* – because of random parts of this recipe and algorithm – so you should build that into your analysis: make sure that any apparent differences aren't due to random choices made while running the code. The strongest contribution should still come from **D** in this example:

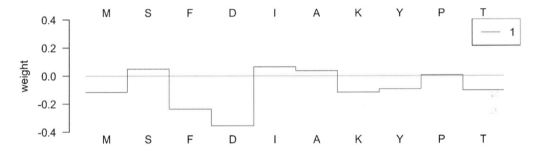

Figure 8.9 – A prediction profile plot for 10 amino acids of a protein sequence

This prediction profile is a simple but effective display of the most important amino acids.

3D structure protein alignment in bio3d

Three-dimensional structural alignments between two molecular models can reveal structural properties that are common or unique to either of the proteins. These can suggest evolutionary or functional commonalities. In this recipe, we'll look at how to get the alignment of two protein sequences in three dimensions and view them in 3D.

Getting ready

For this recipe, we need to install a sequence aligner. We'll take advantage of the fact that the `msa` package comes with a version of **MUSCLE** and install that. You can also use `conda` to install it separately.

We will also need to install a viewer. We will use `PyMOL`, which can be installed into a conda environment as follows:

```
conda install -c conda-forge -c schrodinger pymol-bundle
```

We'll also use the `bio3d` package and some data files in the `rbioinfcookbook` package.

How to do it...

We can predict structure by performing the following steps:

1. Load the necessary library and files:

```
library(bio3d)

f1xwc.pdb <- fs::path_package(
  "extdata",
  "1xwc.pdb",
  package="rbioinfcookbook"
)
f3trx.pdb <- fs::path_package(
  "extdata",
  "3trx.pdb",
  package="rbioinfcookbook"
)

a <- read.pdb(f1xwc.pdb)
b <- read.pdb(f3trx.pdb)
```

2. Carry out the alignment:

```
pdbs <- pdbaln(list("1xwc"=a,"3trx"=b), fit=TRUE,exefile="msa")
```

3. Launch and render the alignment in PyMol:

```
env_path <- function(env, program = ""){

  df <- reticulate::conda_list()
  b <- df$python[which(df$name == env)]

  if (length(b) == 0) {
     stop("no environment with that name found")
  }

  file.path(dirname(b), program)
}

pymol_path <-  env_path("bioinformatics_project", "pymol")

pymol(pdbs, exefile = pymol_path, type = "launch", as="cartoon")
```

These are all the steps we need to perform to get a rendered view of our predicted structure.

How it works...

As usual, *step 1* is to load the library and the input data – two different **protein database (PDB)** files with the `read.pdb()` function. In *step 2*, we do the alignment with the `pbaln()` function. All the PDBs we want to align are put into a list object with an appropriate name. The `fit` argument is set to `TRUE` to carry out the superposition of the structures based on all the aligned sequences. The `exefile` argument tells the function where to find the aligner – here, a value of `msa` tells it to look in the `msa` package we installed.

Once we have an alignment, we want to visualize it in PyMOL. The executable is installed in a `conda` environment so that we can use the custom `env_path()` function defined at the start of *step 3* to extract the path and pass it to `pymol()` as an argument. PyMOL should start and the alignment should render.

There's more...

If you don't want to use *MUSCLE* in `msa`, you can use a path to an alternative executable in *step 2* or replace `exefile` with `web.args="your.email@something.org"` to carry out the alignment over the web at EBI.

Omitting the `type` argument in *step 3* will result in a *PyMOL* script being written that you can use in a separate *PyMOL* session.

9

Phylogenetic Analysis and Visualization

Phylogenetics is the study of the evolutionary relationships among species or other groups of organisms. It involves the use of molecular and computational techniques to construct phylogenetic trees, which depict the evolutionary history of the organisms under study.

In bioinformatics, phylogenetics is studied using various computational tools and methods, including sequence alignment, distance-based methods, maximum likelihood, and Bayesian inference. These methods allow researchers to compare DNA or protein sequences from different organisms and infer their evolutionary relationships based on similarities and differences in their genetic makeup. Phylogenetics has many applications in biology, and is used to help understand the evolutionary history of species, to study the origins and spread of diseases (phylogenetic analysis can be used to trace the origins and spread of infectious diseases), and to inform conservation efforts by identifying species or populations that are evolutionarily distinct and therefore particularly important to preserve.

Phylogenetics has a long history in R and not just in Bioconductor. There are many packages on CRAN for evolutionary analysis. In the recipes in this chapter, we will take a good look at how to work with tree formats from a variety of sources. A key focus will be how to manipulate trees to focus on particular parts and work with visualizations based on `ggplot2`-based packages, and the latter's usefulness in viewing and annotating large trees.

In this chapter, we will cover the following recipes:

- Reading and writing varied tree formats with `ape` and `treeio`
- Visualizing trees of many genes quickly with `ggtree`
- Quantifying and estimating differences between trees with `treespace`
- Extracting and working with subtrees using ape

- Creating dot plots for alignment visualizations
- Reconstructing trees from alignments using `phangorn`
- Finding orthologue candidates using reciprocal BLASTs

Technical requirements

We will use `renv` to manage packages in a project-specific way. To use `renv` to install packages, you will first need to install the `renv` package. You can do this by running the following commands in your R console:

1. Install `renv`:

    ```
    install.packages("renv")
    ```

2. Create a new `renv` environment:

    ```
    renv::init()
    ```

    This will create a new directory called `.renv` in your current project directory.

3. You can then install packages with the following:

    ```
    renv::install_packages()
    ```

4. You can also use the `renv` package manager to install Bioconductor packages by running the following command:

    ```
    renv::install("bioc::package name")
    ```

5. For example, to install the `Biobase` package, you would run this:

    ```
    renv::install("bioc::Biobase")
    ```

6. You can use `renv` to install development packages from GitHub like this:

    ```
    renv::install("user name/repo name")
    ```

7. For example, to install the `danmaclean` user `rbioinfcookbook` package, you would run this:

    ```
    renv::install("danmaclean/rbioinfcookbook")
    ```

You can also install multiple packages at once by separating the package names with a comma. `renv` will automatically handle installing any required dependencies for the packages you install.

Under `renv`, all packages will be installed in the local project directory and not the main central library, meaning you can have multiple versions of the same package, one specific one for each project.

All the sample data you need for this package is in the specially created data package on GitHub, `danmaclean/rbioinfcookbook`. The data will become available in your project after installing that.

For this chapter, we'll need the following packages:

- Regular packages:

    - `adegraphics`

    - `ape`

    - `cowplot`

    - `data.table`

    - `dplyr`

    - `fs`

    - `ggplot2`

    - `phangorn`

    - `readr`

    - `reticulate`

    - `treespace`

- GitHub:

    - `danmaclean/rbioinfcookbook`

    - `evolvedmicrobe/dotplot`

- Bioconductor:

    - `Biostrings`

    - `dotplot`

    - `ggtree`

    - `msa`

    - `treeio`

In addition to these packages, we will also need some R tools, such as `conda`. All these will be described when needed.

Further information

Not all the recipes in this section happen in R; some are command-line-based setups. I generally assume a bash terminal for these bits. Most macOS and Linux machines will have these available in a Terminal application. Windows users will likely not need these specific steps, though various packages for running a Linux subsystem on Windows exist if you wish to search them out.

In R, it is normal practice to load a library and use functions directly by name. Although this is great in short interactive sessions, it can cause confusion when many packages are loaded at once and share function names. To clarify which package and function I am using at a given moment, I will occasionally use the `packageName::functionName()` convention.

Sometimes, in the middle of a recipe, I'll interrupt the code to dive into some intermediate output or to look at the structure of an object. When that happens, you'll see a code block where each line begins with ## (double hash symbols). Consider the following command:

```
letters[1:5]
```

This will give us the following output:

```
## a b c d e
```

Note that the output lines are prefixed with ##.

Reading and writing varied tree formats with ape and treeio

Phylogenetic analysis is a cornerstone of biology and bioinformatics. The programs are diverse and complex, the computations are long-running, and the datasets are often large. Many programs are standalone and many have proprietary input and output formats. This has created a very complex ecosystem that we must navigate when dealing with phylogenetic data, meaning that often the simplest strategy is to use combinations of tools to load, convert, and save the results of analyses in order to be able to use them in different packages. In this recipe, we'll look at dealing with phylogenetic tree data in R. To date, R support for the wide range of tree formats is restricted, but a few key packages have sufficient standardized objects such that workflows can focus on a few types and conversion to those types is streamlined. We'll look at using the ape and treeio packages to get tree data into and out of R.

Getting ready

For this section, we'll need the tree and phylogenetic information provided by the rbioinfcookbook package. One is a Newick format file, the other is a Nexus format file. They each represent the same mammal phylogeny. We'll also need a tree from the BEAST program and a RAxML file. Both these are taken from the treeio package, so we'll need that from Bioconductor and the ape package.

How to do it...

Reading and writing tree formats with `ape` and `treeio` can be executed by following these steps:

1. Load the ape library and a `tree`:

```
library(ape)
newick_file_path <- fs::path_package(
  "extdata",
  "mammal_tree.nwk",
  package="rbioinfcookbook"
)

nexus_file_path <- fs::path_package(
  "extdata",
  "mammal_tree.nexus",
  package="rbioinfcookbook"
)

newick <-ape::read.tree(newick_file_path)
nexus <-ape::read.nexus(nexus_file_path)
```

2. Load the `treeio` library and load in the BEAST/RAxML data:

```
library(treeio)
beast_file_path <- fs::path_package(
  "extdata",
  "beast_mcc.tree",
  package="rbioinfcookbook"
)raxml_file_path <- fs::path_package(
  "extdata",
  "RAxML_bipartitionsBranchLabels.H3",
  package="rbioinfcookbook"
)

library(treeio)
beast <- read.beast(beast_file_path)
raxml <- read.raxml(raxml_file_path)
```

3. Check the object types:

```
class(newick)
class(nexus)
class(beast)
class(raxml)
```

4.   Convert `tidytree` to `phylo` and vice versa:

```
beast_phylo <- treeio::as.phylo(beast)
newick_tidytree <- treeio::as.treedata(newick)
```

5.   Write the output files:

```
treeio::write.beast(newick_tidytree, file = "mammal_tree.beast")
ape::write.nexus(beast_phylo, file = "beast_mcc.nexus")
```

And that's how we can read and write phylogenetic trees in R.

How it works...

In *step 1*, we make use of very straightforward loading functions from `ape` – we use the `read.tree()` and `read.nexus()` functions, which can read the generic format trees in the files. In *step 2*, we repeatedly use the specific format functions from `treeio` for the BEAST and RAxML output. *Step 3* simply confirms the object types that the function returns. Note that `ape` returns `phylo` objects while `treeio` returns `treedata` objects. The two are interconverted using `as.phylo()` and `as.treedata()` from `treeio` in *step 4*. By converting in this way, we can get input in many formats into downstream analyses in R. In *step 5*, we use the file writing functions to write trees to disk.

See also

The loading functions we used in *step 2* are just a couple of those available. Refer to the `treeio` package vignettes for a comprehensive list.

Visualizing trees of many genes quickly with ggtree

Once you have computed a tree, the first thing you will want to do with it is take a look. That's possible in many programs, but R has an extremely powerful, flexible, and fast system in the form of the `ggtree` package. In this recipe, we'll learn how to get into `ggtree` and re-layout, highlight, and annotate tree images in just a few commands.

Getting ready

You'll need the `ggplot2`, `ggtree`, and `ape` packages. You'll also require the `itol.nwk` file from the `rbioinfcookbook` package. The file is a Newick tree of 191 species from the `Interactive Tree of Life` online tool's public dataset. At the time of writing, there is an issue with an upstream dependency that causes this code to fail, though it is correct. We hope this will have gone away by the time you read this. If it hasn't, a workaround is to install the source version of `ggtree` from `Biocmanager`, like this:

```
BiocManager::install("ggtree", force=T, type = 'source')
```

Once those are installed, you'll have everything you need for the chapter.

How to do it...

Visualizing trees of many genes quickly with `ggtree` can be executed using the following steps:

1. Load the libraries and tree:

```
library(ggplot2)
library(ggtree)


tree_file <- fs::path_package(
  "extdata",
  "itol.nwk",
  package="rbioinfcookbook"
)

itol <- ape::read.tree(tree_file)
```

2. Make a basic tree plot:

```
ggtree(itol)
```

3. Make a circular plot:

```
ggtree(itol, layout="circular")
```

4. Rotate and invert the tree:

```
ggtree(itol) + coord_flip() +
scale_x_reverse()
```

5. Add labels to tips:

```
ggtree(itol) +
geom_tiplab(color="blue",size= 2)
```

6. Make a strip of color to annotate a particular clade:

```
ggtree(itol, layout="circular") +
geom_strip(13,14, color="red",barsize=1)
```

7. Make a blob of color to highlight a particular clade:

```
ggtree(itol, layout="unrooted") +

geom_hilight(node = 11, fill="steelblue")
```

The recipe gives us a nicely laid out and highlighted tree.

How it works...

The code does a lot very quickly. It can do this by virtue of its ggplot layer model and syntax.

Step 1 starts by loading a tree from a file. Our tree has 191 tips so is quite large. We pull the file from the data package with fs, then create a phylo object from the Newick file using ape::read.tree(). Note that we don't need to have a *treedata* object for ggtree in subsequent steps; the phylo object is acceptable to ggtree.

Next, in *step 2*, we create a basic plot. The ggtree() function is a wrapper for a longer ggplot-style syntax, so all the usual ggplot functions can be used as extra layers in the plot, which is helpful for styling. The output looks like *Figure 9.1*:

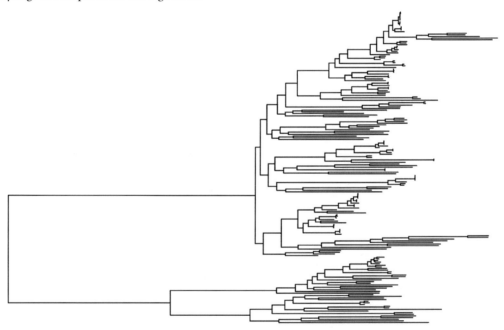

Figure 9.1 – A basic ggtree plot

In *step 3*, we change the layout of the plot. Setting the layout argument to circular gives a round tree, as in *Figure 9.2*. Many other tree layouts are available through this argument:

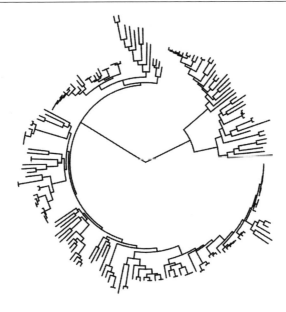

Figure 9.2 – A circular plot

With *step 4*, we re-orient our base plot, changing the left-right direction using the coordinate flip and scale reverse functions, ending up with *Figure 9.3*:

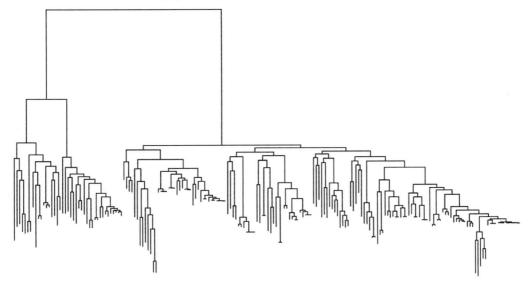

Figure 9.3 – A flipped plot

In *step 5*, we add names to the end of the tips. The `size` argument sets the text size, giving a tree like in *Figure 9.4*:

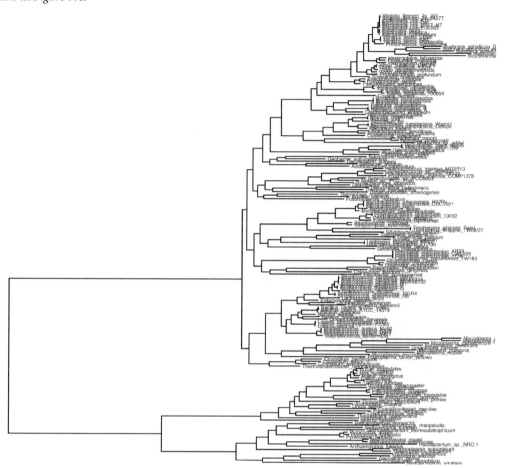

Figure 9.4 – Labeled tips

The final steps add some graphical annotations. *Step 6* adds a strip notation across the span between the start and end nodes of the tree. The first two arguments to `geom_strip()` are the start and end node numbers. The `barsize` argument sets the width of the colored strip (see *Figure 9.5*):

Figure 9.5 – A strip notation mark

Then we add a highlight section. The geom_hilight() function will add a shape of color centered around a particular node. The value for the node argument tells the plot where to place the shape (see *Figure 9.6*):

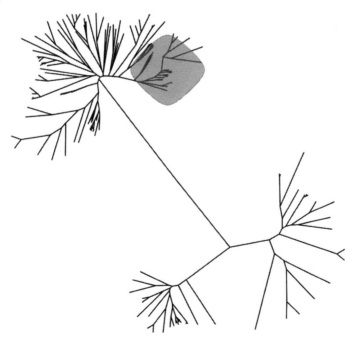

Figure 9.6 – A highlighted node

As we can see, this is a nice package for visualizing trees.

There's more...

Steps 6 and *7* relied on us knowing which nodes in the tree to manipulate. This isn't always obvious as the nodes are identified by number and not name. We can get the node number we want if we use the **Most Recent Common Ancestor (MRCA)** function. Simply pass it a vector of node names and it returns the ID of the node that represents the MRCA:

```
MRCA(itol, tip=c("Photorhabdus_lumenscens", "Blochmannia_floridanus"))
```

It returns the following result:

```
## 206
```

This is the node number we can use to access the clade we are interested in.

Quantifying and estimating the differences between trees with treespace

Comparing trees to differentiate or group them can help researchers to see patterns of evolution. Multiple trees of a single gene tracked across species or strains can reveal differences in how that gene is changing across species. At the core of these approaches are metrics of distances between trees. In this recipe, we'll calculate one such metric to find pairwise differences between 20 different genes in 15 different species, hence 15 different tips with identical names in each tree. Such similarity in trees is needed to compare and get distances, and we can't do an analysis like this unless these conditions are met.

Getting ready

For this recipe, we'll use the `treespace` package to compute distances and clusters. We'll use `ape` and `adegraphics` for accessory loading and visualization functions. The input data will be 20 files of Newick format trees, each of which represents a single gene in each of the 15 species. These are available from the `danmaclean/rbioinfcookbook` package, so install that.

How to do it...

Quantifying the differences between trees with `treespace` can be done with the following steps:

1. Load the libraries:

```
library(ape) library(adegraphics)
library(treespace)
Load all the files into a multiPhylo object:
```

```
file_path <- fs::path_package(
  "extdata",
  "gene_trees",
  package="rbioinfcookbook"
)

treefiles <- list.files(file_path, full.names = TRUE)
tree_list <- lapply(treefiles, read.tree)

class(tree_list) <- "multiPhylo"
```

2. Compute the Kendall-Colijn distances:

```
comparisons <- treespace(tree_list, nf = 3)
```

3. Plot pairwise distances:

```
table.image(comparisons$D, nclass=25)
```

4. Plot **Principal Component Analysis** (**PCA**) and clusters:

```
plotGroves(comparisons$pco, lab.show=TRUE, lab.cex=1.5)

groves <- findGroves(comparisons, nclust = 4)
plotGroves(groves)
```

This is all we need to look at the distances between trees.

How it works...

The short and sweet code here is really powerful – and gives a lot of analysis in a few commands.

Step 1 is to load libraries. *step 2* starts by making a `treefiles` character vector that holds full paths to each of the 20 trees we wish to use. The `list.files()` function that we use takes a filesystem path as its argument and returns the names of the files it finds in that path. As `treefiles` is a vector, we can use it as the first argument to `lapply()`. In case you're not familiar with it, `lapply()` is an iterator function that returns an R list (hence, `lapply()`). Simply put, `lapply()` runs the function named in the second argument over the list of things in the first. The current thing is passed as the target function's first argument. So, in *step 2*, we run the `read.tree()` function on each file named in `treefiles` and receive an R list of `phylo` tree objects in return. The final step is to ensure that the `tree_list` object has the `multiPhylo` class so that we satisfy the requirements of the downstream functions. Helpfully, a `multiPhylo` object is a list-like object anyway, so we can get away with adding the `mulitPhylo` string to the class attribute with the `class()` function.

In *step 3*, the `treespace()` function from the package of the same name does an awful lot of analysis. It first runs pairwise comparisons of all trees in the input and then carries out clustering using PCA. These are returned in a list object with a member, D, containing the pairwise distances for the trees and pco, containing the PCA. The default distance metric, the Kendall-Colijn distance, is particularly suitable for rooted gene trees as we have here, though the metric can be changed. The nf argument simply tells us how many principal components to retain. As our aim is plotting, we won't need more than three.

We plot a distance matrix in *step 4*. This comes from comparisons$D and is done with the `table.image()` function. The nclass argument tells us how many levels of color to use. We get a plot like the one in *Figure 9.7*:

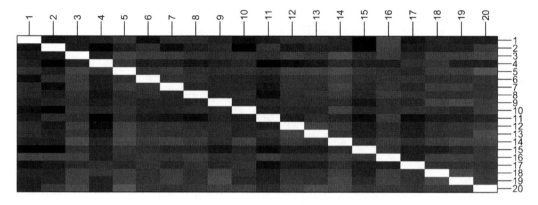

Figure 9.7 – A pairwise tree distance plot

In *step 5*, we use the `plotGroves()` function to plot the PCA, viewed in *Figure 9.8*:

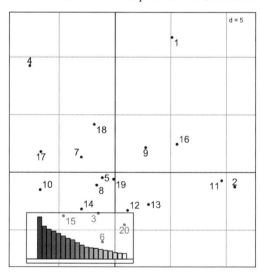

Figure 9.8 – A PCA of the grouped trees

We can use the `findGroves()` function to group the trees in the number of groups given by the `nclust` argument and re-plot to view that, as in *Figure 9.9*:

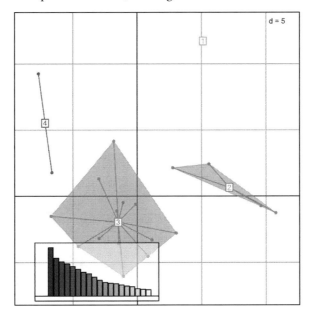

Figure 9.9 – A clustered PCA of the groups

This gives us a full range of options for visualizing clusters of trees.

There's more...

If you have many trees and the plot is crowded, you can create an interactive plot that can be zoomed and panned using the following code:

```
plotGrovesD3(comparisons$pco, treeNames=paste0("species_", 1:10))
```

This can be extremely helpful with large datasets.

Extracting and working with subtrees using ape

A common but often frustrating task is cropping trees to look at a section in a new, clearer context or combining them with another tree in order to present two distant clades more clearly. In this short recipe, we'll look at how easy it can be to manipulate trees- specifically, how to pull out a subtree as a new object and how to combine trees into other trees. We'll use the `ape` package, the phylogenetic workhorse in R that will give us functionality for completing those tasks easily.

Getting ready

We'll need a single example tree – the `mammal_tree.nwk` file in the `rbioinfcookbook` package will be fine. All the functions we require can be found in the `ape` package.

How to do it...

Extracting and working with subtrees in `ape` can be executed using the following steps:

1. Load the library and tree:

```
library(ape)
tree_file <- fs::path_package(
   "extdata",
   "mammal_tree.nwk",
   package="rbioinfcookbook"
)

newick <-read.tree(tree_file)
```

2. Get a list of subtrees:

```
l <- subtrees(newick)
plot(newick)plot(l[[4]], sub = "Node 4")
```

3. Extract a specific subtree:

```
small_tree <- extract.clade(newick, 9)
```

4. Combine two trees:

```
new_tree <- bind.tree(newick, small_tree, 3)
plot(new_tree)
```

These steps create a new tree from sections of two others.

How it works...

The functions in this recipe are really straightforward but extremely useful.

In *step 1*, we just load the example tree, extracting the file from the `rbioinfcookbook` package. We need a `phylo` class tree to progress.

In *step 2*, we use `subtrees()` to extract non-trivial (greater than one node) subtrees and put them in a list. The members of that list are numbered according to the node number in the original tree, and each object in the list is a `phylo` object, like the parent. We can inspect the original tree, *Figure 9.10*, and the subtree at node 4, *Figure 9.11*, using the `plot()` function:

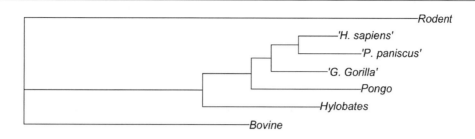

Figure 9.10 – A plotted tree

The subtree looks as shown in *Figure 9.11*:

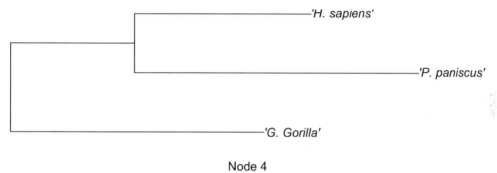

Node 4

Figure 9.11 – A subtree

In *step 3*, we get a single specific subtree using the `extract.clade()` function. The first argument to this function is the tree, while the second is the node that will be extracted. In fact, all nodes downstream of this node are taken and a new `phylo` object is returned.

The last step shows how to use the `bind.tree()` function to combine two `phylo` objects. The first argument is the major tree, which will receive the tree of the second argument. Here, we shall stitch the `small_tree` object onto `newick`. The third argument is the node in the major tree to which the second tree will be joined. Again a new `phylo` object is returned. When we plot the new tree, we can see the repeated segment relative to our original tree, as in *Figure 9.12*:

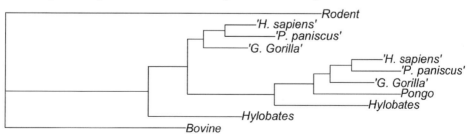

Figure 9.12 – A tree joined to another tree

Together these steps help us build trees with selected nodes.

There's more...

A minor problem with the preceding functions is that they expect us to know the node number we want to work with. A simple way to access this is by using the interactive subtreeplot() function. This subtree(newick) call will generate an interactive plot for the tree provided. By clicking on nodes, the image is updated to show the subtree and clicked node ID.

Creating dot plots for alignment visualizations

Dot plots of pairs of aligned sequences are possibly the oldest alignment visualization. In these plots, the positions of two sequences are plotted on the *x* axis and *y* axis, and for every coordinate in that space, a point is drawn if the letters (nucleotides or amino acids) correspond at that *(x,y)* coordinate. Since the plot can show regions that match that aren't generally in the same region of the two sequences (as lines away from the diagonal), the plot is a good way to visually spot insertions and deletions and structural rearrangements in the two sequences. In this recipe, we'll look at a speedy method for constructing a dot plot using the dotplot package and a bit of code for getting a grid plot of all pairwise dot plots for sequences in a file.

Getting ready

We'll need the bhlh.fa file, which contains three **basic helix-loop-helix (bHLH)** transcription factor sequences from pea, soy, and lotus. The file is provided by the rbioinfcookbook package. We'll also need the Biostrings package and the evolvedmicrobe/dotplot GitHub-hosted package.

How to do it...

Generating dot plots for alignment visualization can be executed using the following steps:

1. Load the libraries and sequences:

    ```
    library(Biostrings)
    library(ggplot2)
    library(dotplot)

    seqfile <- fs::path_package(
      "extdata",
      "bhlh.fa",
    ```

```
        package = "rbioinfcookbook"
    )


    seqs <- readAAStringSet(seqfile)
```

2. Make a basic dot plot:

```
dotPlotg(as.character(seqs[[1]]),
         as.character(seqs[[2]] ))
```

3. Change the dot plot and apply themes and labels:

```
dotPlotg(as.character(seqs[[1]]), as.character(seqs[[2]]
), wsize=7, wstep=5,
        nmatch=4) +   theme_bw() +
   labs(x=names(seqs)[1], y=names(seqs)[2] )
```

4. Make a function that will create a dot plot automatically:

```
make_dot_plot <- function(i=1, j=1, seqs = NULL){
   seqi <- as.character(seqs[[i]])
   seqj <- as.character(seqs[[j]])
   namei <- names(seqs)[i]

   namej <- names(seqs)[j]
   return( dotPlotg(seqi, seqj ) +
  theme_bw() + labs(x=namei, y=namej) )
}
```

5. Set up data structures to run the function:

```
combinations <- expand.grid(1:length(seqs),1:length(seqs))
plots <- vector("list", nrow(combinations) )
```

6. Run the function on all the possible combinations:

```
for (r in 1:nrow(combinations)){
    i <- combinations[r,]$Var1[[1]]
     j <- combinations[r,]$Var2[[1]]
     plots[[r]] <- make_dot_plot(i,j, seqs)
}
```

7. Plot the grid of plots:

```
cowplot::plot_grid(plotlist = plots)
```

That is all we need to do.

How it works...

The first part of this recipe is pretty familiar. In *step 1*, we load in the libraries and use `Biostrings` to load in our protein sequences. Note that our sequences in the `seqs` object are an instance of the `XStringSet` class. In *step 2*, we can create a basic dot plot using the `dotplotg()` function. The arguments are the sequences we want to plot. Note that we can't pass the `XStringSet` objects directly; we need to pass character vectors, so we coerce our sequences into that format with the `as.character()` function. Running this code gives us the dot plot in *Figure 9.13*:

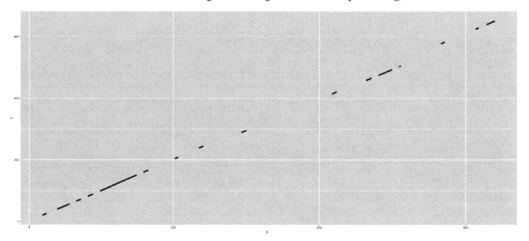

Figure 9.13 – A basic dot plot of two sequences

In *step 3*, we elaborate on the basic dot plot by first changing the way a match is considered. With the `wsize` option, we state that we are looking at 7 residues at a time (instead of the default of 1), the `wstep` option tells the plotter to jump 5 residues at each step, and the `nmatch` option tells the plotter to mark a window as matching if four of the residues are identical. We then customize the plot by adding a `ggplot2` theme to it in the usual manner and add axis names. Note how the results in *Figure 9.14* are different from *Figure 9.13*:

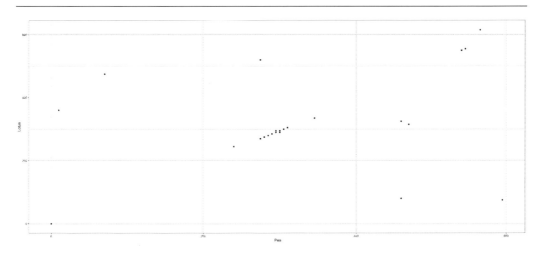

Figure 9.14 – A themed, improved dot plot of two sequences

The custom function, make_dot_plot(), defined in *step 4*, takes two numbers in i and j variables and an XStringSet object in seqs. It then converts the *i*-th and *j*-th sequence in the seqs object to characters and stores those in the seqi and seqj variables. It also extracts the names of those sequences as namei and namej. Finally, it creates and returns a dot plot using the variables created.

To use the function, we need two things: the combinations of sequences to be plotted and a list to hold the results. In *step 4*, the expand.grid() function is used to create a dataframe of all possible combinations of sequences by number, which we store in the combinations variable. The plots variable created from the vector() function contains a list object with the right number of slots to hold the resultant dot plots.

Step 6 is a loop that iterates over each row of the combinations dataframe, extracting the sequence numbers we wish to work with and storing them. The make_dot_plot() function is called and its results are stored in the list we created.

Lastly, in *step 7*, we use the `cowplot::plot_grid()` function with our list of plots to make a master plot of all possible combinations that looks like *Figure 9.15*:

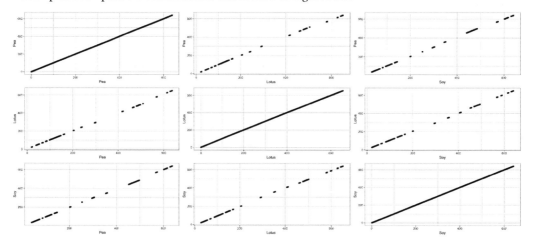

Figure 9.15 – A plot of all pairwise dot plots

That is the full set of dot plots we aimed to make.

Reconstructing trees from alignments using phangorn

So far in this chapter, we've assumed that trees are already available and ready to use. Of course, there are many ways to make a phylogenetic tree and, in this recipe, we'll take a look at some of the different methods available.

Getting ready

For this chapter, we'll use the `abc.fa` file of yeast ABC transporter sequences, the Bioconductor `Biostrings` package, and the CRAN `msa` and `phangorn` packages.

How to do it...

Constructing trees using `phangorn` can be done like this:

1. Load in the libraries and sequences and make an alignment:

```
library(Biostrings)
library(msa)
library(phangorn)

seqfile <- fs::path_package(
```

```
    "extdata",
    "abc.fa",
    package="rbioinfcookbook"
)
seqs <- readAAStringSet(seqfile)
aln <- msa::msa(seqs, method=c("ClustalOmega"))
```

2.   Convert the alignment:

```
aln <- as.phyDat(aln, type = "AA")
```

3.   Make UPGMA and neighbor-joining trees from a distance matrix:

```
dist_mat <- dist.ml(aln)

upgma_tree <- upgma(dist_mat)
plot(upgma_tree, main="UPGMA")
nj_tree <- NJ(dist_mat)
plot(nj_tree,"unrooted", main="NJ")
```

4.   Calculate the bootstraps and plot:

```
fit <- pml(nj_tree, aln)
bootstraps <- bootstrap.phyDat(aln,FUN=function(x) { NJ(dist.
ml(x)) } , bs=100)
plotBS(nj_tree, bootstraps, p = 10)
```

And with that, we should have our plot of a bootstrap tree.

How it works...

Step 1 carries out loading and makes an amino acid sequence alignment, returning an `MsaAAMultipleAlignment` object.

Step 2 uses the `as.phyDat()` function to convert the alignment to a `phyDat` object that can be used by the `phangorn` functions.

In *step 3*, we actually make trees. Trees are made from a distance matrix, which we can compute with `dist.ml()` and our alignment (this is a maximum-likelihood distance measure; other functions can be used here if needed). The `dist_mat` object is passed to the `upgma()` and `NJ()` functions to make trees of those types. These functions return standard `phylo` objects that can be worked with in many other functions. Here we plot directly, giving output like that of *Figure 9.16*:

NJ

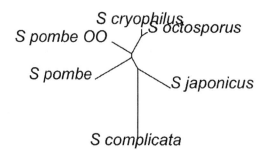

Figure 9.16 – An unrooted neighbor-joining tree

Finally, in *step 4*, we use the `bootstraps.phyDat()` function to compute bootstrap support for the branches in the tree. The first argument to that is the `phyDat` object we created and named, `aln`, and the second argument, `FUN`, requires either the name of a function that can calculate trees or an anonymous in-line function. Here, we use an anonymous function wrapping the `NJ()` method we used earlier. The `bs` argument tells the functions how many bootstraps to compute. Finally, we can plot the resulting bootstrap values onto the tree using the `plotBS()` function, resulting in what's shown in *Figure 9.17*:

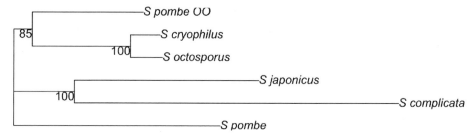

Figure 9.17 – A rooted neighbor-joining tree with bootstraps

This is a plot with bootstraps or reliability measures.

Finding orthologue candidates using reciprocal BLASTs

In genomics, **orthology** refers to the relationship between genes from different species that evolved from a common ancestral gene through speciation. Orthologous genes typically have the same function and structure and play similar roles in different organisms, even if they have diverged over time.

Orthology has many important uses in bioinformatics. Orthology can be used to infer the function of a gene in a newly sequenced genome based on its similarity to known genes in other species. This can be especially useful for identifying genes that are involved in specific biological processes or pathways. Orthologous genes can be used to compare the genomes of different organisms and study the evolution of gene families. By identifying which genes are conserved across different species, researchers can gain insights into the evolutionary history of those genes and the organisms that carry them.

Orthology can be inferred using various computational methods that compare the DNA or protein sequences of genes from different organisms. **Reciprocal best BLAST hit (RBH)** is a simple method that involves searching for the best hit of a gene in one species against all genes in another species, and then searching for the best hit of the gene in the other species against all genes in the first species. If the two best hits are the same genes, then they are considered orthologs.

More complicated and sensitive methods exist, including the Inparalog method, tree-based methods, and Markov-clustering methods. In this recipe, we'll look at the RBH method as implemented in the R OrthologR package.

Getting ready

For this recipe, we'll need the readr and datatable packages. We'll also get a small amount of sample data from danmaclean/rbioinfcookbook. The function we will use relies on an externally installed version of blastp, so we will need to install that in an environment using conda. I assume that it will be called bioinformatics_project in *step 1*. The reticulate package will be needed, too.

How to do it...

Computing RBH to infer orthology can be done as follows:

1. Create a function that will find the path to blast:

```
env_path <- function(env, program = ""){
  df <- reticulate::conda_list()
  b <- df$python[which(df$name == env)]
  if (length(b) == 0) {    stop("no environment with that name
found")
  }
  file.path(dirname(b), program)
}

blast_path <-  env_path("bioinformatics_project")
```

2. Set up a function to make a blast database:

```r
make_blastdb <- function(fasta, blast_path) {
  system(paste0(blast_path, "makeblastdb -in ", fasta,
 "input_type fasta -dbtype prot -hash_index"
                  ))

}
```

3. Set up a function to run `blastp`:

```r
run_blast <- function(query, db, outfile, blast_path,
evalue="1E-5", max_target_seqs=1000) {

  system(paste0(
      blast_path,
      'blastp -db ',
      db,
      ' -query ',
      query,
      ' -evalue ',
      evalue,
      ' -max_target_seqs ',
      max_target_seqs,
      ' -out ',
      outfile,
      ' -outfmt "6',
      ' qseqid sseqid pident nident length mismatch gapopen gaps
positive ppos qstart qend qlen qcovs qcovhsp sstart send slen
evalue bitscore score"'
                                                        )
                                                 )
}
```

4. Run `blastp` in the first direction:

```r
sceres <- fs::path_package(
  "extdata",
  "sceres_100.fa",
  package = "rbioinfcookbook"
)

spombe <- fs::path_package(
  "extdata",
  "spombe_100.fa",
  package = "rbioinfcookbook"
```

```
)

blast_res_a <- "sp_vs_sc.csv"
make_blastdb(sceres, blast_path)
run_blast(spombe, sceres, blast_res_a, blast_path)
```

5. Run `blastp` in the reciprocal direction:

```
blast_res_b <- "sc_vs_sp.csv"
make_blastdb(spombe, blast_path)
run_blast(sceres, spombe, blast_res_b, blast_path)
```

6. Set up a function to parse the `blastp` output:

```
parse_hits <- function(outfile){
col_names <-
  c(
    "query_id", "subject_id",
    "perc_identity", "num_ident_matches",
    "alig_length", "mismatches",
    "gap_openings", "n_gaps",
    "pos_match", "ppos",
    "q_start", "q_end",
    "q_len", "qcov",
    "qcovhsp", "s_start",
    "s_end", "s_len",
    "evalue", "bit_score",
    "score_raw"
  )

hits <-
  data.table::as.data.table(
    readr::read_delim(
      file = outfile,
      delim = "\t",
      col_names = FALSE,
      col_types = readr::cols(
        "X1" = readr::col_character(), "X2" = readr::col_
character(),
        "X3" = readr::col_double(), "X4" = readr::col_integer(),
        "X5" = readr::col_integer(), "X6" = readr::col_
integer(),
        "X7" = readr::col_integer(), "X8" = readr::col_
integer(),
        "X9" = readr::col_integer(), "X10" = readr::col_
double(),
```

```
        "X11" = readr::col_integer(), "X12" = readr::col_
integer(),
        "X13" = readr::col_integer(),
        "X14" = readr::col_double(),
        "X15" = readr::col_double(),
        "X16" = readr::col_integer(),
        "X17" = readr::col_integer(),
        "X18" = readr::col_integer(),
        "X19" = readr::col_double(),
        "X20" = readr::col_number(),
        "X21" = readr::col_double()
      )
    )
  )

data.table::setnames(x   = hits,
                     old = paste0("X", 1:length(col_names)),
                     new = col_names)

data.table::setkeyv(hits, c("query_id", "subject_id"))
return(hits)
}
```

7. Set up a function to filter the best hits:

```
filter_best_hits <- function(x) {

        min_val <- min(x$evalue)
        evalue <- alig_length <- NULL
        res <- dplyr::filter(x, evalue == min_val)
        if (nrow(res) > 1) {
                max_len <- max(res$alig_length)
                res <- dplyr::filter(res, alig_length == max_
len)
        }

        if (nrow(res) > 1)
                res <- dplyr::slice(res, 1)
        return(res)
}
```

8. Apply the best hit function:

```
sp_sc <- parse_hits(blast_res_a)        |>
  dplyr::group_by(query_id) |>
        dplyr::do(filter_best_hits(.))
sc_sp <- parse_hits(blast_res_b)        |>
  dplyr::group_by(query_id) |>
        dplyr::do(filter_best_hits(.))
```

9. Join the IDs on the reciprocal best hits:

```
colnames(sc_sp)[1:2] <- c("subject_id", "query_id")
rbh <- dplyr::semi_join(
                        sp_sc,
                        sc_sp,
                        by = c("query_id", "subject_id")
)
```

And that is how we set up RBH BLAST searches.

How it works...

Step 1 is a familiar one, and uses a custom function on the `reticulate` package to get the path to the BLAST executables that were installed using conda. *Steps 2* and *3* each show how to build a function that will run a system command – `makeblastdb` and `blastp` respectively. The functions work by pasting together fragments of the relevant commands with the values of variables – notably, `blast_path`, and in *step 3*, some BLAST hit options to limit the number of hits returned and to format the output. The very long output string at the end of the `run_blast()` function does nothing more than say which output columns we want in the BLAST results, despite being very verbose. That code is very wide and doesn't print to the page well, so note that it should be entered *without* any line breaks or carriage returns – don't press *Enter* in the middle of that code if transcribing it.

In *step 4* and *step 5*, we just run the BLAST, using the functions we have created. We extract the sequence files from the data package, and in *step 4*, run S.pombe as a query against an S.cerevisiae database, putting the output into a CSV file. In *step 5*, we run the reciprocal search – S.cerevisiae – against S.pombe again, putting the output into a CSV file for reading in. These steps can take a very long time with whole genomes, especially large ones.

With *step 6*, we define our functions for the processing of the BLAST results. The `parse_hits()` function is simple in concept – it just wants to read the BLAST result's CSV file and return a dataframe-style object – but it goes about it in a fashion that is very robust and efficient computationally, to aid in reading extremely large files. First, `col_names` contains a vector of column names for our hit table, then we use `readr` to read in the data, being very careful to explicitly set the column types we expect to load in. Things can easily go wrong somewhere in big files so this seemingly verbose approach can pay off when something does go a bit awry. The `readr` command is wrapped in a call to `as.data.table()`, which converts the object to a robust `data.table` object, optimized for work on very large dataframes. The `col_names` vector is used to name the columns in the data table and keys for fast indexing by `query_id` and `subject_id`. The function returns the prepared data table.

Step 7 defines a filter function that will find the best hit (by `evalue`) for each query protein in the data table. The function actually only receives a section of the data table – all lines with the same query – at each invocation. So, it works by checking for the hits that have the lowest value of the `evalue` variable in the section of the table. If there are equally low E-values, the one with the longest hit length is returned, and if there is still more than one, it returns the first one found (essentially, a random return).

In *step 8*, we use our `parse` and `filter` functions to load in the BLAST results, grouped by each query, and filter out the best hit for each query. We do this for each direction of BLAST, giving us two data tables of best hits for each direction of BLAST.

Finally, in *step 9*, we use the `semi_join()` function from `dplyr` to join the two data tables on query and subject IDs, keeping only rows that are complements in each. The `rbh` object contains the reciprocal best BLAST hits. Note that this is a selected dataset, so all 100 sequences find their best RBH.

See also

All of the functionality here – and more – is included in the GitHub `"HajkD/orthologr"` package. But it does require a central installation of `BLAST` (specifically for `makeblastdb`), and not just a conda-based one. So, if you're happy doing that and messing with system `PATH` variables, give it a go. To get it working, you'll have to manually install these dependencies from Bioconductor: `Biostrings`, `GenomicRanges`, `GenomicFeatures`, `Rsamtools`, and `rtracklayer`. When it's ready, look for the `blast_rec()` function.

10

Analyzing Gene Annotations

Large-scale model organism sequencing projects, such as the *Human Genome Project* or the *1001 plant genomes* sequencing projects, have made a huge amount of genomics data publicly available. Likewise, open-access data sharing by individual laboratories has made the raw sequencing data of genomes and transcriptomes widely available too. Working with this data programmatically can mean having to parse or bring locally some seriously large or complicated files. Much effort has gone into making these resources as accessible as possible through APIs and other queryable interfaces, such as BioMart. In this chapter, we will look at some recipes that will allow us to search annotations without having to download whole genome files and find relevant information across databases. We'll look at how to analyze those annotations for biologically meaningful patterns in gene or protein sets derived from things such as differential expression and proteomics analysis.

In this chapter, we will cover the following recipes:

- Retrieving gene and genome annotations from BioMart
- Getting Gene Ontology information for functional analysis from appropriate databases
- Using AnnotDB packages for genome annotation
- Using ClusterProfiler for determining GO enrichment in clusters
- Finding GO enrichment in an Ontology Conditional way with topGO
- Finding enriched KEGG pathways
- Retrieving and working with SNPs

Technical requirements

We will use `renv` to manage packages in a project-specific way. To use `renv` to install packages, you will first need to install the `renv` package. You can do this by running the following commands in your R console:

1. Install `renv`:

    ```
    install.packages("renv")
    ```

2. Create a new `renv` environment:

    ```
    renv::init()
    ```

    This will create a new directory called `.renv` in your current project directory.

3. You can then install packages with this:

    ```
    renv::install_packages()
    ```

4. You can also use the `renv` package manager to install Bioconductor packages by running the following command:

    ```
    renv::install("bioc::package name")
    ```

5. For example, to install the `Biobase` package, you would run the following:

    ```
    renv::install("bioc::Biobase")
    ```

6. You can use `renv` to install development packages from GitHub like this:

    ```
    renv::install("user name/repo name")
    ```

7. For example, to install the `danmaclean` user `rbioinfcookbook` package, you would run the following:

    ```
    renv::install("danmaclean/rbioinfcookbook")
    ```

    You can also install multiple packages at once by separating the package names with a comma. The `renv` tool will automatically handle installing any required dependencies for the packages you install.

Under `renv`, all packages will be installed into the local project directory and not the main central library, meaning you can have multiple versions of the same package, one specific one for each project.

All the sample data you need for this package is in the specially created data package on GitHub, `danmaclean/rbioinfcookbook`. The data will become available in your project after installing that.

For this chapter, we'll need the following packages:

- Regular packages:

  - `dplyr`

  - `ggplot2`

  - `readr`

- Bioconductor:

  - `biomaRt`

  - `clusterProfiler`

  - `GO.db`

  - `GOplot`

  - `org.Hs.eg.db`

  - `Rgraphviz`

  - `topGO`

- GitHub:

  - `danmaclean/rbioinfcookbook`

In addition to these packages, we will also need some R tools such as Conda; these will be described when needed.

Further information

Not all the recipes in this section happen in R; some are command-line-based setups. I generally assume a Bash terminal for these bits. Most macOS and Linux machines will have these available in a **Terminal** application. Windows users will likely not need these specific steps, though various packages for running a Linux subsystem on Windows exist if you wish to search them out.

In R, it is normal practice to load a library and use functions directly by name. Although this is great in short interactive sessions, it can cause confusion when many packages are loaded at once and share function names. To clarify which package and function I am using at a given moment, I will occasionally use the `packageName::functionName()` convention.

Sometimes, in the middle of a recipe, I'll interrupt the code to dive into some intermediate output or to look at the structure of an object. When that happens, you'll see a code block where each line begins with ## (double hash symbols). Consider the following command:

```
letters[1:5]
```

This will give us the following output:

```
## a b c d e
```

Note that the output lines are prefixed with ##.

Retrieving gene and genome annotations from BioMart

Once a draft of a genome sequence is prepared, a lot of bioinformatics work goes into finding the genes and other functional features or important loci that are in a genome. These are numerous, difficult to perform and verify, typically take lots of expertise and time, and are not something we would want to repeat. Genome project consortia will typically share their annotations in some way, often through public databases of some sort. BioMart is a common data structure and computational interface through which annotation data is made available. In this recipe, we'll look at how to programmatically access such databases so we can get annotations for genes that we are interested in.

Getting ready

For this recipe, we'll need the `biomaRt` Bioconductor package and a working internet connection. We'll also need to know the BioMart server to connect to – there are about 40 worldwide, providing information about all sorts of genomes. The most widely accessed are the Ensembl databases, and these are the defaults in this package. The code we'll develop will apply to any of the BioMarts with a little modification of table names and URLs as appropriate.

How to do it...

Retrieving gene and genome annotations from BioMart can be done using the following steps:

1. List marts in the selected database, `gramene`:

```
library(biomaRt)
listMarts(host = "https://ensembl.gramene.org")
```

2. Create a connection to the selected mart:

```
gramene_connection <- useMart(biomart = "ENSEMBL_MART_PLANT",
                              host = "https://ensembl.gramene.
org")
```

3. List datasets in that mart:

```
data_sets <- listDatasets(gramene_connection)
head(data_sets)
data_set_connection <- useMart("alyrata_eg_gene",
                               biomart = "ENSEMBL_MART_PLANT",
                               host = "ensembl.gramene.org")
```

4. List the datatypes we can actually get in this dataset:

```
attributes <- listAttributes(data_set_connection)
head(attributes)
```

5. Get a vector of all chromosome names:

```
chrom_names <- getBM(attributes = c("chromosome_name"),
                     mart = data_set_connection )
head(chrom_names)
```

6. Create some filters to query data:

```
filters <- listFilters(data_set_connection)
head(filters)
```

7. Get gene IDs on the first chromosome:

```
first_chr <- chrom_names$chromosome_name[1]

genes <- getBM(attributes = c("ensembl_gene_id", "description"),
               filters = c("chromosome_name"),
               values = c(first_chr),
               mart = data_set_connection )

head(genes)
```

This gives us a list of genes and annotations on the first chromosome.

How it works...

The recipe turns on doing a series of different lookups on the database, each time receiving a little more information to work with.

In *step 1*, after loading the biomaRt library, we get a list of marts available at the host URL. You can change the URL as needed. We get a dataframe of the available marts and use that information in *step 2*, which uses the useMart() function to create a connection to gramene stored in gramene_connection.

In *step 3*, we use the connection to retrieve the datasets available using the listDatasets() function, and we get a result like this:

```
##                  dataset                                      description
          version
## 1      aalpina_eg_gene             Arabis alpina genes (A_alpina_
V4)      A_alpina_V4
## 2   achinensis_eg_gene Actinidia chinensis genes (Red5_PS1_1.69.0)
```

```
Red5_PS1_1.69.0
## 3        acomosus_eg_gene                    Ananas comosus genes
(F153)              F153
## 4        ahalleri_eg_gene          Arabidopsis halleri genes
(Ahal2.2)           Ahal2.2
## 5        alyrata_eg_gene           Arabidopsis lyrata genes
(v.1.0)             v.1.0
## 6 aofficinalis_eg_gene     Asparagus officinalis genes (Aspof.
V1)           Aspof.V1
```

Then, select one of the `alyrata_eg_gene` datasets to use in `useMart()` to create a connection to the dataset, storing the connection in `data_set_connection`.

By the end of *step 4*, we're done working out which datasets we can use. We use `data_set_connection` to connect via `listAttributes()` and get a dataframe of the types of information we can get.

In *step 5*, we finally get some information with the main function, `getBM()`. We set the `attributes` argument to the names of the data we want to get back; here, we get all values for `chromosome_name` and store them in `chrom_names`.

In *step 6*, we set up filters to restrict the values we wish to receive. We first ask the `data_set_connection` object which filters we can use with the `listFilters()` function; note that one we can filter on is `chromosome_name` so we'll use that.

In *step 7*, we set up a full query. We intend to get all genes on the first chromosome –we already have a vector of these in the result of *step 5*, so we take the first element of `chrom_names` and perform the query with `getBM()` asking for the `ensembl_gene_id` and `description` attributes; we set to filter on the chromosome name (any value from the attributes list can be used). We also pass the actual connection object defining the BioMart to use. We get back a dataframe of gene IDs and descriptions filtered to be on the first chromosome.

Getting Gene Ontology information for functional analysis from appropriate databases

The **Gene Ontology (GO)** is a very useful restricted vocabulary of annotation terms for genes and gene products that describe the biological process, molecular function, or cellular component of an annotated entity. As such, the terms are helpful as data in gene-set enrichment analysis and other functional *-omic* approaches. In this recipe, we'll look at how we can prepare a list of gene IDs in a genomic region and get the GO IDs and descriptions for them.

Getting ready

We will just need the `biomaRt` package from Bioconductor and an internet connection.

How to do it...

Getting GO information can be done using the following steps:

1. Make connections to Ensembl BioMart and find attributes:

```
library(biomaRt)
ensembl_connection <- useMart(biomart = "ENSEMBL_MART_ENSEMBL")
listDatasets(ensembl_connection)

data_set_connection <- useMart("hsapiens_gene_ensembl", biomart
= "ENSEMBL_MART_ENSEMBL")

att <- listAttributes(data_set_connection)
fil <- listFilters(data_set_connection)
```

2. Get a list of genes and use their IDs to get GO annotations:

```
genes <- getBM(attributes = c("ensembl_gene_id"),
               filters = c("chromosomal_region"),
               value = c("1:200:2000000:1"),
               mart = data_set_connection)

go_ids <- getBM(attributes = c("ensembl_gene_id",
                                "go_id", "goslim_goa_
description"),
                filters = c("ensembl_gene_id"),
                values = genes$ensembl_gene_id,
                mart = data_set_connection )
```

And that gets us our GO terms for the genes we selected.

How it works...

Step 1 replicates the first few steps of the previous recipe, *Retrieving gene and genome annotations from BioMart*, and involves getting the correct values for connection to BioMart, the datasets, attributes, and filters.

In *step 2*, we use the getBM() function to get ensembl_gene_id attributes in a particular chromosome region, saving the result in the genes object. We then use that function again using ensembl_gene_id as a filter, asking it to return ensembl_gene_id, go_id, and goslim_goa_description to get the actual GO annotation for just the selected genes.

Using AnnoDB packages for genome annotation

Bioconductor AnnoDB packages provide a set of software tools and resources for the annotation and functional analysis of genomic data, including DNA sequences, microarray data, and high throughput sequencing data. These packages are designed to help researchers in the field of genomics to better understand the biological significance of their data by providing them with access to a comprehensive database of biological annotations and functional annotations, such as GO pathway analysis, and functional enrichment analysis.

The Bioconductor AnnoDB packages are designed to work with a wide range of genomic data types from various organisms and are regularly updated to include the latest annotations and functional information. Some of the key features of these packages include tools for mapping genomic data to annotated genomic features, tools for retrieving functional annotations for specific genomic regions, and tools for performing various types of functional analyses. In this recipe, we'll look at how to use an example AnnoDB package to get annotations on the human genome assembly.

Getting ready

We'll need the Bioconductor org.Hs.eg.db and GO.db packages, as well as the rbioinfcookbook and dplyr packages.

How to do it...

Annotating a vector of *H. sapiens* gene symbols goes like this:

1. Load the library and check the available data:

    ```
    library(org.Hs.eg.db)
    columns(org.Hs.eg.db)
    ```

2. Check the searchable keys:

    ```
    keytypes(org.Hs.eg.db)
    ```

3. Get a list of one keytype and search columns:

    ```
    library(rbioinfcookbook)
    annots <- select(org.Hs.eg.db,
            keys = hu_gene_symbols,
            keytype = "SYMBOL",
            columns = c("ALIAS",
                        "GO",
                        "UNIPROT")
            )
    ```

4. Expand the GO annotation:

```
library(GO.db)

go_annots <- select(GO.db,
        keys=annots$GO,
        keytype = "GOID",
        columns = "DEFINITION")
```

5. Combine the two:

```
dplyr::left_join(annots, go_annots, by = c("GO" = "GOID"))
```

And that's how we get annotations from AnnoDB.

How it works...

The neat recipe here starts in *step 1* by loading the AnnotDB package for the organism we're interested in and checking out what type of data it can give us using the `columns()` function, which gives us a return something like this:

```
## [1] "ACCNUM"        "ALIAS"        "ENSEMBL"      "ENSEMBLPROT"
"ENSEMBLTRANS"
## [6]
"ENTREZID"      "ENZYME"       "EVIDENCE"     "EVIDENCEALL"  "GENENAME"
## [11]
"GENETYPE"      "GO"           "GOALL"        "IPI"          "MAP"
## [16]
"OMIM"          "ONTOLOGY"     "ONTOLOGYALL"  "PATH"         "PFAM"
## [21]
"PMID"          "PROSITE"      "REFSEQ"       "SYMBOL"       "UCSCKG"
## [26] "UNIPROT"
```

These entries are really just the column header of all the different data types and are not too verbose. For a description of each, we can use the R help system with one of the values, such as `help("ACCNUM")`, and a description should pop up in the R help window.

In *step 2*, we use the `keytypes()` function to check which keys we can use to query with – these are the sorts of things we'll need to provide to the package to get the other annotations out. It returns this:

```
## [1] "ACCNUM"    "ALIAS"      "ENSEMBL"    "ENSEMBLPROT"  "ENSEMBLTRANS"
## [6] "ENTREZID"  "ENZYME"     "EVIDENCE"   "EVIDENCEALL"  "GENENAME"
## [11] "GENETYPE" "GO"   "GOALL"        "IPI"          "MAP"
## [16] "OMIM"      "ONTOLOGY"   "ONTOLOGYALL"  "PATH"       "PFAM"
## [21] "PMID"      "PROSITE"    "REFSEQ"       "SYMBOL"     "UCSCKG
## [26] "UNIPROT"
```

In this case, this is the same as the columns but needn't always be. Now that we know the data we can get out and the type of data we can query with, we need some values for the query keys, which may often come from your analysis, but for this example, we have the `hu_gene_symbols` data from the `rbioinfcookbook` package that contains a vector of 10 symbols. We apply this in *step 3* using the `select()` function, setting the `keytype` argument to `SYMBOL`, and asking for the `ALIAS`, `GO`, and `UNIPROT` IDs associated with the symbols. Note that the returned `annots` dataframe is over 1,000 rows long, indicating one-to-many relationships in the data, particularly in the GO IDs.

In *step 4*, we expand on the GO annotations; we only received an ID in the previous step, but we really want the full description as well. That wasn't in the `org.Hs.eg.db` output columns so we couldn't retrieve it from that annotation package. We can retrieve it from the specialized GO.db GO package, which uses virtually the same syntax, so *step 4* echoes *step 3* with values for keys from the `annots` object and specific columns selected. Finally, in *step 5*, we combine the two search results into one dataframe.

See also

Bioconductor also provides a resource called `AnnotationHub`, which is a web interface to about 80 different online resources. The `AnnotationHub` package provides functions for accessing the data in them easily and programmatically. The data types covered are much more wide-ranging than those in the AnnotDB packages and searching it can save a lot of processing time.

Using ClusterProfiler for determining GO enrichment in clusters

GO analysis involves the use of ontologies to annotate genes based on their biological function, cellular component, and molecular processes. The GO Consortium provides a controlled vocabulary of terms that describe gene function, and these terms are arranged in a hierarchical structure. It aids in the interpretation of high-throughput genomic data, such as microarray and RNA-seq data, by identifying enriched biological themes and pathways among the differentially expressed genes.

In Bioconductor, GO analysis can be performed using various packages such as `org.Hs.eg.db`, `GOstats`, and `clusterProfiler`. These packages allow the user to map gene identifiers to GO terms and perform statistical tests to identify enriched terms in a set of genes.

In this recipe, we will look at how to go from a set of genes in a generic input to assessing them with plots from different GO-related packages.

Getting ready

For this recipe, we'll need the `clusterProfiler` and `GOplot` Bioconductor packages. We will take a dataframe of expression values for some *Magnaporthe oryzae* genes and a dataframe of full GO annotation in the `rbioinfcookbook` data package.

How to do it...

Performing GO enrichment analysis with `clusterProfiler` goes as follows:

1. Set up the mappings between terms, descriptions, and gene names:

```
library(rbioinfcookbook)
  term2gene <- data.frame(
    term = mo_go$`GO term accession`,
    gene = mo_go$`Gene stable ID`
  )

  term2name <- data.frame(
    term = mo_go$`GO term accession`,
    name = mo_go$`GO term name`
  )

  all_genes <- unique(mo_go$`Gene stable ID`)
```

2. Prepare the gene list to investigate:

```
mo_exp_path <- fs::path_package(
  "extdata",
  "mo_gexp.csv",
  package = "rbioinfcookbook"
)

mo_exp <- readr::read_csv(mo_exp_path)
```

3. Do the enrichment analysis:

```
library(clusterProfiler)
enrich_info <- enricher(mo_exp$gene_id,
                        universe = all_genes,
                        TERM2GENE = term2gene,
                        TERM2NAME = term2name)
```

4. Convert to a dataframe:

```
result_table <- as.data.frame(enrich_info)
```

5. Plot the result:

```
dotplot(enrich_info)
```

6. Convert to DAVID format:

```r
enricher_to_david <- function(enrich,terms){
  comma_sep_genes = gsub("/", ", ", enrich@result$geneID)

  terms <- dplyr::mutate(terms,
    short_category = dplyr::if_else(`GO domain` == 'biological_
process', "BP",
                                    dplyr::if_else(`GO domain`
== "molecular_function", "MF", "CC"))
  )

  id_to_category <- terms$short_category
  names(id_to_category) <- terms$`GO term accession`
  fixed_category <- id_to_category[enrich@result$ID]

  data.frame(
    category = fixed_category,
    ID = enrich@result$ID,
    term = enrich@result$Description,
    genes = comma_sep_genes,
    adj_pval = enrich@result$p.adjust
  )


}

david <- enricher_to_david(enrich_info, mo_go)
```

7. Plot in a `GOplot` plot:

```r
library(GOplot)
expr_info <- data.frame(
  ID = mo_exp$gene_id,
  logFC = mo_exp$log2.fc
)
circ <- circle_dat(david, expr_info)

circ <- circ |> dplyr::mutate(term = substr(term, 1, 20))

GOBubble(circ, labels = 10, display='single', table.legend =
TRUE, ID=TRUE) +
  ggplot2::ylim(0, 330)
```

This gives us a nice GO enrichment representation.

How it works...

Step 1 in such an analysis is to set up some GO term definitions and accession mappings to their relevant genes. In the real world, these annotations can come from lots of places, including Bioconductor annotation packages or downloads from model genome websites and BioMarts. In our example, we have a straightforward annotation already in a dataframe, `mo_go`, that contains gene IDs and their GOs. So, ready for `clusterProfiler`, *step 1* uses that and sets up `term2gene`, which contains only the gene ID and GO term accession, and `term2name`, which contains only the GO term accession and the GO description. We also set up a list of unique gene IDs to represent the entire genome. In *step 2*, we extract the list of genes and expression values to analyze with GO; in real analysis, this would likely come from your experiment directly.

Step 3 is where we get to perform the enrichment analysis; we carry out that using the `clusterProfiler` function called `enricher()`, passing it the data we prepared in *step 1* and the gene IDs from the gene expression dataframe. We get back a complicated `enrichResult` object, but we can view that more nicely using the `as.data.frame()` function, as in *step 4*.

With *step 5*, we can start to visualize the result; the `dotplot()` function gives a nice representation as in *Figure 10.1*, and shows clearly that *calcium ion binding* is enriched in these genes:

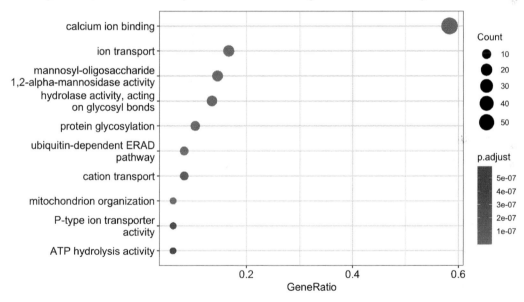

Figure 10.1 – A dot plot representation of a GO analysis

Other packages, such as `GOplot`, offer alternative useful visualizations but need the enrichment result in a different format. In *step 6*, we convert to `DAVID` format by creating a custom function that extracts the gene names from the provided `enrich` object, then converts the term type from words to initials (for example, from `biological_process` to BP) and creates a dataframe from other data in the `enrich` object and returns that. After running that, we move on to *step 7*. To use the `GOBubble()` function, we need to rename the gene ID and expression value columns of our `mo_exp` expression data to `ID` and `logFC`, and prepare a dataframe of the right format from it using the `circle_dat()` function. We pass that the DAVID object and the expression data. We also must trim the GO definitions in the returned `circ` object, as some of them are very long text strings so don't render well in some plot types. Here, with `dplyr::mutate()` and `substr()`, we just take the first 20 characters of the string and use that.

Finally, in *step 7*, we get to plot; we use `GOBubble()` and pass it options to ensure that we get all GO categories in a single panel, the table legend, and that the bubbles are annotated with the GO ID (not the full description). We get a plot as in *Figure 10.2*:

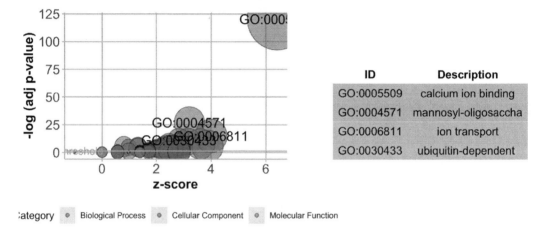

Figure 10.2 – A bubble plot representation of a GO analysis

As we can see, it's a nice representation of the GO terms. It suffers a little for space sometimes, which is why the accompanying table is useful.

Finding GO enrichment in an Ontology Conditional way with topGO

The GO is a hierarchical ontology that describes the biological processes, molecular functions, and cellular components of gene products in a standardized way. The ontology is structured as a **directed acyclic graph (DAG)** with three main categories: **Biological Process (BP)**, **Molecular Function (MF)**, and **Cellular Component (CC)**.

Higher in the GO hierarchy, there are broader terms; for example, in the BP category, terms such as *biological regulation* and *cellular process* exist. As we move down the hierarchy, the terms become more specific and narrower in scope, and *regulation of gene expression* or *protein localization to organelle* are more specific terms within the BP category. Each term has parent terms and child terms.

The hierarchical nature of the GO allows researchers to perform analyses at different levels of specificity. A common need is to *collapse* similar terms into a higher, more general term that captures them all. In this recipe, we'll look at a couple of ways of automating that with the `topGO` package. Specifically, `topGO` implements the hierarchy-aware methods known as `elim` and `parentchild`, as described in *Alexa et al. 2006 (Bioinformatics 22:1600)* and *Grossman et al. 2007 (Bioinformatics 23:3024)*.

Getting ready

For this recipe, we'll need the `topGO` Bioconductor package and some data in the `rbioinfcookbook` package.

How to do it...

Hierarchy-aware GO analysis can be done as follows:

1. Prepare the sets of genes and GO annotations:

```
library(rbioinfcookbook)

mo_ids  <- unique(mo_go$`Gene stable ID`)

geneid2_go <- lapply(mo_ids, function(gene_id){
    df <- dplyr::filter(mo_go, `Gene stable ID` == gene_id)
    unique(df$`GO term accession`)
})

names(geneid2_go) <- mo_ids

mo_exp_path <- fs::path_package(
  "extdata",
  "mo_gexp.csv",
  package = "rbioinfcookbook"
)
mo_exp <- readr::read_csv(mo_exp_path)

gene_list <- factor(as.integer( mo_ids %in% mo_exp$gene_id))
names(gene_list) <- mo_ids
```

2. Build the `topGO` object:

```
library(topGO)

topGO_data <- new("topGOdata",
                  ontology = "MF",
                  allGenes = gene_list,
                  nodeSize = 3,
                  annot = annFUN.gene2GO,
                  gene2GO = geneid2_go
                  )
```

3. Run tests:

```
test_result_elim <- runTest(topGO_data, algorithm = "elim",
statistic = "fisher")
test_result_pc <- runTest(topGO_data, algorithm = "parentchild",
statistic = "fisher")
```

4. Create a `combinedresults` list:

```
results <- GenTable(topGO_data,
                    elim_fisher_pval = test_result_elim,
                    pc_fisher_pval = test_result_pc,
                    orderBy = "elim_fisher_pval",
                    ranksOf="elim_fisher_pval",
                    topNodes = 10)
```

5. Plot the GO trees:

```
showSigOfNodes(topGO_data, score(test_result_elim),
               firstSigNodes = 5,
               useInfo = "all")

showSigOfNodes(topGO_data,
               score(test_result_pc),
               firstSigNodes = 5,
               useInfo = "all")
```

This is all we need to perform the topology-aware GO analysis.

How it works...

The recipe starts off, as many GO analyses do, with the conversion of our data to a new format for analysis. In *step 1*, we take the `mo_go` data object, which contains a data frame of GO annotations of *Magnaporthe oryzae*, and extract the unique IDs to make a vector of all IDs. We then use the `lapply()`

function to loop over all those IDs, and apply `dplyr::filter()` to extract subsets of the GO annotation object, which include the current gene ID and return a vector of GO IDs attached to that gene by collapsing the dataframe column with the GO IDs in. The resulting list, `geneid2go`, contains a mapping in the right format for `topGO`. We next load in a dataframe of IDs and gene expression values and prepare the `sgene_list` object, which must be a named vector of all genes in which the names of the vector are the gene IDs and the values are a factor of `'0'` or `'1'` levels, indicating whether the gene is in the list of interest or not. The code does this by checking logically whether the members of the full gene list (mo_ids) are in the list of interest (mo_exp$gene_id) with `%in%`, then converts that to integers and then a factor, and adds the names to the vector with `names()`.

In *step 2*, we can create the `topGO_data` object using the constructor. We pass `new()` the ontology we're interested in, the list of all genes, and a node size threshold that will only analyze GO IDs with the minimum number of genes (in this case, 3). The `annot` argument gets a constant – a function within the `topGO` package – and `gene2GO` receives the mapping prepared in *step 1*.

By *step 3*, we're all set up and ready to perform statistical tests. The `runTest()` function takes our input data and allows us to define the algorithm and test we want to use. We here first use the `elim` method and the `parentchild` method, analyzing each with Fisher's exact test.

In *step 4*, we combine the results of the tests into a single dataframe for analysis; note that it contains columns of *p*-values for both algorithms and that they give different results.

In *step 5*, we get to visualize the GO tree and each node's level of significance within it. The `firstSigNodes` parameter limits how many significant GO terms to use. The resulting subgraphs are different for each algorithm, as you can see in *Figure 10.3* and *Figure 10.4*:

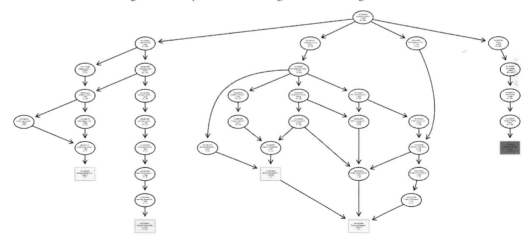

Figure 10.3 – A GO term graph from the elim algorithm

Note the slight difference in the topology of the graph depending on the algorithm:

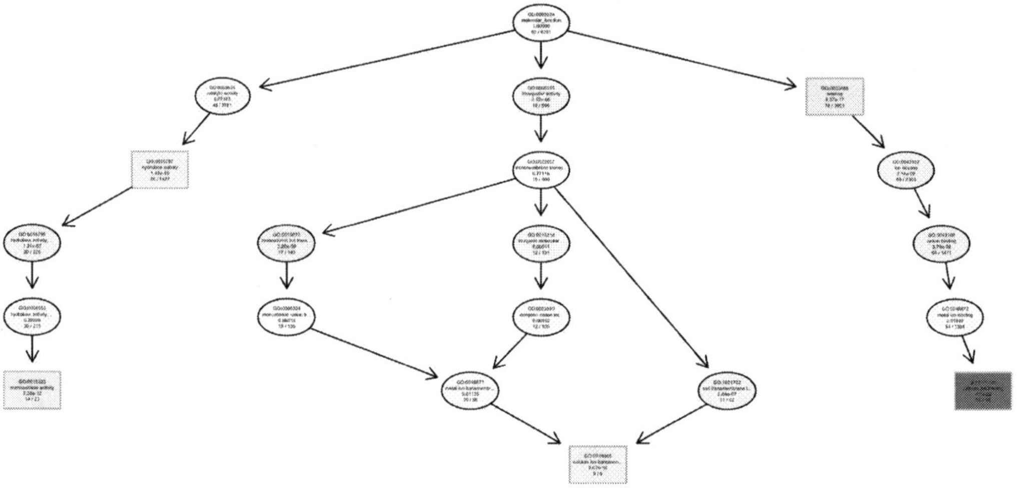

Figure 10.4 – A GO term graph from the parentchild algorithm

In the subgraph, the intensity of color indicates the significance, and the rectangles indicate the significant terms from the analysis. Within each glyph, the GO term info and *p*-value are also shown.

Finding enriched KEGG pathways

Kyoto Encyclopedia of Genes and Genomes (**KEGG**) is a bioinformatics resource that integrates genomic, chemical, and systemic functional information. KEGG contains a comprehensive database of molecular networks that represent various biological systems, such as metabolic pathways, regulatory pathways, and signaling pathways.

KEGG is widely used in bioinformatics analysis to understand the relationships between genes, proteins, and other biomolecules in biological systems. It provides a wealth of information on the molecular mechanisms of various biological processes, such as metabolism, signal transduction, and disease pathways. Researchers can use KEGG to analyze their own datasets, such as gene expression data or protein-protein interaction data, and identify the key pathways that are affected by their experiments.

In this recipe, we'll look at how to examine a gene list derived from experiments in order to find pathways using the free-to-academics website.

Getting ready

We'll use the `clusterProfiler` package and data in the `rbioinfcookbook` package. Some of the code accesses external web resources, so we'll need an active internet connection too.

How to do it...

Searching for enriched pathways in KEGG goes as follows:

1. Find the KEGG code:

```
library(clusterProfiler)
search_kegg_organism('mgr', by='kegg_code')
```

2. Load some genes of interest:

```
library(rbioinfcookbook)
mo_gexp <- fs::path_package(
  "extdata",
  "mo_gexp.csv",
  package="rbioinfcookbook"
)

genes <- readr::read_csv(mo_gexp)
```

3. Perform the enrichment:

```
kegg_result <- enrichKEGG(gene = genes$gene_id, organism="mgr",
pvalueCutoff = 0.05)
as.data.frame(kegg_result)
4. Send the result to the web for visualisation:
browseKEGG(kegg_result,"mgr00513")
```

This is all we need to do for the enrichment of KEGG.

How it works...

This code is a nice variant of the GO enrichment we've already seen, with an important change in *step 1*. Here, we must use KEGG to get a code for our organism of interest. All the codes are listed on the KEGG website at https://www.genome.jp/kegg/catalog/org_list.html. You can also use the search_kegg_organism() function to retrieve information by setting the by option to any of the column names that we get in the output from the function without arguments, as exemplified here:

```
##        kegg_code                      scientific_
name                         common_name
## 599        mgr                     Pyricularia
oryzae                    Pyricularia oryzae
## 1367     mgra                   Mannheimia
granulomatis            Mannheimia granulomatis
## 4015       mgry Magnetospirillum gryphiswaldense MSR-1
Magnetospirillum gryphiswaldense MSR-1
```

```
## 5645        mgro                    Mycobacterium
grossiae                    Mycobacterium grossiae
```

We're looking for `Magnaporthe oryzae` (which is also known as `Pyricularia oryzae`), which we see has the KEGG code of `mgr`.

In *step 2*, we simply create a dataframe of genes of interest from `M.oryzae` for analysis. In *step 3*, we use `enrichKEGG()`, passing it the genes of interest, the KEGG code, and a `p.value` cutoff for the pathways to include. The result can be coerced into a more useful dataframe using `as.dataframe()`.

To visualize the result on the enriched pathway and browse it over the web, we can send `kegg_result` and the pathway ID using the `browseKEGG()` function; the graphic should pop up in a web browser window.

Retrieving and working with SNPs

SNPs and other polymorphisms are important genomic features and we of the want to retrieve know SNPs in particular genomic regions. In this recipe, we will look at doing that in two different BioMarts that hold different types of data. In the first part, we'll use `gramene` to look a retrieving plant SNPs. In the second part, we'll look at how to find information on human SNPs in the main Ensembl database.

Getting ready

As before, we'll need only the `biomaRt` package from Bioconductor and a working internet connection.

How to do it...

Retrieving and working with SNPs can be done using the following steps:

1. Get the list of datasets, attributes, and filters from `gramene`:

```
library(biomaRt)
listMarts(host = "https://ensembl.gramene.org")
gramene_connection <- useMart(biomart = "ENSEMBL_MART_PLANT_
SNP",
                                host = "https://ensembl.gramene.
org")
listDatasets(gramene_connection)
data_set_connection <- useMart("athaliana_eg_snp",
                                biomart = "ENSEMBL_MART_PLANT_
SNP",
                                host = "https://ensembl.gramene.
org")

listAttributes(data_set_connection)
listFilters(data_set_connection)
```

2. Query for the actual SNP information:

```
snps <- getBM(attributes = c("refsnp_id", "chr_name",
                             "chrom_start", "chrom_end"),
              filters = c("chromosomal_region"),
              values = c("1:200:200000:1"),
              mart = data_set_connection
              )
```

This will retrieve the SNPs specified.

How it works...

Step 1 follows the pattern established in the *Retrieving gene and genome annotations from BioMart* recipe at the start of this chapter, in which we made the initial connections with `listMarts()`.

This looks as follows:

```
##                      biomart                    version
## 1      ENSEMBL_MART_PLANT              Plant Genes 66
## 2 ENSEMBL_MART_PLANT_SNP Plant Variation Mart 66
```

We then use them to list the datasets, `listDatasets()`. The *Arabidopsis* `"athaliana_eg_snp"` dataset is used. We use the `list...()` functions to show the filters and attributes we can use and retrieve and pass values from those searches as needed to the `getBM()` function to perform the search. The `chromosomal_region` filter allows us to specify a value describing a particular locus on the genome, the `value` argument gets a `'Chromosome:Start:Stop:Strand'` formatted string – specifically, `'1:200:20000:1'`, which will return all SNPs on chromosome 1, between nucleotides 200 and 20,000 on the positive strand (note the negative strand is `'-1'`).

There's more...

Finding human SNPs from Ensembl follows pretty much the same pattern. The only difference is that, because Ensembl is the default server, we can omit the server information from the `useMart()` function. A similar query for human SNPs would look like this:

```
data_set_connection <- useMart("hsapiens_snp", biomart="ENSEMBL_MART_
SNP")
snps <- getBM(attributes = c("refsnp_id", "chr_name",
                             "chrom_start", "chrom_end"),
              filters = c("chromosomal_region"),
              values = c("1:200:200000:1"),
              mart = data_set_connection
              )
```

The preceding code would return data as described in the main steps.

11
Machine Learning with mlr3

Machine learning (**ML**) is a broad term that covers a wide range of bioinformatic and data science activities including, regression, classification, and data clustering.

The mlr3 package is an open source ML framework for the R programming language. It is designed to provide a unified and efficient interface for building, evaluating, and comparing ML models. mlr3 is built on top of the mlr package, which is one of the most popular ML packages in R.

mlr3 follows a modular design, which means that different components of the ML process, such as data preprocessing, feature selection, model training, and model evaluation, are separated into individual objects. This design allows for greater flexibility and modularity, enabling users to easily customize and extend the functionality of the framework. We will look at this framework through consecutive classification and test steps in this chapter.

In this chapter, we will cover the following recipes:

- Defining a task and learner to implement **k-nearest neighbors** (**k-NN**) in mlr3
- Testing the fit of the model using cross-validation
- Using logistic regression to optimize parameters in a model to classify based on the relative likelihoods of two outcomes
- Classifying using random forest and interpreting it with iml
- Dimension reduction with PCA in ml3 pipelines
- Creating a tSNE and UMAP embedding
- Clustering with k-means and hierarchical clustering

Technical requirements

We will use `renv` to manage packages in a project-specific way. To use `renv` to install packages, you will first need to install the `renv` package. You can do this by running the following commands in your R console:

1. Install `renv`:

    ```
    install.packages("renv")
    ```

2. Create a new `renv` environment:

    ```
    renv::init()
    ```

    This will create a new directory called `.renv` in your current project directory.

    You can then install packages with the following:

    ```
    renv::install_packages()
    ```

3. You can also use the `renv` package manager to install Bioconductor packages by running the following command:

    ```
    renv::install("bioc::package name")
    ```

4. For example, to install the `Biobase` package, you would run the following:

    ```
    renv::install("bioc::Biobase")
    ```

5. You can use `renv` to install development packages from GitHub by writing this:

    ```
    renv::install("user name/repo name")
    ```

6. For example, to install the user `danmaclean` package `rbioinfcookbook`, you would run:

    ```
    renv::install("danmaclean/rbioinfcookbook")
    ```

You can also install multiple packages at once by separating the package names using commas. `renv` will automatically handle installing any required dependencies for the packages you install.

Under `renv`, all packages will be installed into the local project directory and not the main central library, meaning you can have multiple versions of the same package, one specific to each project.

All the sample data you need for this package is in the specially created data package on GitHub: `danmaclean/rbioinfcookbook`. The data will become available in your project after installing that.

For this chapter, we'll need the following packages:

- Regular packages:

  - `DALEXtra`
  - `dplyr`
  - `factoextra`
  - `ggplot2`
  - `iml`
  - `magrittr`
  - `mlbench`
  - `mlr3`
  - `mlr3learners`
  - `mlr3pipelines`
  - `mlr3tunining`
  - `mlr3viz`
  - `palmerpenguins`
  - `purrr`
  - `RColorBrewer`
  - `Rtsne`
  - `tibble`
  - `tidyr`
  - `umap`

- Bioconductor:

  - `Biobase`

- GitHub:

  - `danmaclean/rbioinfcookbook`

In addition to these packages, we will also need some R tools, such as Conda. All of these will be described when needed.

Further information

Not all the recipes in this section happen in R; some are command line-based setups. I generally use a bash terminal for these bits. Most macOS and Linux machines will have these available in a terminal application. Windows users will likely not need to follow these specific steps, though various packages for running a Linux subsystem on Windows exist if you wish to search them out.

In R, it is standard practice to load a library and use functions directly by name. Although this is great in short interactive sessions, it can cause confusion when many packages are loaded at once and share function names. To clarify which package and function I am using at a given moment, I will occasionally use the `packageName::functionName()` convention.

Sometimes in the middle of a recipe, I'll interrupt the code to dive into some intermediate output or to look at the structure of an object. When that happens, you'll see a code block where each line begins with ## (double hash symbols). Consider the following command:

```
letters[1:5]
```

This will give us the following output:

```
## a b c d e
```

Note that the output lines are prefixed with ##.

Defining a task and learner to implement k-nearest neighbors (k-NNs) in mlr3

The **k-nearest neighbors** (**k-NN**) classification is a non-parametric ML algorithm used for classifying data points based on their proximity to other labeled data points. The algorithm determines the class membership of an unlabeled data point by examining the classes of its k-NNs in the feature space. The dataset consists of labeled data points, where each data point has a set of features (attributes) and belongs to a specific class or category. The value of k represents the number of nearest neighbors to consider for classification. It is typically chosen based on cross-validation or other model selection techniques. The algorithm measures the distance between the unlabeled data point and all the labeled data points in the feature space. The most commonly used distance metric is Euclidean distance. The k data points with the shortest distances to the unlabeled point are identified as its nearest neighbors. The algorithm assigns the class label that is most prevalent among the k-NNs to the unlabeled data point. It is a good first algorithm to try when predicting classes in a supervised manner.

The `mlr3` package in R provides a framework for efficiently carrying out many ML tasks, including k-NN. The package allows us to define a task object that describes the data we wish to train models on and create a learner object that defines parameters such as training/test sets and on which sets we can train a model. The package allows us to use the trained learner object with test splits and provides performance measures to evaluate the model.

In this recipe, we'll use `mlr3` to build a classifier for breast cancer tumor data. A set of measurements have been taken from tumors identified as either benign or malignant.

Getting ready

For this recipe, we will need to install the `mlr3`, `kknn`, and `mlr3viz` packages. We will use the `BreastCancer` object from the ML specific data package `mlbench`.

How to do it...

Here's how we begin classifying using kNN with `mlr3`:

1. Load the data and set up the task:

```
library(mlr3)
library(mlr3viz)
library(mlbench)
data("BreastCancer")

selected <- BreastCancer[c("Cl.thickness", "Cell.size", "Cell.
shape",
                           "Marg.adhesion", "Epith.c.size", "Bl.
cromatin",
                           "Normal.nucleoli", "Mitoses", "Class"
                           )]

task <- as_task_classif(selected, target="Class")
autoplot(task)
```

2. Set up the learner:

```
library(mlr3learners)
learner <- lrn("classif.kknn") #install "kknn" package
learner

learner$param_set$set_values(k = 4)
learner
```

3. Specify the train/test data partition:

```
split <- partition(task, ratio=0.8)
```

4. Train the model:

```
learner$train(task, split$train)
learner$model
```

5. Predict on the test data:

```
predictions <- learner$predict(task, split$test)
predictions
autoplot(predictions)
```

6. Specify some measures and assess the model:

```
measures <- msrs(c("classif.precision", "classif.specificity",
"classif.sensitivity"))
predictions$score(measures)
```

From this code, we see we have trained a machine learning model and assessed it.

How it works...

The first part of any data analysis is to clean the dataset. Even though this is a recipe, we still have to do that here. *Step 1* loads the packages we will need and the `BreastCancer` dataset. Some of the columns in `BreastCancer` contain NA values and character data that we can't use, so we select the numeric and factor data columns we need. Then, we use `mlr3::as_task_classif()` to set up the `task` object—this is essentially the dataset wrapped up so that it can be used by other `mlr3` functions. The object knows the sort of task (classification) that is to be carried out with it, so it can warn you if you try to do something inapplicable later. The `autoplot()` function generates a plot of the target data for us, as seen in *Figure 11.1*:

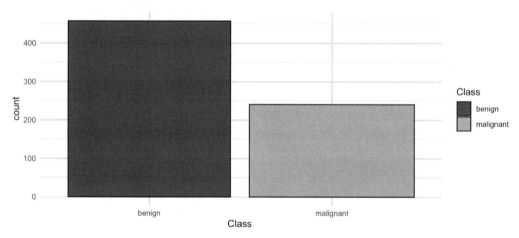

Figure 11.1 – A visualization of the classes in the target of our BreastCancer data

In *step 2*, we specify the learner: the type of ML we will be doing. `mlr3` has roughly two types of learners—classifiers and regressions. The `lrn()` function helps us create this object, but there are only a couple of built-in learners. We must first load the accessory package `mlr3learners` to access a wider range, selecting `classif.kknn` to use the k-NN implementation in the `kknn` package (which also must be installed manually). If we inspect the `learner` object as created by default, we see the following:

```
## <LearnerClassifKKNN:classif.kknn>
## * Model: list
## * Parameters: k=7
## * Packages: mlr3, mlr3learners, kknn
## * Predict Types:  [response], prob
## * Feature Types: logical, integer, numeric, factor, ordered
## * Properties: multiclass, twoclass
```

There is useful information, such as the feature types and the prediction types we can make, that we can use to train a model like this. Inspecting the object is also a quick way to see the parameters we can set. Here, we see that the only parameter for k-NN is `k`, and at the moment it is set to 7. So, we alter the value of `k` using the `$` syntax. Its usage here may be a little unfamiliar to you, so just think of this as meaning that the function we need is stored in the object itself and the `$` lets us drill down to it. This means that the function is automatically set on the object we use it on, that is, `learner`. After using the `learner$param_set$set_values()` function to set k to 4, we see that the contents of the learner are different:

```
## <LearnerClassifKKNN:classif.kknn>
## * Model: list
## * Parameters: k=4
## * Packages: mlr3, mlr3learners, kknn
## * Predict Types:  [response], prob
## * Feature Types: logical, integer, numeric, factor, ordered
## * Properties: multiclass, twoclass
```

In *step 3*, we use the `partition()` function to set up the test/training split of the data. The `ratio` argument sets the proportion of the data to use in training. A random split is made and the row numbers of the set that each row is assigned to are saved.

In *step 4*, we're ready to go. We just have to ask the `learner` object to train itself, which we do with the `$train()` function, passing it the preformed `task` and `split$train` data. We can inspect the model produced here using the `learner$model()` function.

In *step 5*, we can use our newly trained learner to make some predictions on the test set. The `learner$predict()` function takes the task and the test split. We can visualize the result of the test comparing the ground truth against the model prediction using the `autoplot()` function with the predictions, as seen in *Figure 11.2*:

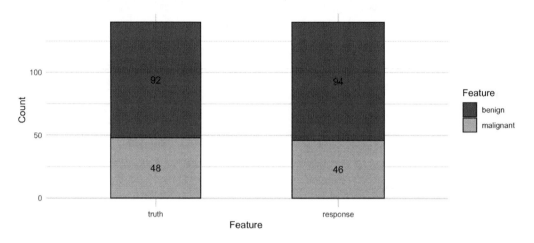

Figure 11.2 – A comparison of predictions from the model against the ground truth

We can improve our evaluation of the model by looking at specific measures of success. In *step 6*, we use the `msrs()` function to select some measures and ask the `predictions` object to use its `$score` function on itself to print accuracy, sensitivity, and specificity.

There's more...

We can get more information on the task data from `autoplot()` using the `type` argument by setting it to `pairs` like so:

```
autoplot(task, type = "pairs")
```

This will return a richer pairwise comparison of the data types.

The types of learners can be listed as follows:

```
mlr_learners$keys()
```

The types of measures can be listed in this manner:

```
mlr_measures$keys("classif")
```

This gives us a nice little set of diagnostics for our object.

See also...

Neural networks are another type of learner that we can use in `mlr3`. There are two broad types: the artificial shallow neural networks and the deep, multi-layer neural networks. The first sort, shallow neural networks, have been around for a very long time, have good implementation in `mlr3`, and can be used as just another type of learner in the way that k-NN was used in this recipe. The deep neural networks are very different, need a lot of computational resources, and require the external **Keras** libraries to work. The interface between Keras and `mlr3` is still in the early stages of development and the authors warn that it is unstable. If I tried to write a recipe about it, there's a strong chance it would be out of date very quickly. If you really want to try **Keras** learners in `mlr3`, you can find them in the `mlr3keras` package here: `https://github.com/mlr-org/mlr3keras`. If you do give it a go and have opinions on it, why not let the developers know what you think and assist in the package development?

Testing the fit of the model using cross-validation

Cross-validation provides a reliable estimate of a model's performance on unseen data. Simulating the model's performance on multiple subsets of the data reduces the effect of random variations in the training and testing data splits, providing a more realistic assessment of its generalizability.

K-fold cross-validation involves dividing a dataset into K equally-sized subsets, or folds, where K is a predefined number typically chosen between 5 and 10. The original dataset is randomly partitioned into K subsets of approximately equal size (folds), and a model is trained on K-1 folds and evaluated on the fold left out. This means that K-separate model training and evaluation cycles are performed. The performance values from the K iterations are then averaged to obtain a single metric that represents the overall performance.

Leave-one-out (**LOO**) cross-validation is a variant of cross-validation where the number of folds is equal to the number of samples in the dataset. In this technique, for each fold, a single sample is withheld as the test set and the remaining samples are used to train the model. This process is repeated for all samples in the dataset, and the performance of the model is evaluated based on the aggregated results. It is particularly useful when working with small datasets where the number of samples is limited.

In this recipe, we'll look at how to implement these schemes in `mlr3`.

Getting ready

For this recipe, we'll use the `mlr3` package, its accessory package `mlr3learners`, and the data package `mlrbench`. We'll also need to install the `mlr3` dependency `kknn` manually.

How to do it...

Cross-validation can be done as follows:

1. Set up the task and learner:

    ```
    library(mlr3)
    library(mlbench)
    library(mlr3learners)
    data("BreastCancer")

    selected <- BreastCancer[c("Cl.thickness", "Cell.size", "Cell.
    shape",
                                "Marg.adhesion", "Epith.c.size", "Bl.
    cromatin",
                                "Normal.nucleoli", "Mitoses", "Class"
                                )]

    task <- as_task_classif(selected, target="Class")
    learner <- lrn("classif.kknn") #install "kknn" package
    learner$param_set$set_values(k = 4)
    ```

2. Set up the resampling object:

    ```
    resamp_kcv <- rsmp("cv")
    resamp_kcv$param_set$values = list(folds = 3)
    ```

3. Perform the resampling experiment:

    ```
    result_kcv <- resample(task, learner, resamp_kcv)
    ```

4. Assess the iterations:

    ```
    measures <- msrs(c("classif.precision", "classif.specificity",
    "classif.sensitivity"))
    result_kcv$score(measures)
    ```

5. Examine the aggregated predictions:

    ```
    pred_kcv<- result_kcv$prediction()
    pred_kcv$confusion
    ```

6. Use the same task and learner in a different validation scheme:

    ```
    resamp_loo <- rsmp("loo")
    result_loo <- resample(task, learner, resamp_loo)
    result_loo$score(measures)
    ```

That's all we need to cross cross-validate the model.

How it works...

Recalling that the aim in this recipe is to assess the generalizability of a model to wider data sets, we begin in *step 1* by setting up the same task (i.e. the `BreastCancer` data) as in the *Defining a task and learner to implement k-nearest neighbors (k-NNs) in mlr3* recipe, and the same learner with the same parameters.

In *step 2*, we can set up the resampling scheme, defining the type with the `rsmp()` function, passing it the value `"cv"` for `'cross-validation'` and using the `$param_set` method to set the number of folds. We will do three folds.

We perform the resampling in *step 3* using the `resample()` function. The returned `result_kcv` object carries the resulting predictions from each of the folds that were done. If we print the object we can also see if any errors or warnings were generated during that process.

Now that the resampling is performed, we can assess the differences between all the different sets of models produced here as we did previously for a single model. In *step 4*, we create a vector of measures to look at from the `msrs()` function and pass them to the `result_kcv$score()` method. The right-hand side of the output looks something like the following (though note that randomness within the selection process and the algorithm itself will mean there are variations):

```
## iteration classif.precision classif.specificity classif.sensitivity
## 1              0.9565217           0.9041096           0.9625000
## 2              0.9183673           0.8695652           0.9574468
## 3              0.9622642           0.9210526           0.9745223
```

In these folds, it looks like the metrics are usually quite close together. Though specificity varies somewhat, the second fold is a distance behind. Together, these give us a view of the general usefulness of our model, it does seem to be a bit data-dependent from this, which is usually a feature of a model we would want to avoid.

In *step 5*, we use the `$prediction()` method to get a combined prediction over all models, printing the resulting confusion matrix, which looks as follows:

```
##              truth
## response     benign malignant
##   benign        444        30
##   malignant      14       211
```

The next thing to do is to repeat the evaluation using a different resampling technique. In *step 6*, we use LOO quite easily, recycling the task and learner and measuring objects. We really just have to respecify the resampler using `rsmp()` and rerun it. Everything else is the same. We get a similar output table, though note that some of the metrics we chose to score don't make as much sense as they are proportional. This means you get some NA when working on single rows as in LOO.

The approach of `mlr3` is shown well in this recipe. The modular object-based design allows us to try new metrics easily.

There's more...

For the `rsmp()` function we used in *steps 2* and *6*, we seemed to pull the values for the different resampling schemes out of nowhere (`"cv"` and `"loo"`). The `mlr_resamplings` dictionary shows a full list of all that are implemented in the package.

Using logistic regression to classify the relative likelihood of two outcomes

Logistic regression is a statistical modeling technique used to predict categorical outcomes, particularly in binary classification situations where the outcome can take one of two possible values. It aims to find the relationship between a set of input variables and the probability of a certain outcome occurring. Logistic regression estimates the relationship between these input variables and the probability of the outcome. It tries to find the best-fit line or curve that represents this relationship. Unlike linear regression, which predicts continuous values, logistic regression predicts the probability of a specific outcome. We set a probability threshold (usually 0.5) to decide the class label. If the predicted probability is above the threshold, the outcome is predicted as one class, and if it is below the threshold, the outcome is predicted as the other class. Once the model is trained, it can be used to predict the outcome for new instances by calculating the probabilities based on the input variables and applying the probability threshold.

The logistic regression model is trained using maximum likelihood estimation, which finds the optimal coefficients for the input variables that maximize the likelihood of the observed outcomes based on the predicted probabilities. This method takes more parameters than the simple k-NN we've used previously, so we will also take advantage of mlr3's tuner objects, which let us iterate through various values to find the best set for our data. That will be the object of this lesson: to assess the model performance at different parameter values so that we can find the best combinations with which to build a final model.

Getting ready

For this recipe, we'll use the `mlr3` package, it's accessory packages `mlr3learners`, `mlr3viz`, and `mlr3tuning`, and the data package `mlrbench`.

How to do it...

Performing a logistic regression and optimizing it using tuner objects can be done as follows:

1. Set up the task, learner, and resampler:

```
library(mlr3)
library(mlbench)
library(mlr3learners)
data("BreastCancer")

selected <- BreastCancer[c("Cl.thickness", "Cell.size", "Cell.
shape","Marg.adhesion", "Epith.c.size", "Bl.cromatin","Normal.
nucleoli", "Mitoses", "Class")]

task <- as_task_classif(selected, target="Class")
learner <- lrn("classif.log_reg")
resamp_kcv <- rsmp("cv")
resamp_kcv$param_set$values = list(folds = 3)
measure <- msr("classif.acc")
```

2. Inspect the parameters we can optimize:

```
as.data.table(learner$param_set)
```

3. Set dynamic limits on parameters:

```
library(mlr3tuning)
learner$param_set$set_values(epsilon = to_tune(0, 10),
                             maxit = to_tune(1, 10) )
```

4. Decide how the optimization task should terminate:

```
terminate <- trm("run_time", secs = 5)
```

5. Compile the information into a tuning problem object:

```
tunit <- ti(
  task = task,
  learner = learner,
  resampling = resamp_kcv,
  measures = measure,
  terminator = terminate
)
```

6. Run the tuner:

```
tuner <- tnr("random_search")
tuner$optimize(tunit)
tunit$result
```

7. Plot the result metric against the values of the parameters chosen:

```
library(mlr3viz)
autoplot(tunit)
```

This code lets us build and evaluate the logistic regression.

How it works...

This recipe condenses the familiar creation of the task, learner, resampling strategy, and evaluation measure into *step 1*. The data are loaded and the objects are created, specifying a logistic regression classif.log_reg learner and a three-fold cross-validation resampling strategy (cv). The measure on which we will assess the models is singular and specified by the msr() function as classification accuracy (classif.acc). All these will be used repeatedly as we go through the different values of parameters for the logistic regression learner.

With the learner set up, we can examine it to see what parameters could be optimized. We do that in *step 2* by coercing the object to a data.table object. The output (truncated a little) looks like this:

```
##                id    class lower upper       levels nlevels is_bounded
special_vals
## 1:   dispersion
ParamUty    NA    NA                 Inf       FALSE    <list[0]>
## 2:       epsilon
ParamDbl  -Inf   Inf                 Inf       FALSE    <list[0]>
## 3:      etastart
ParamUty    NA    NA                 Inf       FALSE    <list[0]>
## 4:         maxit ParamDbl  -Inf   Inf
```

We can see that the epsilon and maxit parameters are numeric double parameters ParamDbl and can take values from +/- infinity. We will optimize those in this example.

In *step 3*, we load the package mlr3tuning to access tuning/optimization objects and functions and set up the selected parameters in the learner object using learner$param_sets$set_values(), to which we pass the range of possible values we wish to store using to_tune() functions. This means the values here will be changed each run according to our chosen optimization scheme, which will be defined later.

In *step 4*, we need to define when the optimization will terminate. Optimizations can run over many thousands of combinations of parameters, so it's a good idea to decide how it should end. In mlr3, terminator objects define the stopping criteria. We use the `trm()` function with the `run_time` criteria set to five seconds for this brief example. Many other stopping criteria, including *n* iterations and failure to improve after *n* attempts, can be set up. Check the `mlr3` terminator documentation for a list.

By *step 5*, we have all the information needed to define the task to be run at each tuning/optimization step. The objects we've created are compiled using the `ti()` into a container called a tuning problem that represents the whole set of things we need to build and tune the learner.

The tuning/optimization strategy is decided next. There are many ways to vary the values of the parameters. We can choose to do it completely at random, via a structured grid search that tries every value in a range, or follow genetic/evolutionary strategies that explore the space in a targeted way. `mlr3` has many built-in strategies. For simplicity in this example, in *step 6*, we set up the tuner using the `tnr` function set to randomly search. We then call the `optimize()` function on the `tuner` object, which runs the optimization on the `tunit` tuning problem we set up. The stopping criterion was to stop after five seconds, so the optimization should be over quickly. When it is done, the best model score metric is stored in the optimized tuning problem under `tunit$result`, giving us an idea of the performance of the models.

In order to see the effect of the values of the parameters on the performance metric, we can use the `autoplot()` function to generate a basic visualization. In *step 7*, we pass the `tunit` object to the plotter and get something similar to *Figure 11.3*:

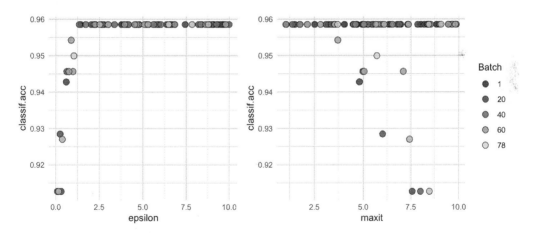

Figure 11.3 – A visualization of the effect of varying the values
of two parameters in a learner on classification accuracy

We can see the values of the parameters that give the best classification accuracy, and we can use the values in subsequent model builds.

See also

We selected a simple optimization strategy here. There are other more involved and perhaps more applicable ones. Check out the documentation at `https://mlr3book.mlr-org.com/optimization.html`.

Classifying using random forest and interpreting it with iml

Random forest is a versatile ML algorithm that can be used for both regression and classification tasks. It is an ensemble learning method that combines multiple decision trees to make predictions. Decision trees split the data based on the values of features to create subsets with similar target variable values. Random forest combines multiple decision trees to create a more robust and accurate model. The algorithm randomly selects a subset of the training data (bootstrapping) and a subset of features at each tree's node to create a diverse set of decision trees. The random subsets of the training data are used to train individual decision trees in the forest. The bootstrapping technique allows each tree to see a slightly different variation of the data, reducing the risk of overfitting.

Random forest assesses feature (variable) importance by evaluating how much each feature contributes to reducing error in the model. The feature importance values are calculated based on the average error weighted by the probability of reaching that node. We can use this to interpret the model and assess which features are most informative. Model effectiveness can also be visualized with the **receiver operating characteristic** (**ROC**) curve. This is a graphical representation used to assess the performance of a binary classification model. It illustrates the trade-off between the true positive rate and the false positive rate at various classification thresholds and provides insights into the model's ability to discriminate between positive and negative classes, regardless of the chosen classification threshold. It allows you to assess the model's sensitivity to different levels of specificity.

In this recipe, we'll build a `RandomForest` model in mlr3 in the way that we've done before and look at how to perform a feature importance analysis and develop the ROC curve.

Getting ready

We'll need the `mlr3`, `mlr3learners`, `mlrbench`, and `ranger` packages to build the model. We'll also need the `iml` and `DALEXtra` packages to run the model through feature importance and ROC curves.

How to do it...

We begin building a `RandomForest` as follows:

1. Load the data and train learners:

    ```
    library(mlr3)
    library(mlr3learners)
    library(mlbench)
    data("BreastCancer")

    selected <- BreastCancer[c("Cl.thickness", "Cell.size", "Cell.
    shape",
                                "Marg.adhesion", "Epith.c.size", "Bl.
    cromatin",
                                "Normal.nucleoli", "Mitoses", "Class"
                                )]

    task <- as_task_classif(selected, target="Class")
    split <- partition(task, ratio=0.5)

    learner <- lrn("classif.ranger", predict_type = "prob")
    ##install ranger
    learner$train(task, row_ids = split$train)
    ```

2. Demonstrate the prediction using the trained learner:

    ```
    predict(learner, selected[1:5,] )
    ```

3. Build a standard `iml` predictor object:

    ```
    library(iml)
    cancer_x <- task$data(rows = split$train, cols = task$feature_
    names)
    cancer_y <- task$data(rows = split$train, cols = task$target_
    names)
    predictor <- Predictor$new(learner, data = cancer_x, y =
    cancer_y)
    ```

4. Run the feature importance analysis:

    ```
    imp <- FeatureImp$new(predictor, loss="ce")
    imp$plot()
    ```

5. Run the ROC analysis:

```
library(DALEXtra)
model <- explain_mlr3(learner,
                      data = cancer_x,
                      y = as.numeric(cancer_y$Class ==
"malignant"))
mod_perf <- model_performance(model)
mod_perf
plot(mod_perf, geom = "roc")
```

This code builds the model and gives us a feature analysis.

How it works...

In *step 1*, we carry out the familiar data cleaning and task definition processes before building the trained model in the `learner` object. You can read about this in more detail in the first recipe in this chapter *Defining a task and learner to implement k-nearest neighbors (k-NNs) in mlr3*. *Step 2* is a quick demonstration of how to use the `predict()` function to use the model to classify unseen data. Here, we simply pass it the model in `learner` and a new set of data formatted like that which the model was trained on. In this case, we use a small subset of the data the model was trained on. The result is a simple vector of class names:

```
## [1] benign    malignant benign    malignant benign
## Levels: benign malignant
```

The next objective is to perform feature importance analysis. We have decided to use the nice methods in the `iml` package, but that means we need to get our current model and data into the right shape for that. *Step 3* does this, creating two reformats of our training data and saving them in the variables `cancer_x` and `cancer_y`. These can then be passed to the `Predictor` constructor of `iml` along with the model in `learner` that creates the `predictor` object.

In *step 4*, we can run and plot the feature importance analysis using the `FeatureImp$new()` function, then run the `plot()` method on the resulting `imp` object. That gives us *Figure 11.4*:

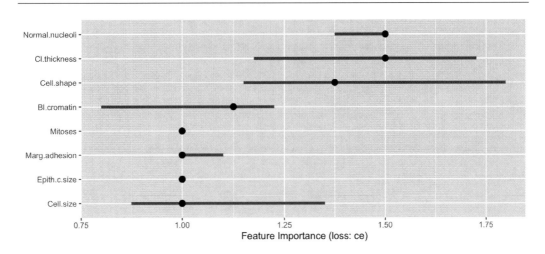

Figure 11.4 – A feature importance plot on the RandomForest model of the BreastCancer data

By *step 5*, we can move on to the ROC curve, which is done with methods from the DALEXtra package. Again, we first need to reformat the data, as we do in explain_mlr3() function. We can inspect the model object to get a summary of performance that looks like this:

```
## Preparation of a new explainer is initiated
##    -> model label      :  R6  (  default  )
##    -> data             :  209  rows  8  cols
##    -> target variable  :  209  values
##    -> predict function :  yhat.LearnerClassif  will be used
(  default  )
##    -> predicted values :  No value for predict function target
column. (  default  )
##    -> model_info       :  package mlr3 , ver. 0.16.0 , task
classification (  default  )
##    -> predicted values :  numerical, min =  9.428846e-05 , mean
=  0.3414915 , max =  1
##    -> residual function :  difference between y and yhat
(  default  )
##    -> residuals        :  numerical, min =  -0.7269598 , mean
=  0.003006121 , max =  0.8061695
##   A new explainer has been created!
## Measures for:  classification
## recall     : 0.9861111
## precision  : 0.9594595
## f1         : 0.9726027
## accuracy   : 0.9808612
## auc        : 0.9984286
```

The resulting `model` object can now be passed to the `model_performance()` function and the result of that can be passed to the generic `plot()` function, specifying the `roc` geom. The resulting plot looks similar to *Figure 11.5*:

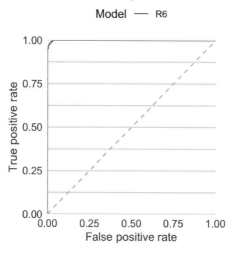

Figure 11.5 – A ROC curve on the RandomForest model of the BreastCancer data

The plot is the ROC curve we were hoping to see.

Dimension reduction with PCA in mlr3 pipelines

Principal Component Analysis (**PCA**) is a dimensionality reduction technique commonly used in bioinformatics to analyze and interpret high-dimensional biological data, such as gene expression data, protein profiles, or genomic data.

The main goal of PCA is to find a lower-dimensional representation of the data while preserving the most important patterns and variability present in the original data. It achieves this by transforming the data into a new set of uncorrelated variables called principal components. These principal components are ordered in such a way that the first component captures the maximum amount of variance in the data, the second component captures the second maximum variance, and so on.

PCA is useful in bioinformatics for various applications, including visualization, as it reduces data to two or three dimensions for use in plots. PCA has an important role in feature selection in ML, as it can be used to select the most informative features (genes, proteins, etc.) in a training set by assessing their contributions to the principal components. This helps in reducing the dimensionality of the data while retaining the most relevant variables and making the task more computationally tractable.

In this recipe, we'll look at how to build a pre-processing step such as PCA into an `mlr3` pipeline rather than as an external step.

Getting ready

For this recipe, we'll use the `mlr3` package, it's accessory packages `mlr3learners`, `mlr3pipelines`, and `mlr3tuning`, and the data package `mlrbench`. We'll also need the `magrittr` package.

How to do it...

To build a pipeline with a PCA preprocessing step, we proceed as follows:

1. Build the pipeline component for scaling and PCA:

```
library(mlr3pipelines)
scale <- po("scale")
pca <- po("pca")
```

2. Build the start of the pipeline:

```
library(magrittr)
pipel <- scale %>>%
  pca

pipel$plot()
```

3. Add a learner as a pipeline object:

```
library(mlr3learners)

learner = lrn("classif.kknn")
learner$param_set$set_values(k = 4)
pipel <- pipel %>>%
  po("learner", learner = learner)
pipel$plot()
```

4. Convert the pipeline to a learner:

```
p_learner <- as_learner(pipel)
```

5. Use the pipeline learner as usual:

```
library(mlbench)
data("BreastCancer")

selected <- BreastCancer[c("Cl.thickness", "Cell.size", "Cell.
shape","Marg.adhesion", "Epith.c.size", "Bl.cromatin","Normal.
```

```
nucleoli", "Mitoses", "Class")]

task <- as_task_classif(selected, target="Class")

resamp_kcv <- rsmp("cv")
resamp_kcv$param_set$values = list(folds = 3)

result_kcv <- resample(task, p_learner, resamp_kcv)
measures <- msrs(c("classif.precision", "classif.specificity",
"classif.sensitivity"))
result_kcv$score(measures)
```

This code gives us the results of a PCA.

How it works...

Step 1 is to start creating pipeline objects—the parts of the pipeline we will string together. We can do this with the po function and the name of the object. For the preprocessing step, we have chosen a "scale" and a "pca". These have no further options, though many of the pipeline objects we could create do. In *step 2*, we string the parts into a pipeline using the magrittr pipeline %>>% operator. The resulting pipeline pipel object has a $plot method we can use to view the pipeline, as seen in *Figure 11.6*:

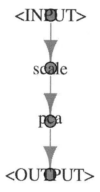

Figure 11.6 – A basic pre-processing pipeline

In *step 3*, we build the k-NN learner using the `learner()` function, set it's parameters as usual, and then add it to the end of the existing pipeline to give us the pipeline seen in *Figure 11.7*:

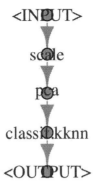

Figure 11.7 – The pipeline with the learner

In *step 4*, we take the whole pipeline and convert it into an object equivalent to a learner. The `as_learner()` function does this, and we can now proceed to use the pipeline as we have done before.

With *step 5*, the longest step, we produce the datasets, task, and resampling strategy (as we did in the earlier recipe in this chapter) and run it. Then, we again assess the result with selected measures. Printing the results gives us something like the following:

```
##       task_id             learner_id resampling_id iteration classif.
precision
## 1: selected scale.pca.classif.
kknn             cv           1           0.9341317
## 2: selected scale.pca.classif.
kknn             cv           2           0.9354839
## 3: selected scale.pca.classif.
kknn             cv           3           0.972973
```

The `learner_id` column confirms that this learner was preprocessed by scaling and PCA and that three-fold cross-validation was performed.

There's more...

Lots of the components of the mlr3 ecosystem can be used as pipeline components. To get a list from within R, try inputting the following:

```
library("mlr3pipelines")
as.data.table(mlr_pipeops)
```

That should give you a list of components you can use in the pipeline.

Creating a tSNE and UMAP embedding

t-Distributed Stochastic Neighbor Embedding (t-SNE) and **Uniform Manifold Approximation and Projection (UMAP)** are both dimensionality reduction techniques commonly used in ML and data visualization.

t-SNE is a non-linear technique that aims to visualize high-dimensional data in a lower-dimensional space while preserving the local structure of the data. t-SNE is particularly useful for revealing clusters or groups of data points that may not be immediately apparent in the original high-dimensional space.

UMAP is another non-linear dimensionality reduction technique that has gained popularity due to its scalability and efficiency. UMAP also focuses on preserving local structures and employs a different mathematical method based on graph theory and optimization techniques. UMAP is often used for visualizing large datasets with millions of data points.

Both algorithms suffer from being computationally expensive, especially when dealing with large datasets. UMAP was developed to address this issue and is generally faster than t-SNE, but it can still be slower than other linear techniques such as PCA. Both algorithms are sensitive to the random initialization of the embedding, which means running the same algorithm with different random seeds can produce different results. It's important to be aware of this when interpreting the visualizations.

Crucially, the resulting lower-dimensional representations may not have a direct correspondence to the original features. The focus is on capturing the relationships between data points rather than preserving the global structure. Both techniques have several parameters that need to be set, such as the perplexity in t-SNE and the number of neighbors in UMAP. Choosing appropriate parameter values can significantly affect the quality and interpretability of the embeddings, making it important to experiment and tune these parameters.

Nonetheless, t-SNE and UMAP are useful for exploratory data analysis, pattern recognition, and visualization tasks, helping researchers and data scientists gain insights from complex and high-dimensional data. The visualizations should not be considered equivalent to the clusters and clades we are more familiar with in bioinformatics.

In this recipe, we will look at how to perform a visualization in t-SNE and UMAP and how to tune the most important parameters.

Getting ready

For this recipe, we'll use familiar data from the `palmerpenguins`, the `tidyr`, `dplyr`, and `tibble` packages to manipulate that data. For analysis and visualization, we'll use the `Rtsne`, `umap`, `purrr`, and `ggplot2` packages.

How to do it...

We start creating these embeddings by preparing the data:

1. Load libraries and data:

```
library(palmerpenguins)
library(tidyr)
library(dplyr)
library(tibble)

penguins_filtered <- penguins |>
  drop_na() |>
  select(-year) |>
  mutate(ID=row_number())

penguins_scaled <- penguins_filtered |>
  select(where(is.numeric)) |>
  column_to_rownames("ID") |>
  scale()
```

2. Define the parameter space and embedding function:

```
library(Rtsne)
space <- expand.grid(perp = seq(5, 50, by = 10), dim = 1:3)

tsne <- function(p, d) {
  tsn <- Rtsne(penguins_scaled, perplexity = p, dimensions = p)
  data.frame(
  SNE1 = tsn$Y[,1],
  SNE2 = tsn$Y[,2],
  perplexity = p,
  dimensions = d,
  species = penguins_filtered$species
)

  }

res <- purrr::map2(space$perp, space$dim, tsne) |>
  purrr::list_rbind()
```

3. Plot the results:

```
library(ggplot2)
  ggplot(res) +
  aes(SNE1,SNE2 ) +
  geom_point(aes(colour = species)) +
  facet_grid(perplexity ~ dimensions) +
    theme_minimal()
```

4. Repeat the whole thing with UMAP and specific parameters:

```
library(umap)

space <- expand.grid(n_neighbours = c(5,25,50) , min_dist =
c(0.01, 0.1, 0.5, 0.99))

do_umap <- function(n, m) {
  map <- umap(penguins_scaled, n_neighbours = n, min_dist = m)
  data.frame(
  UMAP1 = map$layout[,1],
  UMAP2 = map$layout[,2],
  n_neighbours = n,
  min_dist = m,
  species = penguins_filtered$species
)

}

purrr::map2(space$n_neighbours, space$min_dist, do_umap) |>
  purrr::list_rbind() |>
  ggplot() +
  aes(UMAP1,UMAP2) +
  geom_point(aes(colour = species)) +
  facet_grid(n_neighbours ~ min_dist) +
    theme_minimal()
```

This code gives us two different plots of our data.

How it works...

The first step is to make sure that we have cleaned and scaled the data, so in *step 1*, we use a tidyverse style pipeline to remove observations with NA (using `drop_na()`), remove the uninformative year column using `select(-year)`, and add a row number-based ID column. We keep this as `penguins_filtered` in order to retain the species data should we need to. We go on to extract the numeric columns to a new dataframe, move the `ID` column to the `rownames` attribute (so really, out of the actual dataframe), and then when we have just numeric columns that we want to visualize, we can apply the `scale()` function to bring all the data into similar ranges and prevent the algorithm from giving one variable more weight than others.

In *step 2*, we start t-SNE by loading the library and preparing a data structure to hold the values of the parameter search space. The `expand.grid()` function returns a dataframe of all combinations of the vectors passed to it, so we get a `perp` column (for perplexity) with values 5 to 50 in increments of 10 and a `dim` column (for dimension) with values 1 to 3. Next, we define a function that will conduct t-SNE using passed values for the perplexity and dimension parameters. The resulting `tsn` object is parsed into a dataframe to record the parameters and results. After the function is defined, we run it on the search space using `purrr::map2` function, which will iterate over two equal-sized vectors—here, the two columns in `space`—and send their values to the named function, `tsne`. The resulting list of data frames from that is condensed into a single dataframe.

Step 3 is a standard `ggplot2` plot of the data, showing in each facet the visualization for each combination of the two parameters we varied. We get a result like the one in *Figure 11.8*:

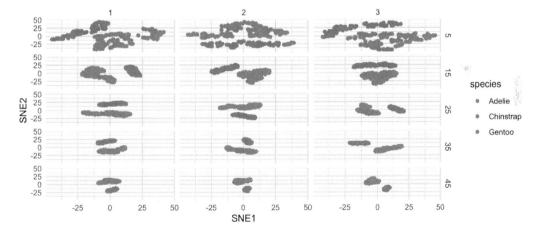

Figure 11.8 – A t-SNE visualization showing the effect of perplexity and dimension parameters

Note the really massive changes in the relationships between groups that make it inappropriate for interpretation as a cluster in the same way we do for other clustering's in bioinformatics.

The whole process is repeated in *step 4* for the UMAP algorithm. The process is virtually identical save for some renaming and choosing different values for the parameters most important in UMAP—n_neighbours and `min_dist`. The result looks like those in *Figure 11.9*:

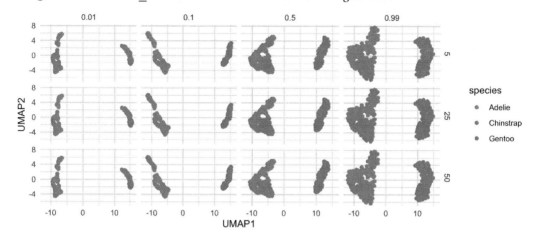

Figure 11.9 – A UMAP visualization showing the effect of n_neighours and min_dist

Again, note the effect of the parameters on clustering.

Clustering with k-means and hierarchical clustering

It is common in bioinformatics to want to classify things into groups without first knowing what or how many groups there may be. This process is usually known as clustering and is a type of unsupervised ML. This is commonly used in genomics experiments, particularly RNAseq and related count-based technologies. In this recipe, we'll start with a large gene expression dataset with around 150 samples. We'll learn how to estimate how many groups of samples there are and apply a method to cluster them based on the reduction of dimensionality with PCA followed by a k-means cluster.

Getting ready

We'll need the `factoextra`, `RColorBrewer`, and Bioconductor `biobase` libraries. We'll also use the `modencodefly_eset` object from the `rbioinfcookbook` package.

How to do it...

We can cluster with the following code

1. Load the data and run a PCA:

    ```
    library(factoextra)
    library(Biobase)
    library(rbioinfcookbook)
    expr_pca <- prcomp(exprs(modencodefly.eset), scale = TRUE,
    center=TRUE)
    fviz_screeplot(expr_pca)
    ```

2. Extract the principal components and estimate the optimal clusters:

    ```
    main_components <- expr_pca$rotation[, 1:3]
    fviz_nbclust(main_components, kmeans, method = "wss")
    ```

3. Perform k-means clustering and visualize:

    ```
    kmean_clus <- kmeans(main_components, 5, nstart=25, iter.
    max=1000)
    fviz_cluster(kmean_clus, data = main_components,
                palette = RColorBrewer::brewer.pal(5, "Set2"),
                ggtheme = theme_minimal(),
                main = "k-Means Sample Clustering"
                )
    ```

This code gives us the clustering we want.

How it works...

In *step 1*, we load libraries, including the `rbioinfcookbook` library that provides us with `modencodefly.eset` to work on. We use it in the `Biobase` function `exprs()`, which extracts the expression measurements as a rectangular matrix and passes that to the `prcomp()` function, which performs PCA and returns a PCA object, `expr_pca`. We then plot the PCA with the `factoextre` function `fviz_screeplot()` and see the result in *Figure 11.10*:

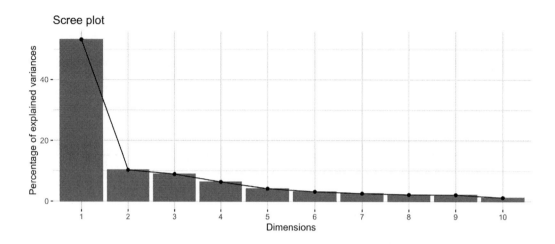

Figure 11.10 – A screenplot showing the variance captured by each principal component

This shows how much of the variance within the data is captured by each principal component. The first three components capture over 70% of the variance. We can use these three instead of the whole 150-column dataset, simplifying the process and speeding up the analysis greatly.

In *step 2*, we extract the main components using subsetting on the rotation slot of the `expr_pca` object, extracting the first three columns. These correspond to the three components. We save these in a variable called `main_components` and use the `fviz_nbclust()` function on it and the `kmeans()` function to create the following diagram:

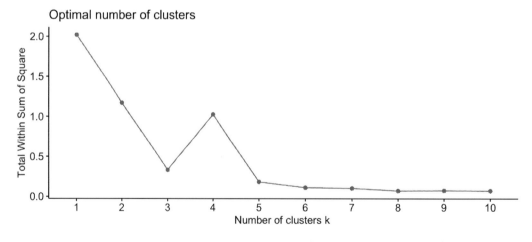

Figure 11.11 – An elbow plot showing the variability reduction in increasing numbers of clusters tested

In this function, the data are divided into increasing numbers of clusters and the **Within Sum of Squares (wss)** is computed—this being a measure of the variability within each cluster. It decreases greatly up to about five clusters, after which it levels off and not much improvement is seen. This indicates that the data contains about five clusters.

In *step 3*, we perform a k-means cluster using the kmeans() function, providing main_components as the data for the first argument and setting the number of clusters to five. The values of nstart and iter.max arguments are reasonable options for most runs of the algorithm. We pass the kmeans_clust result object to fviz_cluster() and set some display options. You should see something like *Figure 11.12*:

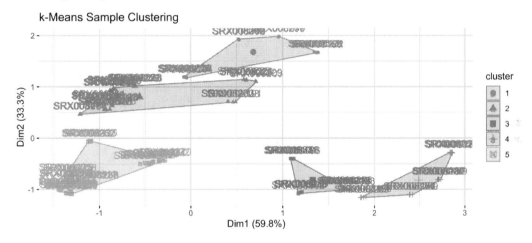

Figure 11.12 – A clustered PCA

That's all we intended to do in this recipe!

12

Functional Programming with purrr and base R

Functional programming is a programming paradigm that emphasizes immutability, pure functions, and declarative programming, treating computation as the evaluation of mathematical functions and avoiding shared state and side effects. It focuses on composing functions and working with immutable data to create robust and predictable programs. In terms of our day-to-day work, this means focusing on using functions to solve problems and avoiding changing data. We also emphasize writing clear, reusable code that is easier to understand and predictable in its behavior. This style helps us as programmers, especially when code becomes complex or must be maintained over a longer period of time.

R has several base functions, including the `apply` family, as well as external packages that support functional programming, including `purrr`, and `tidyverse`. These tool kits provide functions and operators that facilitate working with data using a functional programming paradigm, allowing for concise and expressive code that focuses on transformations and operations on data. At the center of this way of working is the dataframe object, but not all, indeed not even most, R functions return a handy dataframe object. Therefore, we'll look at ways of converting objects to dataframes and extending them so that they can be a more complex data type, without compromising the streamlined functionality we've come to understand from packages such as `dplyr`. We will learn how to take advantage of the functional programming available in R by converting base objects to tidy formats, and then we'll work with them in reproducible and scalable pipelines with streamlined code. By the end of the chapter, you'll have a good handle on how to build code that is concise and easier to maintain through functional programming.

In this chapter, we will cover the following recipes:

- Making base R objects tidy
- Using nested dataframes for functional programming
- Using the `apply` family of functions

- Using the `map` family of functions from `purrr`
- Working with lists in `purrr`

Technical requirements

We will use `renv` to manage packages in a project-specific way. To use `renv` to install packages, you will first need to install the `renv` package. You can do this by running the following commands in your R console:

Install `renv`:

```
install.packages("renv")
```

Create a new `renv` environment:

```
renv::init()
```

This will create a new directory called `.renv` in your current project directory.

You can then install packages with the following:

```
renv::install_packages()
```

You can also use the `renv` package manager to install Bioconductor packages by running the following command:

```
renv::install("bioc::package name")
```

For example, to install the Biobase package, you would run the following:

```
renv::install("bioc::Biobase")
```

You can use `renv` to install development packages from GitHub like this:

```
renv::install("user name/repo name")
```

For example, to install the `danmaclean` user `rbioinfcookbook` package, you would run the following:

```
renv::install("danmaclean/rbioinfcookbook")
```

You can also install multiple packages simultaneously by separating the package names with a comma. `renv` will automatically handle installing any required dependencies for the packages you install.

Under `renv`, all packages will be installed in the local project directory and not the main central library, meaning you can have multiple versions of the same package, specifically for each project.

All the sample data you need for this package is in the specially created data package on GitHub, `danmaclean/rbioinfcookbook`. The data will become available in your project after installing that.

For this chapter, we'll need the following packages:

- Regular packages:

  - `broom`

  - `dplyr`

  - `purrr`

  - `tidyr`

- GitHub:

  - `danmaclean/rbioinfcookbook`

- Bioconductor:

  - `Biobase`

  - `biobroom`

In addition to these packages, we will also need some non-R tools, such as conda; all these will be described at the point of use.

Further information

Not all the recipes in this section happen in R; some are command-line-based setups. I generally assume a bash terminal will be used for these tasks. Most macOS and Linux machines will have these available in a **Terminal** application. Windows users will likely not need these specific steps, although various packages to run a Linux subsystem on Windows exist if you wish to search them out.

In R, it is normal practice to load a library and use functions directly by name. Although this is great in short interactive sessions, it can cause confusion when many packages are loaded at once and share function names. To clarify which package and function I am using at a given moment, I will occasionally use the `packageName::functionName()` convention.

Sometimes, in the middle of a recipe, I'll interrupt code to dive into some intermediate output or to look at the structure of an object. When that happens, you'll see a code block where each line begins with ## (double hash symbols). Consider the following command:

```
letters[1:5]
```

This will give us the following output:

```
## a b c d e
```

Note that the output lines are prefixed with ##.

Making base R objects "tidy"

The `tidyverse` packages (including `dplyr`, `tidyr`, and `ggplot2`) have had a huge influence on data processing and analysis in R, through their application of the "tidy" way of working. In essence, "tidy" means that data is kept in a particular format, in which each row holds a single observation of some variable , and columns specify the variables recorded and contain all values for those variables across all observations. Such a structure means that analytical steps have predictable input and output and can be built into complex pipelines with relative ease. Most base R objects are not tidy, and it can often take significant programming work to extract the parts that are needed downstream. In this recipe, we will look at some functions to automatically convert some common base R objects into a tidy dataframe.

Getting ready

We'll need `tidyr`, `broom`, and also `biobroom` from Bioconductor. For data, we'll use the `danmaclean/rbioinfcookbook` package and the built-in `mtcars` and `iris` datasets.

How to do it...

Making base R objects tidy can be done using the following steps:

1. Tidy an `lm` object:

    ```
    library(broom)
    model <- lm(mpg ~ cyl + qsec, data = mtcars)
    tidy(model)
    augment(model)
    glance(model)
    ```

2. Tidy a `t.test` object:

    ```
    t_test_result <- t.test(x = rnorm(20), y = rnorm(20) )
    tidy(t_test_result)
    ```

3. Tidy an ANOVA object:

    ```
    anova_result <- aov(Petal.Length ~ Species, data = iris)
    tidy(anova_result)
    post_hoc <- TukeyHSD(anova_result)
    tidy(post_hoc)
    ```

4. Tidy a Bioconductor `ExpressionSet` object:

    ```
    library(biobroom)
    library(Biobase)
    library(rbioinfcookbook)
    ```

```
tidy(modencodefly.eset, addPheno=TRUE)
```

This demonstrates a range of options to tidy common R objects.

How it works...

We will start with *step 1* by examining some functions to tidy the common lm object, created by the lm() function. The first task is to create the object, so we perform a multiple regression using the mtcars data, and then we use the tidy() function on the model to return an object summary of the components of the model. It looks like this:

```
##   term          estimate std.error statistic    p.value
##   <chr>          <dbl>     <dbl>     <dbl>        <dbl>
## 1 (Intercept)    47.4      8.81       5.38 0.00000882
## 2 cyl            -3.14     0.398     -7.88 0.0000000109
## 3 qsec           -0.442    0.398     -1.11 0.276
```

The augment() function returns per-observation data for the model, should we want that. It looks like this:

```
##          .rownames      mpg   cyl  qsec .fitted  .resid   .hat ...
##          <chr>          <dbl> <dbl> <dbl>  <dbl>   <dbl>  <dbl> ...
## 1 Mazda RX4              21     6  16.5   21.3 -0.292  0.0665 ...
## 2 Mazda RX4 Wag          21     6  17.0   21.0 -0.0447 0.0453 ...
```

The glance() function inspects the model and returns summaries in a tidy format, as follows:

```
##   r.squared adj.r.squared sigma statistic      p.value   df ...
##      <dbl>       <dbl>   <dbl>    <dbl>        <dbl> <dbl> ...
## 1    0.737       0.719   3.19     40.7 0.00000000382     2 ...
```

The function returns an object that is useful when we want to compare models. Consider comparing all these dataframe-based objects with the default objects.

Step 2 shows the same process for the t.test object. First, we run a t-test on some random numbers, just to get the object, and then we run tidy() on it. The output looks like this:

```
##    estimate estimate1 estimate2 statistic p.value parameter   ...
##      <dbl>     <dbl>     <dbl>     <dbl>   <dbl>     <dbl>   ...
## 1   0.201    -0.158    -0.359     0.577   0.567      37.8   ...
```

With *step 3*, we run ANOVA on the iris data using the aov() function to look at the effect of species on petal length – in this case, when we use tidy(), we get a model-level summary, perhaps not what we were expecting, so we instead run tidy() on the result of a post hoc test from TukeyHSD().

Step 4 moves on to Bioconductor, and we use the `Biobroom` version of `tidy()` on the `ExpressionSet` object. This turns the square matrix of expression values into a tidy dataframe, along with columns for sample data and other data types. The extra argument, `addPheno`, is specific to this type of object and inserts the phenotype metadata from the object. Note that the resulting dataframe is over 2 million lines long – biological datasets can be large and can generate very large dataframes.

Using nested dataframes for functional programming

Functional programming is a programming style that focuses on using functions to solve problems. It avoids changing data and emphasizes writing clear, reusable code that is easier to understand and predictable in its behavior.

The dataframe is at the core of the tidy way of working, and we tend to think of it as a spreadsheet-like rectangular data container, with only a single value in each cell. In fact, dataframes can be nested – they can hold other dataframes in specific single cells. This is achieved internally by replacing a dataframe's vector column with a list column so that each cell becomes a member of a list, and any sort of object can be held within the now conceptual single cell of the outer dataframe.

In this recipe, we'll look at ways to make a nested dataframe and ways of working with it using a functional style, with the aim that it will simplify working with large or multifaceted data.

Getting ready

We will use the `tidyr`, `dplyr`, `purrr`, and `broom` libraries. We'll also use the built-in `mtcars` data.

How to do it...

Using nested dataframes can be done with the following steps:

1. Create a nested dataframe:

```
library(tidyr)
nested_mt <- nest(mtcars, -cyl)
```

2. Add a new list column, holding the results of a linear model:

```
library(dplyr)
library(purrr)
nested_mt_list_cols <- nested_mt |>
  mutate(
    model = map(data, ~ lm(mpg ~ wt, data = .x))
  )
```

3. Add a new list column, holding the results of tidying the linear model:

```
library(broom)
nested_mt_list_cols <- nested_mt_list_cols |>
    mutate(tidy_model = map(model, tidy))
```

4. Unnest the dataframe:

```
simple_df <- unnest(nested_mt_list_cols, tidy_model)
```

This is how we work with nested dataframes.

How it works...

First, we create a nested dataframe in *step 1*. We use the nest() function from tidyr to nest the mtcars dataframe. The - option tells the functions which columns to exclude from being collapsed into the nested part of the dataframe. This effectively makes the cyl column a factor on which different subsets are created. It's conceptually similar to the dplyr::group_by() function, which you may be already familiar with. Inspecting the object clarifies what has happened:

```
## # A tibble: 3 × 2
##     cyl data
##   <dbl> <list>
## 1     6 <tibble [7 × 10]>
## 2     4 <tibble [11 × 10]>
## 3     8 <tibble [14 × 10]>
```

The nested dataframe contains a new column called data, into which the nested data has been collapsed. Each nested dataframe contains the rows from the original dataframe that had the value of each cyl displayed.

In *step 2*, we create a new column on our nested dataframe by using mutate(). Within the mutate() call, we must use the map() function from purrr to iterate over each of the sub-dataframes in the named column and apply the named function. The call is map(data ~ lm(...)), so we iterate over each mini-dataframe in the larger one and apply lm() to the mini-dataframe. Within the function call, the new .x variable is just idiomatic, indicating the thing we're currently working on – the mini-dataframe. The nested dataframe now looks like this:

```
## # A tibble: 3 × 3
##     cyl data                model
##   <dbl> <list>              <list>
## 1     6 <tibble [7 × 10]>  <lm>
## 2     4 <tibble [11 × 10]> <lm>
## 3     8 <tibble [14 × 10]> <lm>
```

A new column called model contains an lm() object at each value of cyl.

Having established the pattern of using `mutate` and `map()` to add complex objects to a single cell, we can use that pattern to tidy up the complex object to a dataframe. In *step 3*, we use the `broom::tidy()` function to turn the `lm()` object into a tibble (a type of dataframe). The nested dataframe now looks like this:

```
## # A tibble: 3 × 4
##     cyl data                 model  tidy_model
##   <dbl> <list>               <list> <list>
## 1     6 <tibble [7 × 10]>    <lm>   <tibble [2 × 5]>
## 2     4 <tibble [11 × 10]>   <lm>   <tibble [2 × 5]>
## 3     8 <tibble [14 × 10]>   <lm>   <tibble [2 × 5]>
```

Step 4 uses the `unnest()` function to return everything to a simpler dataframe; the second argument, `tidy_model`, is the column we wish to unpack. We end up with the following result:

```
## # A tibble: 6 × 8
     cyl data                model  term         estimate std.error
  statistic     p.value
   <dbl> <list>              <list>
  <chr>            <dbl>    <dbl>     <dbl>        <dbl>
  1       6 <tibble [7 ×
  10]> <lm>    (Intercept)     28.4        4.18       6.79 0.00105
  2       6 <tibble [7 ×
  10]> <lm>    wt             -2.78        1.33      -2.08 0.0918
  3       4 <tibble [11 × 10]>
  <lm>    (Intercept)     39.6         4.35       9.10 0.00000777
  4       4 <tibble [11 × 10]>
  <lm>    wt             -5.65        1.85      -3.05 0.0137
  5       8 <tibble [14 × 10]>
  <lm>    (Intercept)     23.9         3.01       7.94 0.00000405
  6       8 <tibble [14 × 10]>
  <lm>    wt             -2.19        0.739     -2.97 0.0118
```

We now have a dataframe with the model unpacked. Note that should we wish, we can use normal `tidyverse` functions to remove the list-based column, `column`. The operations are all compatible with the pipe operator and can be combined into a single pipeline command, without having to save intermediate steps, as we have here.

See also

The `unnest()` function will only work when the nested list-based column members are compatible and can be sensibly aligned and recycled, according to the normal rules. In many cases, this won't be true, so you will need to manually manipulate the output with a function of your own devising. For help, refer to the map family of functions, described in the *Using the map family of functions in purrr* recipe later in this chapter.

Using the apply family of functions

Programming in R can sometimes seem a bit tricky; indeed, most of us first use R in a very non-programmatic way at the console, invoking commands but not often using flow control or process logic to make dynamic decisions. The control flow and loop structures that it has initially seem a bit basic and underpowered. Many R functions are vectorized (i.e., they operate on collections); the language takes advantage of this by providing features ensuring we don't need to take the low-level approach we may have learned in Python and other places.

Base R provides the `apply()` functions to assist with common looping tasks. These functions allow you to apply a specified function to elements of an object, such as a matrix, list, or array. `apply()` applies a function to either rows, columns, or both of a matrix or array. The result is a simplified vector, matrix, or array. `lapply()` applies a function to each element of a list and returns a list of results. This function is particularly useful when you want to apply a function to multiple objects contained within a list. `sapply()` is similar but attempts to simplify the result into a vector, matrix, or array if possible. It automatically simplifies output when the result is a list of length one. These apply functions eliminate the need for explicit loops and enable a more functional programming approach by abstracting away the iteration process.

In this recipe, we'll learn how to differentiate the different functions in the family and how to use them to act as concise code for iteration over objects.

Getting ready

We will only need base R functions and data for this recipe, so you are good to go!

How to do it...

Making use of the `apply()` family of functions can be done with the following steps:

1. Create a matrix and use `apply()`:

```
m <- matrix(rep(1:10, 10, replace=TRUE), nrow=10)
apply(m,1, sum)
apply(m,2, mean)
apply(m,2, function(x){max(x * 2)})
```

2. Use `lapply()` over a vector:

```
numbers <- 1:3
number_of_numbers <- function(x){rnorm(x)}
my_list <- lapply(numbers, number_of_numbers)
```

3. Use `lapply()` and `sapply()` over the list:

```
lapply(my_list, mean)
sapply(my_list, mean)
```

4. Use `lapply()` over a dataframe:

```
list_from_data_frame <- lapply(iris, mean, trim=0.1, na.rm=TRUE)
unlist(list_from_data_frame)
```

This describes all the main ways we can use this family of functions.

How it works...

Step 1 begins with the creation of a 10 x 10 matrix, with the rows holding the same numbers and columns, running from 1 to 10. Inspecting it makes it clear, as shown in the snippet:

```
##      [,1] [,2] [,3] [,4] [,5] [,6] [,7] [,8] [,9] [,10]
## [1,]   1    1    1    1    1    1    1    1    1    1
## [2,]   2    2    2    2    2    2    2    2    2    2
## [3,]   3    3    3    3    3    3    3    3    3    3
```

We then use `apply()`, with which the first argument is the object to loop over (m), the second is the direction in which to take sections from the object (or `margin` – 1 is for rows, and 2 is for columns), and the third is the code to apply. For this example, the third argument is the name of a function, the built-in `sum` or `mean`, but, as in the third example, it could be an anonymous function with arbitrary code or any other custom function by name. Contrast the three calls:

```
> apply(m,1, sum)
## [1]   10  20  30  40  50  60  70  80  90 100
> apply(m,2, mean)
## [1]  5.5 5.5 5.5 5.5 5.5 5.5 5.5 5.5 5.5 5.5
> apply(m,2, function(x){max(x * 2)})
## [1]  20 20 20 20 20 20 20 20 20 20
```

We can clearly see the different sections of the data that the `margin` argument chooses. Note that for the third example, the anonymous function takes just one argument; we call it x, but it is just the section of data chosen by `margin`.

In *step 2*, we move on to using `lapply()`, which can loop over many types of data structures, but it always returns a list with one member for each iteration. As it's a list, each member can be a different type or length, so this is a more flexible `loop` function than others. We start the step by creating a vector, (1, 2, 3), and a function that creates a vector of random numbers of a given length. We then use `lapply()` to loop over that vector. The first argument is the thing to iterate over, and the second is the code to apply. Note that the current value of the vector we loop over is passed automatically to the called function as the argument. Inspecting the resulting list, we get the following:

```
> my_list
## [[1]]
## [1] -0.0283512
```

```
##
## [[2]]
## [1] 0.6221370 0.3282322
##
## [[3]]
## [1] -0.6004408  0.3351182 -0.1146729
```

We get a list with a first element of one random number, a second element of two random numbers, and a third element of three, reflecting the value from the original vector that was passed to the function and highlighting that lists can have different- sized and different-typed objects at each element.

In *step 3*, we can see the difference between `lapply()` and `sapply()` when looping over the same structure. Recall that `lapply()` always returns a list, and `sapply()` will always try to simplify it (hence, `l` and `s` apply). We execute `l/s-apply` on the mean function, which returns a single value. The results are like this:

```
> lapply(my_list, mean)
## [[1]]
## [1] -0.0283512
##
## [[2]]
## [1] 0.4751846
##
## [[3]]
## [1] -0.1266651
> sapply(my_list, mean)
## [1] -0.0283512  0.4751846 -0.1266651
```

Note that the answers are the same, but the output structure is different.

In *step 4*, we use `lapply()` over a dataframe – the `iris` data. By default, it works on columns when given a dataframe, applying the `mean()` function to each in turn. Note that the last two arguments (`trim` and `na.rm`) are not options for `lapply()`, although it does look like it. In all these functions, the arguments after positions 1 and 2 are all passed to the code being run, so these two are options for `mean()`. In the output, the column names are used as the element names of the resulting list. With a simple list, as we get here, we can use the `unlist()` function to convert the results to a vector, where possible. If names are present, the vector is named:

```
> unlist(list_from_data_frame)
## Sepal.Length  Sepal.Width Petal.Length  Petal.Width      Species
##     5.808333     3.043333     3.760000     1.184167           NA
```

These steps show how to iterate over objects in a functional way.

Using the map family of functions in purrr

R's base functional programming tool kit is a little sparse. The `purrr` package was created in order to extend it and create a complete and consistent set of tools for working with functions and data structures. `purrr` provides a set of functions for functional programming, including the widely used map family of functions. The `map` functions allow you to iterate over a collection (such as a list or vector) and apply a function to each element, returning the results as a new list or vector.

The functions vary according to what they expect as input, what they iterate over, and what types and structures they return. Like the `apply` functions, they can simplify repetitive tasks, such as data manipulation or model fitting, by automatically handling the iteration process for you but by ensuring they always return the specified types and structures they help us to build more streamlined and effective code that is less prone to bugs.

In this recipe, we'll look at some examples of the map family in use.

Getting ready

For this recipe, we just need the `purrr` package.

How to do it...

Using the map family of functions can be done as in the following examples:

1. Use the basic `map()` to get back a list iterating over different inputs:

```
library(purrr)
df <- data.frame(
   small_nums = 1:3,
   big_nums = c(100, 200, 300)
)


means <- map(df, mean, na.rm=TRUE)

norm <- map2(df, means, function(o, m){o / m} )

result <- pmap(list(df, means, norm), function(o, m, n){
   data.frame(original_value = o,
              means = m,
              normalised = n)
   } )
```

2. Use the suffixed forms to force a return type:

```
map_dbl(df, mean)
map_chr(df, mean)
map_lgl(df, mean)
```

3. Examine other forms:

```
map_dfc(df, log)
walk_result <- walk(df, print,)
```

That is all we need to know to use map functions.

How it works...

Step 1 uses the most common forms of map (). At the start of this step, we set up a data frame as a structure to work on, then first use map () to iterate over that dataframe, calling the mean () function on each element. In this case, the element is each column of the dataframe. We get back a list, which looks like this:

```
## $small_nums
## [1]  2
##
## $big_nums
## [1]  200
```

Each list element is named according to the original dataframe and contains the result of the function.

We use this means list (m) as one input to map2 (), which iterates over two things, the second being the original dataframe (o). We ask text to apply a custom function that divides the original values by the mean (o / m), thereby normalizing the data to give us norm, which looks like this:

```
## $small_nums
## [1]  0.5 1.0 1.5
##
## $big_nums
## [1]  0.5 1.0 1.5
```

In the last line of *step 1*, we use pmap () to iterate over an arbitrary number of things by wrapping them in a list first. We can then apply any function to them and the elements are taken from them in turn and used in the function. Here, we simply use the data.frame () function to make a dataframe of the results:

```
## $small_nums
##    original_value means normalised
## 1               1     2        0.5
```

```
## 2                    2    2       1.0
## 3                    3    2       1.5
##
## $big_nums
##   original_value means normalised
## 1            100   200       0.5
## 2            200   200       1.0
## 3            300   200       1.5
```

Step 2 shows us the suffixed forms of the map() function. These work as map() does but force a particular return type. The map_dbl() ensures a double number is returned:

```
## small_nums  big_nums
##         2       200
```

map_chr() ensures character data is returned:

```
## small_nums       big_nums
## "2.000000" "200.000000"
```

Note that the third example, map_lgl(), tries to return logical (TRUE/FALSE) values, but will fail on the data since they can't logically be co-erced.

Suffixed versions of map2() and pmap() also exist.

Step 3 finishes this recipe by showing some other map() family functions. The map_dfc() function applies the log functionas expected, but instead of returning a list, it returns a dataframe of bound columns (hence _dfc):

```
##   small_nums big_nums
##        <dbl>    <dbl>
## 1          0     4.61
## 2      0.693     5.30
## 3       1.10     5.70
```

A function called map_dfr() for row binding also exists.

Finally, we use walk(), which iterates over the dataframe, but does nothing to it. It returns the input completely unchanged. The usefulness, though, is in that it allows us to carry out a *side-effect* type action (such as writing to file or printing to screen) for each element without messing up the data.

Working with lists in purrr

Lists are incredibly useful data structures that allow you to store and organize various types of objects, such as vectors, matrices, dataframes, and even other lists. Unlike vectors, matrices, or dataframes, lists can accommodate different data types and structures within a single object. This flexibility makes them a powerful tool for data manipulation and analysis in R.

As a result the `purrr` package provides lots of functions for working with lists, and in this short recipe, we'll look at a few for summarizing, simplifying, and extracting data.

Getting ready

We'll just need the `purrr` package.

How to do it...

We can manipulate lists in `purrr` using the following functions:

1. Filter a list of elements:

```
set.seed(2345)
l <- list(
    a = rnorm(10, mean = 1),
    b = rnorm(10, mean = 10),
    c = rnorm(10, mean = 20)
)

library(purrr)

keep(l, function(x) mean(x) >= 10)
keep(l, ~ mean(.x) >= 10)
detect_index(l, ~ mean(.x) >= 10)
every(l, ~ mean(.x) >= 10)
some(l, ~ mean(.x) >= 10)
```

2. Rework the list:

```
names <- c("ones", "tens", "twenties")
l <- set_names(l, names)

short_l <- modify(l, function(x) x[1:3])
transpose(short_l)
```

These are short and sweet steps to work well with lists.

How it works...

Step 1 looks at functions that filter lists and begins by defining a simple list of vectors to work with and a random seed. Then we load `purrr` and use the `keep()` function. This takes a list and a function to apply to each element. Any element on which the function returns `TRUE` is retained. The second form of `keep()` shows a short-hand version using a formula such that the topic variable `.x` stands for the element currently under consideration. From each version, we get the following:

```
## $b
##   [1]  12.055349 10.910236   9.616023 11.241007 10.197379  ...

## $c
##   [1]  20.73866 20.05183 19.50086 20.81962 19.45682 ...
```

Next, in *step 1,* we use `detect_index()`, which will return the index of *the first* element passing the test in the second argument of the function, so we get the following:

```
## [1] 2
```

Finally, in *step 1,* we see the `every()`, which returns `TRUE` if all elements in the list pass a test, and `some()` tests, which returns `TRUE` if only some elements pass a test.

Step 2 focusses on modifying lists and begins by defining a vector of names and using the `set_names()` function to apply them, returning the following:

```
## $ones
##   [1]  -0.191424643   1.549300549   0.937594857   1.265441500 ...
##
## $tens
##   [1]  12.055349 10.910236   9.616023 11.241007 10.197379  ...
##
## $twenties
##   [1]  20.73866 20.05183 19.50086 20.81962 19.45682 1    ...
```

The `modify()` function modifies each element and returns the modified list. Here, the function we apply simply extracts the first numbers from the vector at each list element.

The last function, `transpose()`, rotates the list with its contents, where possible, so makes a nested list in which the first list is named after the indices of the vectors and each element of the inner list is named from the original names in the input list. This makes more sense when visualized and looks like the following truncated output when printed to screen. The inspector in RStudio will be your friend in studying this too:

```
## [[1]]
## [[1]]$ones
## [1] -0.1914246
##
## [[1]]$tens
## [1] 12.05535
##
## [[1]]$twenties
## [1] 20.73866
##
##
## [[2]]
## [[2]]$ones
## [1] 1.549301
...
```

The output is long so is truncated, but the head of it is shown.

13

Turbo-Charging Development in R with ChatGPT

ChatGPT speeds up development in R for bioinformatics by providing rapid code generation, problem-solving guidance, package recommendations, code review and debugging, and documentation assistance. Developers can quickly generate R code snippets for common bioinformatics tasks, saving time in searching for examples. When facing challenges, they can describe the problem to ChatGPT and receive suggestions and insights. ChatGPT's knowledge of bioinformatics packages enables it to recommend relevant tools for specific tasks. Developers can also receive code review and debugging assistance from it, helping catch errors early. ChatGPT can provide information and explanations about bioinformatics functions, algorithms, and data formats, facilitating better utilization of bioinformatics tools, and it can accelerate development by providing valuable support and guidance throughout the whole process. Despite the hype, ChatGPT still isn't very good at solving logical problems, so it can't generate high-level solutions for you. Instead, we'll concentrate on using it for what it's good at: automating repetitive work, solving syntax and programming issues, and explaining pre-existing code. You'll learn how to do all these in this chapter.

In this chapter, we will cover the following recipes:

- Interpreting complicated code with ChatGPT assistance

- Debugging and improving code with ChatGPT

- Generating code with ChatGPT

- Writing documentation for R functions with ChatGPT

- Writing unit tests for R functions with ChatGPT

- Finding R packages to build a workflow with ChatGPT

Technical requirements

We will use `renv` to manage packages in a project-specific way. To use `renv` to install packages, you will first need to install the `renv` package. You can do this by running the following commands in your R console:

1. Install `renv`:

    ```
    install.packages("renv")
    ```

2. Create a new `renv` environment:

    ```
    renv::init()
    ```

    This will create a new directory called `.renv` in your current project directory.

3. You can then install packages with the following:

    ```
    renv::install_packages()
    ```

For this chapter, we'll need the following packages:

-   Regular packages:

    -   `ggplot2`

    -   `tidyr`

Further information

Not all the recipes in this section happen in R; in fact, most happen in the chat window of ChatGPT. Make an account for this at `https://chat.openai.com/`. I'll include results from ChatGPT inline in the recipe steps.

Interpreting complicated code with ChatGPT assistance

ChatGPT can be used to interpret R code by leveraging its natural language processing capabilities and its understanding of the R programming language. It's important to note that while ChatGPT can assist in interpreting and explaining R code, it's still just an AI language model and may not have knowledge of the most recent updates or specific domain-specific intricacies. Double-checking information with official documentation and consulting experienced developers or experts is always necessary. It is massively useful for simplifying and getting a good first-level understanding in most cases.

In this recipe, we'll look at how to take an arbitrary bit of complex code and explain it in plain English.

Getting ready

We need some code to interpret – we'll use a function from the `besthr` Github hosted package at `https://github.com/TeamMacLean/besthr/blob/master/R/functions.R` and an account with ChatGPT from `https://chat.openai.com/`.

How to do it...

Here's how to work in a ChatGPT session and get it to explain some code to you:

1. Paste the following code into the ChatGPT prompt box:

```
explain this R code to me:

#' Convert named columns to factors
#'
#' \code{factorise_cols} returns a copy of the passed data frame
in which all
#' explicitly named columns are converted to factors with \
code{as.factor}
#' All columns with only NA values are ommitted.
#'
#' @param df data frame
#' @param col_list vector of quoted column names
#' @keywords internal
#'
factorise_cols <- function(df, col_list ){
  not_all_na <- function(x) any(!is.na(x))

  for ( i in col_list){
    df <- df %>% dplyr::mutate(!!(i) := as.factor(!!(i)) )
  }
  df %>% dplyr::select_if(not_all_na)
}
```

2. Read the response:

```
This R code defines a function called `factorise_cols` that
converts explicitly named columns of a data frame into factors
using the `as.factor` function. The function takes two
parameters:

1. `df`: This is the data frame that contains the columns to be
converted.
```

```
2. `col_list`: This is a vector of quoted column names. It
specifies which columns in the data frame should be converted to
factors.

The function uses a helper function called `not_all_na` to
filter out columns that have only `NA` values. This helper
function checks if there are any non-NA values in a column using
the `any` and `is.na` functions.

Inside the main function, a loop iterates over each column
name in the `col_list`. For each column, the function uses the
`mutate` function from the `dplyr` package to create a new
column in the data frame (`df`) with the same name, but with the
values converted to factors using the `as.factor` function. The
`!!(i)` syntax is used to unquote the column name.

After the loop, the function uses the `select_if` function from
`dplyr` to select only the columns that pass the `not_all_na`
condition, effectively removing columns that contain only `NA`
values. The resulting data frame is then returned as the output
of the function.

Overall, this function allows you to convert specific columns of
a data frame into factors while excluding columns that contain
only `NA` values.
```

3. Ask for a clarification on a certain point:

```
You said 'The !!(i) syntax is used to unquote the column name.'
Can you go into more depth?
```

4. Read the response:

```
Certainly! In the given code, the `!!` (bang-bang) syntax is
used for unquoting the column name within the context of the
`mutate` function. Let's break it down step by step:

1. In the loop, the variable `i` represents each element (column
name) of the `col_list` vector.

2. Within the `mutate` function, the column name `i` needs to
be unquoted and evaluated as an expression. This is necessary
because `mutate` expects column names to be provided as
expressions rather than strings.

3. The `!!` (bang-bang) operator is used to perform this
unquoting. It is part of the tidy evaluation framework provided
by the `dplyr` package.

4. By wrapping `i` with `!!`, it instructs `mutate` to evaluate
`i` as an expression, resulting in an unquoted column name.
```

```
To illustrate with an example, suppose `col_list` contains
the column names `col1` and `col2`. During the loop iteration,
when `i` is `"col1"`, the line `!!(i)` would be evaluated
as `!!("col1")`, which unquotes the string to yield `col1`.
Similarly, when `i` is `"col2"`, `!!(i)` would be evaluated as
`!!("col2")`, resulting in `col2`.

This unquoting operation is necessary in this context because
the `mutate` function expects column names to be provided as
unevaluated expressions so that it can perform the necessary
data manipulation operations. The `!!` operator allows us to
achieve this unquoting within the `mutate` function call.
```

Note that the response from ChatGPT will be somewhat different depending on context and you may not get exactly what was generated here. That is the nature of the thing, but you should get something with the same meaning.

How it works...

The code in this example comes from a package called `besthr` that creates estimation statistic plots for visual scoring data. The tool must take in arbitrary column names and work within the tidyverse, so it uses some advanced coding techniques to allow that to happen. We first go and get the code from the repository on GitHub (`https://github.com/TeamMacLean/besthr/blob/master/R/functions.R`) and paste that into ChatGPT's prompt box asking it for an explanation.

In *step 2*, we can see the explanation provided (note that the one you get if you try may be different as the model is not guaranteed to reproduce its predictions). The detail is largely correct; certainly, it is sufficient to give us a clear idea of what the code attempts to do and how it does it.

Some parts of the explanation aren't clear, so in *step 3*, we ask for clarification of a tricky bit, again by typing into the prompt box. And in *step 4*, we see a more in-depth description of that part.

In this way, we can get a clear and readable, plain English description of the job done by a particular piece of code very quickly.

There's more...

Other sites can do this, such as Google's Bard. ChatGPT Plus – a subscription service –also has special plug-ins that help make working with code much easier.

Debugging and improving code with ChatGPT

ChatGPT is capable of debugging code due to its extensive training on programming-related text. It has acquired knowledge of common programming patterns and errors, allowing it to understand code snippets, identify potential issues, and provide suggestions or improvements. It can identify minor errors by highlighting syntax issues such as missing brackets, incorrect function calls, and invalid variable assignments. ChatGPT helps troubleshooting by asking clarifying questions to better understand the problem and guide developers toward the root cause, and can aid in code optimization by suggesting efficiency improvements, identifying performance bottlenecks, and proposing more optimized implementations. Lastly, the debugging process with ChatGPT can foster learning and exploration, enabling developers to discover new concepts, programming techniques, or functionalities of specific libraries or packages. In this recipe, we'll walk through an example debugging session with ChatGPT and look at how it helps us to reflect better on our own code.

Getting ready

We just need an account at ChatGPT: `https://chat.openai.com/`.

How to do it...

We can debug some code as follows:

1. Set up some code that we expect to work and try it:

    ```
    data <- data.frame(
      predictor = c(1, 2, 3, 4, NA),
      response = c("A", "B", "C", "D", "E")
    )

    model <- lm(response ~ predictor, data = data)
    ```

2. Send the broken code to ChatGPT:

    ```
    Help me fix the following code:

    data <- data.frame(
      predictor = c(1, 2, 3, 4, NA),
      response = c("A", "B", "C", "D", "E")
    )

    model <- lm(response ~ predictor, data = data)
    ```

3. Read and run the resulting response in R:

```
To fix the code, you need to handle the missing value (NA) in
the predictor column. Here's the corrected code:
# Fixing the code
data <- data.frame(
    predictor = c(1, 2, 3, 4, NA),
    response = c("A", "B", "C", "D", "E")
)

# Replace NA in the predictor column with the mean value
data$predictor[is.na(data$predictor)] <- mean(data$predictor,
na.rm = TRUE)

# Convert the response variable to a factor
data$response <- as.factor(data$response)

# Perform linear regression
model <- lm(response ~ predictor, data = data)
summary(model)
```

```
In the fixed code, I replaced the NA value in the predictor
column with the mean value of the remaining numeric values
using the mean() function with na.rm = TRUE argument. Then,
I converted the response variable to a factor using the
as.factor() function. Finally, the linear regression model is
computed with the corrected data, and summary(model) displays
the model summary.
```

4. Tell ChatGPT the code *still* doesn't work:

```
It still doesn't work - Im getting thie error:
Error in as.character.factor(x) : malformed factor
In addition: Warning message:
In Ops.factor(r, 2) : '^' not meaningful for factors
```

5. Read the response and run the code:

```
Apologies for the oversight. The error is occurring because the
^ operator is not applicable to factors in the formula used in
the linear regression. To fix this, we can convert the factor to
a numeric representation using numeric codes or dummy variables.
Here's the updated code:
# Fixing the code
data <- data.frame(
    predictor = c(1, 2, 3, 4, NA),
    response = c("A", "B", "C", "D", "E")
)
```

```
# Replace NA in the predictor column with the mean value
data$predictor[is.na(data$predictor)] <- mean(data$predictor,
na.rm = TRUE)

# Convert the response variable to a factor
data$response <- as.factor(data$response)

# Convert the factor to numeric codes
data$response <- as.numeric(data$response)

# Perform linear regression
model <- lm(response ~ predictor, data = data)
summary(model)
```

In the updated code, I've used as.numeric() to convert the response factor variable to numeric codes. This allows the regression model to treat it as a numerical response. Now, the lm() function should run without the error, and summary(model) will display the model summary.

6. Ask it to check whether the original code was appropriately analyzed:

```
Were the original data suitable for a linear model?
```

7. Read the response:

No, the original data provided in the code were not suitable for a linear model. Here's why:

1. The `predictor` variable was numeric, which is suitable for a linear model.

2. The `response` variable, however, was categorical with values "A", "B", "C", "D", and "E". Categorical variables cannot be directly used as the response variable in a linear regression model because they do not represent continuous numeric values.

To use a categorical variable as the response variable in a linear model, you typically need to encode it into dummy variables or use techniques like multinomial logistic regression. Dummy variable encoding represents each category as a separate binary variable (0 or 1). Once the categorical variable is properly encoded, it can be used as the response variable in a linear regression model.

Again, that's how the process goes though the output can be different from user to user but the meaning should be the same.

How it works...

In *step 1*, we set up a data frame of some data as a test set to use in a linear model; we wish to examine the relationship between the two variables so assume that a linear model will work. When we run the code in R, we get this:

```
Error in lm.fit(x, y, offset = offset, singular.ok = singular.ok, ...)
:
  NA/NaN/Inf in 'y'
In addition: Warning message:
In storage.mode(v) <- "double" : NAs introduced by coercion
```

This is a typically confounded R error message. We want help, so in *step 2*, we ask ChatGPT to fix the code.

Step 3 shows us ChatGPT's response, which suggests fixing the NA values that are in the `predictor` column. That seems reasonable, and, as it explains, ChatGPT gives us some code that imputes a new value from the mean of all the other values – again, a reasonable value to impute. When we run the code, it still doesn't work and we get a new error, so in *step 4*, we tell ChatGPT about it and ask it to fix the new errors.

In *step 5*, we see an apologetic language model attempt to correct the error. It gives us a confusing reason for doing some strange text/number conversion and fixed code. When we run this new code in the console, we get output like this:

```
## Call:
## lm(formula = response ~ predictor, data = data)
##
## Residuals:
##    1    2    3    4    5
## -0.5 -0.5 -0.5 -0.5  2.0
##
## Coefficients:
##             Estimate Std. Error t value Pr(>|t|)
## (Intercept)   0.5000     1.5546   0.322    0.769
## predictor     1.0000     0.5774   1.732    0.182
##
## Residual standard error: 1.291 on 3 degrees of freedom
## Multiple R-squared:    0.5,  Adjusted R-squared:  0.3333
## F-statistic:    3 on 1 and 3 DF,  p-value: 0.1817
```

This looks a bit strange – the residuals are weird and the rest of the values look poor. We start to question whether this was the right thing to do in the first place.

In *step 6*, we ask ChatGPT whether the linear model was the right sort of analysis. It responds as in *step 7*, telling us quite clearly that it was not appropriate.

This recipe highlights that we can use ChatGPT to fix code that doesn't work, but shows also that ChatGPT will not reason without prompting. Here, it let us pursue a piece of code that wasn't right for the task. As a language model, it can't know that, even though we believe it would be evident from the question setup. It didn't try to correct our flawed assumptions or logic. We still need to be responsible for the logic and applicability of our code.

Generating code with ChatGPT

ChatGPT is useful for generating R code because it has been trained on a vast amount of programming-related text, including R code examples and best practices. With this knowledge, ChatGPT can understand user queries and provide accurate and contextually relevant R code suggestions. It can generate code snippets for tasks such as data manipulation, visualization, statistical analysis, and package usage. ChatGPT's ability to leverage its training to generate syntactically correct and efficient R code helps users save time, improve their coding skills, and explore different approaches to problem-solving. It serves as a valuable resource for both novice and experienced R programmers seeking code generation assistance.

In this recipe, we'll ask ChatGPT to develop a plot for us. Specifically, we'll be looking for a pairs-style scatter plot of all samples against each other. As we'll see, it doesn't get it right but it does help us to find and construct a lot of the code we need and does a lot of the heavy lifting for us.

Getting ready

For this recipe, we'll need the `ggplot2` and `tidyr` packages installed. We also need a ChatGPT account at `https://chat.openai.com/`.

How to do it...

To get ChatGPT to generate some code to create a plot, we can proceed like this:

1. Give it the example data and an instruction:

    ```
    Write me an R function to load and plot this data as a pairs
    style plot:

           sample1 sample2 sample3
    1        2.85    3.61    16.7
    2        2.78    1.58    16.6
    3        2.09    2.75    17.2
    4        1.22    3.56    16.0
    5        4.29    2.89    16.2
    6        2.48    1.77    16.5
    7        3.48    3.66    15.0
    ```

```
 8    1.07    3.47    17.1
 9    4.25    3.74    14.5
10    4.19    3.35    16.3
```

2. Read and run the response:

> Sure! Here's an R function that loads and plots the given data using a line plot:
>
> ```r
> plot_sample_data <- function() {
>   # Define the data
>   sample1 <- c(2.85, 2.78, 2.09, 1.22, 4.29, 2.48, 3.48, 1.07,
> 4.25, 4.19)
>   sample2 <- c(3.61, 1.58, 2.75, 3.56, 2.89, 1.77, 3.66, 3.47,
> 3.74, 3.35)
>   sample3 <- c(16.7, 16.6, 17.2, 16.0, 16.2, 16.5, 15.0, 17.1,
> 14.5, 16.3)
>
>   # Create a data frame
>   data <- data.frame(sample1, sample2, sample3)
>
>   # Plot the data
>   plot(data$sample1, type = "l", col = "blue", ylim =
> range(data), xlab = "Index", ylab = "Value", main = "Sample
> Data")
>   lines(data$sample2, col = "red")
>   lines(data$sample3, col = "green")
>
>   # Add a legend
>   legend("topright", legend = c("Sample 1", "Sample 2", "Sample
> 3"), col = c("blue", "red", "green"), lty = 1)
> }
> ```
>
> You can call the function `plot_sample_data()` to load and plot the data. It will generate a line plot with three lines representing the three samples. The x-axis represents the index, and the y-axis represents the corresponding values. The plot will have a legend indicating the sample colors.

3. Update the prompt to be more clear:

> Thats fine, but I'd like a ggplot2 plot of all sample against the others in a point plot

4. Read and run the response:

> Certainly! Here's an updated version of the function that uses `ggplot2` to create a point plot comparing all the samples against each other:
>
> ```r
> library(ggplot2)
> ```

```
plot_sample_data <- function() {
  # Define the data
  sample1 <- c(2.85, 2.78, 2.09, 1.22, 4.29, 2.48, 3.48, 1.07,
4.25, 4.19)
  sample2 <- c(3.61, 1.58, 2.75, 3.56, 2.89, 1.77, 3.66, 3.47,
3.74, 3.35)
  sample3 <- c(16.7, 16.6, 17.2, 16.0, 16.2, 16.5, 15.0, 17.1,
14.5, 16.3)

  # Create a data frame
  data <- data.frame(sample1, sample2, sample3)

  # Convert the data to long format
  data_long <- tidyr::gather(data, key = "Sample", value =
"Value")

  # Plot the data using ggplot2
  ggplot(data_long, aes(x = Sample, y = Value, color = Sample))
+
    geom_point() +
    labs(x = "Sample", y = "Value", title = "Sample Data") +
    theme_minimal()
}
```

You can call the function `plot_sample_data()` to load
and plot the data. It will generate a point plot where
each point represents a value from one of the samples. The
x-axis represents the samples, and the y-axis represents the
corresponding values. Each sample is color-coded for easy
identification.

5. Try again, adding more detail to the prompt:

That's not what I meant! I want a faceted plot of sample 1 vs
sample2, sample1 vs sample3, sample2 vs sample 3.

6. Read and run the response:

Apologies for the misunderstanding. Here's an updated version
of the function that uses `ggplot2` to create a faceted plot
of sample 1 vs sample 2, sample 1 vs sample 3, and sample 2 vs
sample 3:

```
library(ggplot2)

plot_sample_data <- function() {
  # Define the data
  sample1 <- c(2.85, 2.78, 2.09, 1.22, 4.29, 2.48, 3.48, 1.07,
4.25, 4.19)
```

```
    sample2 <- c(3.61, 1.58, 2.75, 3.56, 2.89, 1.77, 3.66, 3.47,
3.74, 3.35)
    sample3 <- c(16.7, 16.6, 17.2, 16.0, 16.2, 16.5, 15.0, 17.1,
14.5, 16.3)

    # Create a data frame
    data <- data.frame(sample1, sample2, sample3)

    # Convert the data to long format
    data_long <- tidyr::gather(data, key = "Sample", value =
"Value")

    # Plot the data using ggplot2 with facets
    ggplot(data_long, aes(x = sample1, y = sample2)) +
        geom_point() +
        labs(x = "Sample 1", y = "Sample 2") +
        facet_wrap(~Sample, nrow = 3) +
        theme_minimal()

    ggplot(data_long, aes(x = sample1, y = sample3)) +
        geom_point() +
        labs(x = "Sample 1", y = "Sample 3") +
        facet_wrap(~Sample, nrow = 3) +
        theme_minimal()

    ggplot(data_long, aes(x = sample2, y = sample3)) +
        geom_point() +
        labs(x = "Sample 2", y = "Sample 3") +
        facet_wrap(~Sample, nrow = 3) +
        theme_minimal()
}
```

Calling the function `plot_sample_data()` will generate a faceted plot with three panels, each showing the relationship between two samples. The x-axis and y-axis represent the respective samples. Each panel is labeled with the corresponding sample names.

And that is how we get ChatGPT to attempt to draw plots with code for us. Note the difficulty in explaining and understanding what we want. If we can't explain something very clearly and ChatGPT doesn't have an internal representation of what the response should be for our description, it's going to give something not quite right that needs a lot of work.

How it works...

In *step 1*, we give ChatGPT some sample data to draw a plot with. The prompt isn't very specific though and the code that we receive in *step 2*, while working, generates *Figure 13.1*, which isn't what we're after:

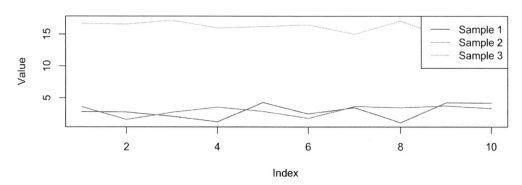

Figure 13.1 – ChatGPT's first attempt, with a minimal prompt

In *step 3*, we generate a more detailed instruction and get the response and code in *step 4*. When we run that, we get the plot in *Figure 13.2*:

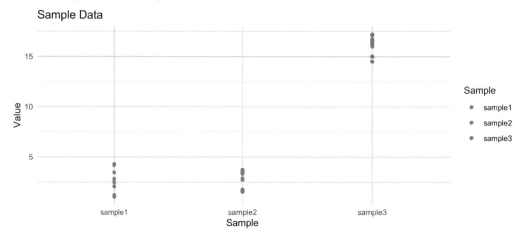

Figure 13.2 – ChatGPT's second attempt, with a more detailed prompt

The plot is a bit better but still not as we wanted. We try again in *step 5*, mentioning `facets` to try and get a small multiple-style plot but end up with generated code in *step 6* that actually errors out.

The recipe shows that ChatGPT can generate code, but it does take a combination of factors for it to be accurate code that does what we want. If the topic of the code is sufficiently covered in tutorials on the internet, we will have the best chance of getting working code. If the topic is not well covered or is absent, then ChatGPT will not be able to *work out* what you meant – it can't be creative and create an interpretation based on your idea. This is because it's a model that knows about the structure of language and not a general-purpose intelligence. ChatGPT just generates the most likely answer from all the things it has been trained on.

The code is not without value though; we do now have a good starting point and can develop things from there using ChatGPT and other sources to assist us in our reading and research.

There's more...

ChatGPT and others are developing code-specific plug-ins and extensions that will be available to paid subscribers of ChatGPT Plus. At the time of writing, these are in beta test and there is a waiting list, but could be worth checking out if you really need that extra help.

Writing documentation for R functions with ChatGPT

ChatGPT is valuable for generating R documentation because it has been trained on a wide range of text sources, including programming documentation. It can understand user queries related to R functions, packages, and concepts, and generate informative and accurate documentation snippets. With its language understanding capabilities, ChatGPT can provide descriptions, parameter details, usage examples, and even explanations of complex concepts in R. This assists developers in quickly accessing relevant information, clarifying doubts, and understanding the functionality of R functions or packages. ChatGPT serves as a handy tool for enhancing the accessibility and comprehensibility of R documentation, supporting users in their programming and analysis tasks.

In this recipe, we'll use ChatGPT to help us with the normally very tedious task of generating documentation and examples for our own function.

Getting ready

We just need an account at ChatGPT: `https://chat.openai.com/`.

How to do it...

To make ChatGPT assist you with code documentation, proceed as follows:

1. Write a prompt and paste in the code:

    ```
    Write Roxygen2 styled documentation for the following R
    function:
    ```

```
factorise_cols <- function(df, col_list ){
  not_all_na <- function(x) any(!is.na(x))

  for ( i in col_list){
    df <- df %>% dplyr::mutate(!!(i) := as.factor(!!(i)) )
  }
  df %>% dplyr::select_if(not_all_na)
}
```

2. Check the response:

```
#' Factorise Selected Columns
#'
#' This function factorises the selected columns in a data
frame.
#'
#' @param df A data frame.
#' @param col_list A character vector specifying the names of
the columns to be factorised.
#' @return A modified data frame with the selected columns
factorised.
#' @export
#'
#' @examples
#' df <- data.frame(
#'   col1 = c("A", "B", "C", NA),
#'   col2 = c(1, 2, NA, 4),
#'   col3 = c("X", "Y", "Z", NA)
#' )
#' factorise_cols(df, c("col1", "col3"))
#'
#' @import dplyr
#' @importFrom base as.factor
factorise_cols <- function(df, col_list) {
  not_all_na <- function(x) any(!is.na(x))

  for (i in col_list) {
    df <- df %>% dplyr::mutate(!!(i) := as.factor(!!(i)))
  }
  df %>% dplyr::select_if(not_all_na)
}
```

And that's all we need to create documentation.

How it works...

In this really simple recipe, we take advantage of ChatGPT's ability to predict documentation from defined code. This works well and plays to ChatGPT's statistical strengths as the documentation follows an extremely structured format that is quite predictable. In *step 1*, we simply ask for Roxygen2 format documentation since this is what is most widely used in R, and then paste the function to be documented.

Step 2 shows the output from one run; we have a nicely formatted and clear description, and ChatGPT has created usage examples for the user. A nice time saver for us.

There's more...

You can go one step further with this and ask ChatGPT to make the code more *readable* for humans with a prompt like this:

```
Tidy up the following R function for ease of human readability:
factorise_cols <- function(df, col_list ){
  not_all_na <- function(x) any(!is.na(x))

  for ( i in col_list){
    df <- df %>% dplyr::mutate(!!(i) := as.factor(!!(i)) )
  }
  df %>% dplyr::select_if(not_all_na)
}
```

We get the following response:

```
#' Factorise Selected Columns
#'
#' This function factorises the selected columns in a data frame.
#'
#' @param df A data frame.
#' @param col_list A character vector specifying the names of the
columns to be factorised.
#' @return A modified data frame with the selected columns factorised.
#' @export
#'
#' @examples
#' df <- data.frame(
#'   col1 = c("A", "B", "C", NA),
#'   col2 = c(1, 2, NA, 4),
#'   col3 = c("X", "Y", "Z", NA)
#' )
#' factorise_cols(df, c("col1", "col3"))
```

```
#'
#' @import dplyr
#' @importFrom base as.factor
factorise_cols <- function(df, col_list) {
  # Helper function to check if any value is not NA
  not_all_na <- function(x) any(!is.na(x))

  # Factorise selected columns
  for (col_name in col_list) {
    df <- df %>% dplyr::mutate(!!col_name := as.factor(!!col_name))
  }

  # Select columns with non-NA values
  df %>% dplyr::select_if(not_all_na)
}
```

In this instance, it refactors some obscure variables and adds inline comments for the reader. Both of these help the reader of the code make easier sense of it. ChatGPT also generates documentation as before, though this may be a hangover from the previous prompt.

Remember that when ChatGPT generates altered code, it isn't guaranteed to work as before. It's your job to check it works as intended.

Writing unit tests for R functions with ChatGPT

ChatGPT is beneficial for generating R unit tests because of its knowledge of programming patterns and best practices. It can understand code snippets, including functions and their expected behaviors, and generate relevant unit tests. By leveraging its training on diverse programming contexts, ChatGPT can assist in creating comprehensive test cases that cover different scenarios and edge cases. It helps ensure code correctness, identify potential bugs, and improve code reliability. ChatGPT's ability to generate unit tests saves developers time and effort, promotes software quality, and contributes to building robust and well-tested R code. In this recipe, we'll learn how to get ChatGPT to do the tedious work of generating test cases for code that we are working on.

Getting ready

We just need a ChatGPT account: https://chat.openai.com/.

How to do it...

To write unit tests for an R function with ChatGPT, do the following:

1. Paste the following request into ChatGPT:

```
write unit tests for the following R code

factorise_cols <- function(df, col_list ){
  not_all_na <- function(x) any(!is.na(x))

  for ( i in col_list){
    df <- df %>% dplyr::mutate(!!(i) := as.factor(!!(i)) )
  }
  df %>% dplyr::select_if(not_all_na)
}
```

2. Read and check the output:

```
library(dplyr)
library(testthat)

# Create a test data frame
test_df <- data.frame(
  col1 = c("A", "B", "C", NA),
  col2 = c(1, 2, NA, 4),
  col3 = c("X", "Y", "Z", NA)
)

# Define the expected output for the test data frame
expected_df <- data.frame(
  col1 = factor(c("A", "B", "C", NA)),
  col3 = factor(c("X", "Y", "Z", NA))
)

# Start defining the unit tests
test_that("factorise_cols correctly factorises selected
columns", {
  # Call the factorise_cols function
  result_df <- factorise_cols(test_df, c("col1", "col3"))

  # Check if the selected columns are factorised
  expect_equal(result_df$col1, expected_df$col1)
  expect_equal(result_df$col3, expected_df$col3)
```

```
  # Check if other columns are not modified
  expect_equal(result_df$col2, test_df$col2)
})

test_that("factorise_cols returns a data frame with non-NA
columns", {
  # Call the factorise_cols function
  result_df <- factorise_cols(test_df, c("col1", "col3"))

  # Check if the returned data frame only contains non-NA
columns
  expect_true(all(!is.na(result_df$col1)))
  expect_true(all(!is.na(result_df$col3)))
  expect_true(all(is.na(result_df$col2)))
})
```

And with that, we should have an output that can test some of the facets of our code at least and a good start to a more dependable and workable code base.

How it works...

The recipe here takes advantage of ChatGPT's representations of the structure of the R programming language in order to write code that will effectively test some example code. In *step 1*, we simply define the function we wish to test and ask for tests.

In *step 2*, we see the output that ChatGPT generated in this instance. It has given us a pretty good set of unit tests. As with everything to do with ChatGPT, there isn't a guarantee that they are correct, but we can read and verify them very easily – certainly in much less time than it would take to write them. One thing to note is that, in this case at least, ChatGPT hasn't generated tests for the case with only NA in a column, which we may decide we need. It is true that this isn't clear in the initial code, so generating the test has given us a new thought on the safe running of this function.

Finding R packages to build a workflow with ChatGPT

ChatGPT is valuable for suggesting R packages for specific problems due to its extensive training on programming-related text and its understanding of various R packages and their function. By analyzing user queries and problem descriptions, ChatGPT can recommend relevant R packages that address specific needs or tasks. It can consider factors such as data manipulation, visualization, statistical analysis, machine learning, or specialized domains. ChatGPT's knowledge allows it to suggest popular and widely-used R packages as well as more specialized or niche packages that may be suitable for the given problem. This capability helps users explore and discover appropriate R packages, saving time and effort in the package selection process and enabling them to leverage the rich ecosystem of R packages available for their specific requirements.

Getting ready

We just need a ChatGPT account: `https://chat.openai.com/`.

How to do it...

To get ChatGPT to suggest a workflow, start as follows:

1. Ask for a set of packages:

    ```
    suggest a workflow of packages in R that would enable me to do
    single cell RNAseq analysis
    ```

2. Read the response:

    ```
    For single-cell RNA sequencing (scRNA-seq) analysis in R, here's
    a suggested workflow of packages that can be used:

    1. Data Import and Preprocessing:
        - `Seurat`: A popular package for scRNA-seq data analysis,
    providing functions for quality control, normalization, and data
    integration.
        - `readr`: For efficient and flexible data import from
    various file formats.
        - `tidyverse`: A collection of packages (e.g., `dplyr`,
    `tidyr`, `ggplot2`) for data manipulation, transformation, and
    visualization.

    2. Quality Control and Filtering:
        - `scater`: Provides functions for quality control metrics
    calculation, visualization, and filtering of low-quality cells
    and genes.
        - `scran`: For normalization and batch effect removal in
    scRNA-seq data.

    3. Cell Clustering and Visualization:
        - `Seurat`: Offers a range of methods for cell clustering,
    dimensionality reduction (e.g., PCA, t-SNE, UMAP), and
    visualization of clusters.
        - `ggplot2`: A powerful package for creating high-quality
    visualizations.
        - `dplyr`: For efficient data manipulation and filtering
    during the clustering process.

    4. Differential Expression Analysis:
        - `Seurat`: Provides methods for identifying differentially
    expressed genes (DEGs) between clusters or groups of cells.
        - `limma`: A widely-used package for differential expression
    analysis, including functionality for linear modeling and
    ```

empirical Bayes methods.

5. Trajectory Inference and Pseudotime Analysis:

- `Monocle3`: Enables trajectory inference and pseudotime analysis to explore cellular dynamics and developmental processes.

- `slingshot`: Another package for trajectory inference and pseudotime analysis.

6. Functional Enrichment Analysis:

- `clusterProfiler`: Offers functions for functional enrichment analysis, including Gene Ontology (GO) and pathway analysis.

- `enrichR`: A package for accessing and visualizing gene set enrichment analysis (GSEA) results from the Enrichr database.

These are just a few examples of packages commonly used in scRNA-seq analysis. Depending on your specific analysis goals and requirements, you may need to explore additional packages and methods. It's also important to consult the documentation and tutorials provided by each package to understand their functionality and usage.

3. Ask for a workflow:

Can you suggest a workflow for using these packages, what would be a good starting point?

4. Get a response:

Certainly! Here's a suggested workflow for scRNA-seq analysis using the mentioned packages:

1. Data Import and Preprocessing:

- Use `readr` or other relevant packages to import the scRNA-seq data from the raw file format into R, creating a suitable data structure (e.g., a matrix or a specialized object like a `SingleCellExperiment` object).

- Perform initial data preprocessing steps such as removing low-quality cells, filtering out low-expressed genes, and performing basic quality control checks.

2. Quality Control and Filtering:

- Use the `scater` package to calculate quality control metrics (e.g., number of genes, number of counts per cell) and visualize them to identify any outliers or problematic cells.

- Apply filtering steps to remove low-quality cells and uninformative genes based on appropriate criteria such as gene expression thresholds, mitochondrial gene content, or library size.

3. Normalization and Batch Effect Removal:

 - Normalize the scRNA-seq data to adjust for sequencing depth and library size differences using methods like "size factors" or "total-count scaling" available in packages like `scran`.

 - Address batch effects, if present, using methods such as `ComBat` from the `sva` package or other relevant methods in `Seurat` for integration and batch effect correction.

4. Cell Clustering and Visualization:

 - Use `Seurat` to perform dimensionality reduction techniques (e.g., PCA, t-SNE, UMAP) to visualize the scRNA-seq data in a lower-dimensional space.

 - Perform clustering analysis on the reduced dimensions using algorithms like graph-based clustering (`FindClusters` function in `Seurat`) to identify distinct cell populations.

 - Visualize the clusters using `Seurat` and `ggplot2` for exploration and interpretation.

5. Differential Expression Analysis:

 - Use `Seurat` or `limma` to identify differentially expressed genes (DEGs) between clusters or groups of cells.

 - Perform statistical tests (e.g., t-tests, Wilcoxon rank-sum tests) and multiple testing correction (e.g., Bonferroni, FDR) to obtain significant DEGs.

 - Visualize the DEGs using volcano plots, heatmaps, or other relevant visualizations.

6. Trajectory Inference and Pseudotime Analysis:

 - If your scRNA-seq data represents a developmental or time-dependent process, use packages like `Monocle3` or `slingshot` to infer cellular trajectories and pseudotime ordering.

 - Visualize the trajectories using plotting functions provided by these packages.

7. Functional Enrichment Analysis:

 - Use `clusterProfiler` or `enrichR` to perform functional enrichment analysis on gene sets derived from differential expression analysis or gene clusters.

 - Identify enriched Gene Ontology (GO) terms, pathways, or other biological annotations associated with the differentially expressed or clustered genes.

 - Visualize the enrichment results using appropriate visualization methods provided by these packages.

It's important to note that this workflow is a general guideline and may need to be adapted based on the specific characteristics and goals of your scRNA-seq analysis. It's recommended to consult the documentation, tutorials, and vignettes provided

```
by each package to gain a deeper understanding of their
functionalities and how to effectively utilize them in your
analysis.
```

These steps represent a long discussion with ChatGPT giving us some long answers, though our input is somewhat briefer.

How it works...

In *step 1*, we just ask ChatGPT to suggest R packages for a problem on `scRNA-seq`. The ability of ChatGPT to suggest R packages is derived from its training on a diverse corpus of programming-related text, including discussions, tutorials, and documentation related to R and its packages. During its training, ChatGPT learns patterns, relationships, and associations between problem descriptions, programming tasks, and the R packages commonly used to solve them.

When presented with a user query or problem description, ChatGPT applies its understanding of the R package ecosystem to analyze the problem context and identify relevant keywords or concepts. It then uses this information to generate suggestions by matching the problem description with known associations between problem types and appropriate R packages. This is how it generates the text seen in *step 2*; they are the packages most matched with the problem description. Therefore, note that it is only a rough guide.

In *step 3*, we ask ChatGPT to come up with suggestions for tying the packages into a draft workflow. It responds with the text in *step 4*. The training data allows ChatGPT to capture the relationships between problem scenarios, solution approaches, and the R packages commonly employed in those contexts. This knowledge enables ChatGPT to provide meaningful recommendations and workflows by using its understanding of the purpose, functionality, and capabilities of various R packages.

It's important to note that while ChatGPT can provide valuable suggestions based on its training, the final selection of R packages should consider specific requirements, user preferences, package documentation, and additional research. The response is only ever a guide and a suggestion for further reading, not a fixed, expert-based answer.

Index

Symbols

3D structure protein alignment
predicting, in bio3d 231-233

A

AllelicImbalance
used, for finding allele-specific
expression (ASE) 166-169

analysis of variance (ANOVA) 97
using, to compare multiple groups
in multiple variable 111-114
using, to compare multiple groups
in single variable 108-110

AnnoDB packages
using, for genome annotation 272-274

ape package 238
tree formats, reading and writing 239, 240
used, for extracting and working
with subtrees 249-251

apply() functions
using 327-329

arbitrary functions
applying, using mutate() function 36-38

autoplot() function 294

B

base R objects
making tidy 322, 323

basic helix-loop-helix (bHLH) 252

batch effects
estimating, with SVA 164-166

bio3d
3D structure protein alignment,
predicting 231-233
used, for finding protein domains 211-214

bioconda
using, to install external tools 19-21

Bioconductor packages 18
managing 18
renv 18, 19

Biological Process (BP) 278

BioMart
gene annotation, retrieving 268-270
genome annotation, retrieving 268-270

bumphunter
used, for finding regions with high
expression ab initio 159-161

busy plots
selected values, highlighting
with gghighlight 58-60

www.packtpub.com

Subscribe to our online digital library for full access to over 7,000 books and videos, as well as industry leading tools to help you plan your personal development and advance your career. For more information, please visit our website.

Why subscribe?

- Spend less time learning and more time coding with practical eBooks and Videos from over 4,000 industry professionals

- Improve your learning with Skill Plans built especially for you

- Get a free eBook or video every month

- Fully searchable for easy access to vital information

- Copy and paste, print, and bookmark content

Did you know that Packt offers eBook versions of every book published, with PDF and ePub files available? You can upgrade to the eBook version at packtpub.com and as a print book customer, you are entitled to a discount on the eBook copy. Get in touch with us at customercare@packtpub.com for more details.

At www.packtpub.com, you can also read a collection of free technical articles, sign up for a range of free newsletters, and receive exclusive discounts and offers on Packt books and eBooks.

Other Books You May Enjoy

If you enjoyed this book, you may be interested in these other books by Packt:

Bioinformatics with Python Cookbook - Third Edition

Tiago Antao

ISBN: 978-1-80323-642-1

- Become well-versed with data processing libraries such as NumPy, pandas, arrow, and zarr in the context of bioinformatic analysis

- Interact with genomic databases

- Solve real-world problems in the fields of population genetics, phylogenetics, and proteomics

- Build bioinformatics pipelines using a Galaxy server and Snakemake

- Work with functools and itertools for functional programming

- Perform parallel processing with Dask on biological data

- Explore **Principal Component Analysis** (**PCA**) techniques with scikit-learn

Healthcare Analytics Made Simple

Vikas "Vik" Kumar

ISBN: 978-1-78728-670-2

- Gain valuable insight into healthcare incentives, finances, and legislation
- Discover the connection between machine learning and healthcare processes
- Use SQL and Python to analyze data
- Measure healthcare quality and provider performance
- Identify features and attributes to build successful healthcare models
- Build predictive models using real-world healthcare data
- Become an expert in predictive modeling with structured clinical data
- See what lies ahead for healthcare analytics

Packt is searching for authors like you

If you're interested in becoming an author for Packt, please visit `authors.packtpub.com` and apply today. We have worked with thousands of developers and tech professionals, just like you, to help them share their insight with the global tech community. You can make a general application, apply for a specific hot topic that we are recruiting an author for, or submit your own idea.

Share Your Thoughts

Now you've finished *R Bioinformatics Cookbook*, we'd love to hear your thoughts! Scan the QR code below to go straight to the Amazon review page for this book and share your feedback or leave a review on the site that you purchased it from.

`https://packt.link/r/1-837-63427-0`

Your review is important to us and the tech community and will help us make sure we're delivering excellent quality content.

Download a free PDF copy of this book

Thanks for purchasing this book!

Do you like to read on the go but are unable to carry your print books everywhere?

Is your eBook purchase not compatible with the device of your choice?

Don't worry, now with every Packt book you get a DRM-free PDF version of that book at no cost.

Read anywhere, any place, on any device. Search, copy, and paste code from your favorite technical books directly into your application.

The perks don't stop there, you can get exclusive access to discounts, newsletters, and great free content in your inbox daily

Follow these simple steps to get the benefits:

1. Scan the QR code or visit the link below

https://packt.link/free-ebook/9781837634279

2. Submit your proof of purchase
3. That's it! We'll send your free PDF and other benefits to your email directly

Made in the USA
Columbia, SC
09 April 2024

34136599R00217